# A DERVISH TEXTBOOK

عوارف المعارفِ شيخ

# شهاب الدين عمر بن محمدِ سهروردي

متجرمه

# محمود بن علي الكاشاني

From the perfume of (His wine-) dregs, wise this one becometh;
From its pure colour, a traditionist that one becometh:

From half a draught, pure this one becometh;
From (drinking) a goblet, a lover that one becometh:

At one draught, another swalloweth—
The jar, the wine-house, the **Sáḳī**, and the wine-drinker:

All swallowed,—yet open remaineth his mouth!
O ocean-heart, mighty drinker! well done!

Gulshan-i-Raz̤, c. 832-836 (ans. 14).

# A DERVISH TEXTBOOK
# FROM THE 'AWARIFU-L-MA'ARIF,
## WRITTEN IN THE THIRTEENTH CENTURY

BY

شيخ

شهاب الدين عمر بن محمد سهروردي

مترجمه

محمود بن علي الكاشاني

***Shaikh Shahābu-d-Dīn 'Umar bin Muḥammad-i-Sahrwardī,***

***translated (out of the Arabic into Persian) by***

***Maḥmūd bin 'Alī al Kāshānī,***

---

***Companion in Ṣūfī,ism to the Dīvān-i-Khwāja Ḥāfiẓ.***

---

TRANSLATED FOR THE FIRST TIME OUT OF THE PERSIAN INTO ENGLISH,

BY

LIEUT.-COL. H. WILBERFORCE CLARKE,

ROYAL (late Bengal) ENGINEERS,

LIFE-MEMBER OF THE ROYAL ASIATIC SOCIETY OF GREAT BRITAIN AND IRELAND; MEMBER OF THE ASIATIC SOCIETY OF BENGAL.

AUTHOR OF "THE PERSIAN MANUAL;" FIRST TRANSLATOR (OUT OF THE PERSIAN) OF "THE BUSTĀN-I-SA'DĪ;" OF "THE SIKANDAR NĀMA-I-NIẒĀMĪ"; AND OF "THE DIVĀN-I-ḤĀFIẒ." AUTHOR OF "NOTES ON ELEPHANTS"; OF "THE SEXTANT;" OF "LONGITUDE BY LUNAR DISTANCES;" AND OF "THE TRANSVERSE STRENGTH OF A RAILWAY-RAIL."

THE OCTAGON PRESS
LONDON

ISBN 0 900860 73 1

**Published for The Sufi Trust by**

**The Octagon Press**

First impression in this edition 1980
Reprinted 1990

Printed and bound in Great Britain by
Redwood Press Limited, Melksham, Wiltshire

# PREFACE.

THE sources, whence this note on sūfī,ism has been derived are :—

i. The introduction (pp. 1—13).
   (*a*) Disquisition on ṣūfī,ism by Sir W. Jones.
   (*b*) "Soofies" (History of Persia) by Malcolm.
   (*c*) The Gulshan-i-Rāz.
   (*d*) Other sources.

ii. The definition of sixty-nine terms used in ṣūfī,ism (pp. 14—158).
   The Miṣbāḥu-l-Hidāyat
   by
   Maḥmūd bin 'Alī al Kashānī,
   being a translation (in Persian) of the Arabic work—
   'Awārif-u-l-Ma'ārif*
   by
   Shaikh Shahābu-d-Dīn 'Umar bin Muḥammad-i-Sahrwardī (*b.* 1145, *d.* 1234).

iii. The performances of darvīshes (pp. 159—168).
   The Darvīshes by Brown.

---

2. Neither the Miṣbāḥu-l-Hidāyat (in Persian), nor the 'Awārifu-l-Ma'ārif (in Arabic),—has ever before been translated into English. What is here given to the Reader comprises more than a half† of the Miṣbāḥu-l-Hidāyat. Shaikh Shahābu-d-Dīn Muḥammad-i-Sahrwardī (*b.* 1145, *d.* 1234), the son of Abū Najīb, was born at Sharward ; and he died at Baghdād.

He was a pious Shaikh, assiduous in spiritual exercises and in the practice of devotion. He is author of

the 'Awārifu-l-Ma'ārif } in Arabic.
,, Ḥikmatu-l-Assār }

and many other works.

The matter (ten pages) taken from Brown's Darvīshes has been arranged, corrected, collected, and greatly condensed.

---

* Otherwise called the 'Awārif-u-l-Ḥaḳā,iḳ.

† That is, out of 343 pages of the Persian Text, 221 pages have been translated into English ; and are herein given.

3. Those who wish further to pursue the subject of ṣūfī,ism will find useful the table of authorities on ṣūfī,ism, English and Persian (pp. iv—v).

4. Unless ṣūfī,ism be understood, the Dīvān-i-Ḥāfiẓ cannot be understood.

In Vol. IV (pp. 196-211) of the works of Emerson (1882), wholly wrong is the view given of the work of Ḥāfiẓ; and mistranslated and misunderstood are the passages there given.

It is unnecessary to give instances; easily may the student verify this statement by referring either to my translation of Ḥāfiẓ, or to the original Persian. Let one instance suffice :—

| Emerson's Works, Vol. IV, p. 205. | Clarke's translation of the Dīvan-i-Ḥāfiẓ, Ode 371. |
|---|---|
| Oft have I said, I say it once more.<br>I, a wanderer, do not stray from myself. | Times I have said; and again I say :—<br>That, heart-bereft, not of myself, have I gone this Path (of love). |
| I am a kind of parrot; the mirror is holden to me.<br>What the Eternal says, I stammering say again. | Behind the (pure) mirror (of the holy traveller's heart), me, they have kept like the parrot.<br>What the Teacher of eternity without beginning said :—" Say "; I say. |
| Give me what you will: I eat thistles as roses,<br>And, according to my food I grow and I give: | Whether, the thorn I be or whether the rose, there is a sward-adorner (God).<br>By whose hand as (it) cherished me, I grew. |
| Scorn me not; but, I know I have the pearl.<br>And am only seeking one to receive it. | O friends, me heart-bereft, astonied, censure not :<br>A great jewel, I have; and the master of vision (the jeweller, God) I seek. |

Emerson (p. 201) says :—

> We do not wish to make mystical divinity out of the Songs of Solomon, much less out of the erotic and bacchanalian songs of Ḥāfiẓ.
>
> Ḥāfiẓ himself is determined to defy all such hypocritical interpretation, and tears off his turban and throws it at the head of the meddling dervis, and throws his glass after the turban.
>
> Nothing is too high, nothing too low for his occasion. Love is a leveller, and Allah becomes a groom, and heaven a closet in his daring hymns to his mistress or to his cupbearer. This boundless charter is the right of genius.

To this statement, would agree no one who had, in the original Persian, read Ḥāfiẓ; and had understood him.

Despite the fact that Emerson wholly fails to understand Ḥāfiẓ as the mystic poet, divine, immortal—strangely he admires him. For at p. 239, he says :—

> You shall not read newspapers, nor politics, nor novels, nor Montaigne, nor the newest French book.

> You may read Plutarch, Plato, Plotinus' Hindu mythology and ethics. You may read Chaucer, Shakespeare, Ben Johnson, Milton; read Collins and Gray; read **Ḥāfiẓ** and the Trouveurs — fact-books which all geniuses prize as raw material and as antidote to verbiage and false poetry.

5. At the head of the various sections, the figures refer to the Persian text of the Miṣbāḥu-l-Hidāyat—

Roman figures to chapters.
Arabic „ „ sections (of chapters).

6. To special notice, I wish to bring Maulavī Mīrzā Muḥammad-i-Bisravī, who rendered me much help in this difficult work.

7. This translation was made in a tropical country, in leisure moments, amidst the pressure and the stress of professional duties most exacting; and under special circumstances of harass and worry that it is not permissible to describe.*

For these reasons, the reader's indulgence is solicited.

---

* See Clarke's ṣūfī,istic translation of the Divān-i-Ḥāfiẓ, Preface, para. 18 (p. xvi).

H. WILBERFORCE CLARKE.

CALCUTTA;
*January 1891.*

## Authorities on Ṣūfī,ism.

| Date. | |
|---|---|
| 1787 | Asiatic Miscellany, vol. ii, pp. 50—53; 131—150. |
| 1809 | Descriptive Catalogue (pp. 34—45), Oriental Library of Tippū Sulṭān, by C. Stewart. This gives 115 excellent Persian works on Ṣūfī,ism. |
| | De Bode's Bukhārā. |
| 1818 | History of Muḥammadanism by C. Mills (p. 473). |
| 1829 | History of Persia, Malcolm—vol. i, pp. 322, 324, 400; vol. ii, pp. 382—426. |
| | Works of Sir W. Jones, ii, pp. 131—150. |
| 1856 | Journal, Asiatic Society, Bengal, vol. xxv, pp. 133—150. 1857. |
| | Note by Sprenger on the earliest work on Ṣūfī,ism. |
| | Sind (chap. viii), Burton. |
| | Modern Egyptians (chap. iii), Lane. |
| | Die Morgenlandische mystik, by Tholuck. |
| 1863 | Ḳanūn-i-Islām, Herklot, pp. 187—200. |
| 1868 | The Darvishes, Brown. |
| 1875 | Notes on Muḥammadanism (p. 227), C. E. Hughes. |
| 1878 | Islām (p. 201), Stobart. |
| 1880 | Gulshan-i-Rāz, translated by Whinfield. |
| 1881 | Catalogue, Oriental Manuscripts (pp. 35—45), British Museum (Quaritch). |
| ? | Paper on the Ṣūfīs by Captain Graham, Bombay. |

| Date. | Author. | Name of Work. |
|---|---|---|
| 911 | Shaikh Junīd-i-Baghdādī. | |
| 1037 | Shaikh Abū Sinā (Avicenna) . . . . . | Maḳāmātu-l-Ārifīn. |
| 1049 | Abū-l-Ḳāsim-i-'Ansarī. | |
| 1166 | Shaikh 'Abdu-l-Ḳadir-i-Gilānī . . . . | Malfūẓāt-i-Jalālī.<br>Sharḥ-i-ghauṣiya va ghaira. |
| 1230 | Shaikh Farīdu-d-Dīn 'Aṭṭār . . . . . . | Asrār-Nāma. |
| 1234 | Shaikh Shahābu-d-Dīn 'Umar bin Muḥammad-i-Sahrwardī. | 'Awārifu-l-Ma'ārif,* otherwise called 'Awārifu-l-Ḥaḳā,iḳ. |
| 1239 | Shaikh Muḥyu-d-Dīn bin Arabī. | |
| 1273 | Maulāna Jalālu-d-Dīn-i-Rūmī . . . . . | The Maṣnavī. |
| 1292 | Shaikh Sa'dī-i-Shīrāzī . . . . . . . | Marghūbu-l-Ḳulūb. |
| 1317 | Sa'du-d-Dīn Maḥmūd-i-Shabistarī . . . | Gulshan-i-rāz.<br>Ḥaḳḳu-l-Yaḳīn.<br>Risāla-i-Shāhid. |
| 1382 | Kamālu-d-Dīn Abū-l-ghanīm 'Abdu-r-Razzāḳ . | Iṣṭilāḥāt-i-ṣūfiya.† |
| 1389 | Khwāja Shamsu-d-Dīn-i-Ḥāfiẓ . . . . . | The Dīvān. |
| 1492 | Nūru-d-Dīn 'Abdu-r-Raḥmān-i-Jāmī . . . | Lawā,iḥ. |
| 1591 | Maulāna 'Urfī . . . . . . . . . . | Ḳaṣā,id. |
| 1610 | Ḳāẓī Nūru-l-lāh-i-Shustarī . . . . . . | Majālisu-l-Muminīn. |
| 1659 | Shāhzāda Dārā Shikūh-i-Ḳādirī . . . . . | Mushāhida-i-sulūk va tarjuma-i-wāsiṭī. |

* See the Preface, para. 1.

† Arabic text (p. 167) edited by Dr. Aloys Sprenger, M.D., 1845, entitled——"Dictionary (in Arabic) of the technical terms of the Ṣūfīs."

| Date. | Author. | Name of Work. |
|---|---|---|
| 1669 | Mīrzā Muḥammad 'Alī-i-Tabrīzī-i-Ṣā,ib . . . | ? |
| 1670 | Shaikh Muḥammad Muḥsin-i-Fānī . . . | The Dābistān. |
| | Shaikh Farīdu-d-Din Shakarganj . . . . | Asrāru-l-Auliya. |

# CONTENTS.

# ṢŪFĪ,ISM.

Said Muḥammad :—

In Islām, is no monachism.*

Nevertheless, in 623 A.D.,† forty-five men of Makka joined themselves to as many others of Madīna; took an oath of fidelity to the doctrines of the prophet (Muḥammad); and formed a fraternity——to establish community of property, and to perform daily certain religious practices by way of penitence.

They took the name of ṣūfī, a word derived from :—

(*a*) صوف (ṣūf) wool, woolly; a hair cloth used by penitents in the early days of Islām.

(*b*) صوفي (ṣūfīy) wise, pious.

(*c*) صوفي (ṣūfī) woollen.

(*d*) صفا (ṣafā) purity.‡

(*e*) صفي (ṣafī) pure.

To the name of ṣūfī, they added the title of فقير (faḳīr), because they renounced the chattels of the world and its joys.

Said Muḥammad :—

" Al faḳru fakhrī, poverty is my glory.

During the life of Muḥammad, Abu Bakr (the first Khalīfa), and 'Alī (the fourth Khalīfa, *b.* 599, *d.* 661), established جماعت (assemblies) wherein vows were made and exercises practised.

In 657 A.D., Uvais-i-Karānī (*d.* 657) established the first religious order of the greatest austerity.

In honour of Muḥammad, who, at the battle of Uhud, 625 A.D., had lost two of his teeth, he drew out his own teeth; and required his followers to do the same.

The term ṣūfī was first adopted by Abū Hāshim, a Syrian Zāhid (*d.* 780 A.D.); in his time was built the first takya (convent). But some say that the seed of ṣūfī,-ism :—

| | in the time of | | in the time of |
|---|---|---|---|
| was sown . . . | Ādam. | began to develop . | Mūsā. |
| germed . . . | Nūh. | reached maturity . | Christ. |
| budded . . . | Ibrāhīm. | produced pure wine . | Muḥammad. |

* The Ḳurān, v. 89.

† The Hijra dates from the 15th July 622 A.D.

‡ Some add صفا (ṣafā), a station near the Kāba, Makka. The man, who wore the blue woollen garment, was esteemed to be pure (ṣafī).

Those who loved this wine have so drunk of it as to become self-less. They exclaim :—

> "Praise be mine! greater than I, is any?
> "The truth (God), am I: there is no other God than I."

One of the earliest ṣūfīs was the woman Rābi'a mentioned by Ibn Khāllikān (*b.* 1211, *d.* 1282). At night, she used to go to the house-top, and to say:—

> "O God! hushed is the day's noise; with his beloved is the lover. But, Thee, I have for my lover; and alone with Thee, I joy."

In Volume I of his works, Sir W. Jones says :—

> There is a species of Persian poetry that consists almost wholly of a mystical religious allegory, though on a transient view it seems to contain only the sentiments of a wild and voluptuous libertinism.
>
> Admitting the danger of a poetical style in which the limits between vice and enthusiasm are so minute as to be hardly distinguishable, we must beware of censuring it severely; for an ardent grateful piety is congenial to the undepraved nature of man, whose mind, sinking under the magnitude of the subject, and struggling to record its emotions, has recourse to metaphors, extending sometimes beyond the bounds of cool reason.

Ṣūfīs believe :—

> That the souls of men differ infinitely in degree but not at all in kind from the divine spirit whereof they are particles, and wherein they will ultimately be absorbed; that the spirit of God pervades the universe, ever present to His work and ever in substance; that He alone is perfect benevolence, perfect truth, perfect beauty; that love for Him is true love, ('ishḳ-i-ḥaḳiḳi), while love of other objects is illusory love ('ishḳ-i-majāzī); that all the beauties of nature are faint resemblances like images in a mirror of the divine charms; that, from eternity without beginning to eternity without end, the supreme benevolence is occupied in bestowing happiness; that men can only attain it by performing their part of the *primal covenant* between them and the Creator; that nothing has a pure absolute existence but *mind* or *spirit;* that material substances are no more than gay pictures presented continually to our minds by the sempiternal artist; that we must beware of attachment to such phantoms and attach ourselves exclusively to God, who truly exists in us as we solely exist in Him; that we retain, even in this forlorn state of separation from our Beloved, the idea of heavenly beauty and the remembrance of our primeval vows; that sweet music, gentle breezes, fragrant flowers, perpetually renew the primary idea, refresh our fading memory, and melt us with tender affections; that we must cherish those affections, and by abstracting our souls from vanity (that is, from all but God) approximate to this essence, in our final union with which will consist our supreme beatitude.

Sprenger* says :—

> The mysticism of the ṣūfīs is a hypertrophy of the religious feeling; and a monomania in which man blasphemously attempts to fathom the depths of the essence of God.
>
> The mystics give up worldly affairs; devote themselves to austerity; and are a nuisance to the world.
>
> This disease attacks every nation after it has passed the meridian of its grandeur.

---

* See Preface to Abd-u-r-Razẓāk's Dictionary of ṣūfī,istic terms, 1845; the Journal, Asiatic Society, Bengal, Volume XXV, of 1856 (p. 145).

The mysticism of :—

(*a*) the Zeoplatonists marked the fall of Rome.
(*b*) „ Ṣūfīs „ „ the Khalīfat.
(*c*) „ later Fathers „ the darkness of the middle ages.

Because the noblest feelings of man are morbidly exalted by this disease it has produced sublime poetry. Nothing can equal the beauty of the poems of :—

Muḥyu-d-Dīn.
Ḥāfiẓ.
Jalālu-d-Dīn-i-Rūmī.

Ṣūfī,ism is not due to the introduction of systems of philosophy from India, or from Greece. It is the result of the development of Islām ; and is well worthy of the attention of the student.

Many consider Pantheism and Ṣūfī,ism to be identical.

The Shaikhs and Ṣūfī-poets profess :—

The most ardent, although Platonic, attachment for individuals of their own sex, remarkable for beauty or for talent, declaring that they are adoring the Creator whilst admiring His beautiful handiwork (corporeal or intellectual) ; and boasting that their love is the more pure in being unmixed with carnal sensuality, such as it must be if bestowed on individuals of the other sex.

Maulāna Jalālu-d-Dīn-i-Rūmī (*b.* 1207, *d.* 1273), says :—

Ṣūfīs profess eager desire but with no carnal affection ; and circulate the cup but no material goblet.
Since in their order, all things are spiritual——all is mystery within mystery.

Modern ṣūfīs believe in the Ḳūrān ; and in an express covenant on the day of eternity without beginning (the day of Alast) between the assemblage of the souls (of men) and the supreme soul (of God), wherefrom they were detached.

In ṣūfī,ism are four stages, which must be passed before man's corporeal veil can be removed ; and his emancipated soul, mixed with the glorious essence, whence it has been separated but not divided :—

i شريعت (sharī'at*)

The murīd (disciple) observeth the shar' and the rites of Islām ; ever beareth his shaikh in mind ; in him effaceth himself through meditation ; maketh him his shield against evil thoughts ; and regardeth his spirit as his guardian spirit.
This is "effacement in the shaikh."

ii طريقت (ṭarīḳat)

The murīd attaineth power ; entereth ṣūfī,ism ; and abandoneth the observance of religious form, exchanging outward for inward worship.
Without great piety, virtue, and fortitude (based on a knowledge of the dignity of the soul of man) he cannot attain this stage.
The shaikh passeth the murīd to the influence of the Pīr (long since deceased) ; and then, in all things, the murīd seeth the Pīr.
This is "effacement in the Pīr."

---

* Some call this nāsūt.

iii معرفت (marifat)*
The murid hath attained to supernatural knowledge; and is, therein, equal to the angels.
By the shaikh, he is led to Muḥammad, whom, in all things, he seeth.
This is "effacement in the Prophet."

iv حقيقت (truth)
The murid hath become joined to truth (God), whom, in all things, he seeth.
This is "effacement in God."

Many reach the second stage; few the fourth.

Some make eleven stages:—

موافقت Muwāfiḳat.
The murid beareth enmity to the Friend's enemy—the world, shaiṭān, imperious lust; and love for the Friend (God).

ميل ma,il.
The murid inclineth to God; and from the heart's page, effaceth "other than God."

موانست muwānisat.
The murid fleeth from all, and seeketh God.

مودت mawaddat.
The murid engageth in submission, in lamentation, in affection, and in agitation in the heart's chamber.

هوا hawā.
The murid keepeth the heart in austerity and in strife (against sin); and maketh it water (soft).

خلت khullat.
The murid maketh all the limbs full of recollection of God; and of aught else void.

الفت ulfat.
The murid maketh himself void of despicable qualities, and joined to laudable qualities.

شغف shaghf.
The murid, through ardency of desire, rendeth the heart's veil; and considereth the revealing of the mystery of love for God—infidelity, save under the mastery of wajd (ecstasy).

تيم taym.
The murid maketh himself the slave of love, and joineth himself to tajrid (outward separation), and to tafrid (inward solitude).

ولش walsh.
The murid keepeth the heart's mirror before God's glory; and becometh intoxicated with its wine).

عشق ishḳ.
The murid keepeth so engaged the tongue in ẕikr (creation of God), the heart in fikr (thought of God), and the soul in mushāhida (viewing God's glory)—that he considereth himself non-existent.

Some consider 'ishḳ to be:—

(*a*) effacing one's self in the essence of Absolute Unity (God).
(*b*) the deposit of faith (Ḳurān, xxxiii, 72).

The following are terms used in ṣūfī,ism:—

| | | | | | |
|---|---|---|---|---|---|
| ṣūfi | the ṣūfī. | ahl-i-taṣawwuf | | | one of mysticism. |
| 'ārif | „ knower. | „ | ḥāl | „ „ | (mystic) state. |
| sālik | „ traveller (to God). | „ | ṭarīḳat | „ „ | the Path (to God). |
| ṭālib | „ seeker (of God). | „ | mārifat | „ „ | (divine) knowledge. |
| 'āshiḳ-i-sādiḳ | „ sincere lover (of God). | „ | ḥakīḳat | „ „ | truth. |

* Some call this 'urf.

| | |
|---|---|
| ahl-i-ḥaḳḳ | one of God. |
| „ sharʿiat | „ „ the sharʾ. |
| taṣawwuf | ṣūfī,ism. |
| mutaṣawwif | sufī,istic. |
| ʿabd, ʿābid | the servant (of God). |
| ʿabūdiyat | „ service „ |
| maʿrifat | „ knowledge „ |
| ṭarīḳat | „ path „ |
| jaẓb | „ attraction „ |
| jamʾ wiṣāl | „ union (with God). |
| sukūnat | „ dwelling „ |
| **sāḳī** | „ cup-bearer. |
| maḳām | degree. |
| manzil | stage. |
| ḥāl | the (mystic) state. |
| wajid | rapture. |
| shauḳ | desire. |
| ẓauḳ | delight. |
| muḥabhat | affection. |
| ʿishḳ | love. |

| | |
|---|---|
| ṣāḥib-i-dil | one possessed of heart, a ṣūfī. |
| „ maʿrifat | „ „ (divine) knowledge. |
| ʿishḳu-l-lāh | love for God. |
| firāḳ | separation (from God). |
| dair, takyat | the convent. |
| zāhid | „ man of (dry) austerity. |
| aṣḥāb-i-ʿilm-i-ẓāhirī | the companions of outward knowledge. |
| „ „ baṭini „ | companions of inward knowledge. |
| ishtyaḳ | ardour. |
| mast | intoxicated. |
| bī khud | void of self, selfless. |
| Pīr | the founder of a religious order. |
| shaikh | „ chief of a convent. |
| khalīfa, naḳīb | „ deputy shaikh. |
| murshid | „ spiritual guide, the shaikh. |
| murīd | „ disciple. |

| | |
|---|---|
| ṣaḥāba | companions in the 1st generation after Muḥammad. |
| tābiʿīn | followers „ 2nd „ „ |
| zāhidān, ʿābidān | devotees „ 3rd „ „ |

The beginning of taṣawwuf (ṣūfīʾism) is īmān (faith), which consists of "six columns" (principles):—

(1) The existence of God.
(2) „ unity „
(3) „ angels.
(4) The prophets.
(5) „ day of resurrection.
(6) Good and evil, through God's predestination.

The end of taṣawwuf lieth in pronouncing the six principles; and in conforming thereto with the heart.

The īmān of common folk (ʾāmm) is:—

ʾilm (knowledge), which is only an imitation of "the six columns" learned from the ʾulamā or from the imāms. They know not why it is necessary to believe in these "six columns"; nor how thereby salvation can be obtained.

Many pursue the ʾilm-i-ṭarīḳat (knowledge of the Path) and wander into error, becoming:—

| | |
|---|---|
| ahl-i-jabrī | one disbelieving freedom of will. |
| „ ḳadrī | „ believing in predestination. |
| „ mujassamī | „ „ only in the body. |
| „ mushabbīa | „ „ in portraits of God. |
| „ mutaẓalī | „ sated (with God). |

In all are seventy-three orders, whereof the true order is only one, the firḳat-i-najāt (the party of salvation).

Manifest is their īmān (faith). Proceeding with only a lamp, they have reached the resplendent sun; at first only imitation, they have reached truth (God).

They find that the ṭariḳat (of the darvīsh) and the sharī'at (of Islām) agree; and that whoever is imperfect in sharī'at is also imperfect in ḥaḳīḳat (truth).

The Ḳuran (lxxviii, 18) says:—

"In the eternal life, my people will rise as monkeys, as hogs, &c., &c.

These, in life, outwardly bore the form of man; but inwardly were brutes.

From these evils, repentance before death will free one.

Give thyself to a murshid (spiritual guide) who, by his prayers, will show thee in dreams the evil parts of thy character till they shall pass away. As the lover delights in his beloved, so doth the darvīsh in his murshid.

The darvīshes say:—

"Neither fear we hell, nor desire we heaven."

By this, they mean:—

"O God, thou bargainest with none; for purity of heart and love for Thee, is our devotion.
Be not heaven nor hell—we adore Thee.
Put us into heaven—'tis through thy excellence; into hell,—through thy justice."

The ṣūfīs are divided into innumerable orders. The two original* orders are:—

1. حلوليه (ḥulūliya) the inspired.
This order believes that God has entered into them; and that the divine spirit entereth all who are devout.
2. اتّحاديه (ittiḥādiya) the unionist. This order believes that God is joined with every enlightened being; that He is as flame, and the soul as charcoal (ready to flame); and that the soul, by union with God, becometh God.

From these two orders are derived the five following orders:—

واصيله (wāṣiliya) the joined (to God).
عشاقيه ('ashāḳiya) „ lovers (of God).
تلقينيه (talḳīniya) „ instructed.
ذاقيه (zakiya) „ penetrated.
واحديه (wāḥidiya) „ solitary.

For full information regarding the many orders of the ṣūfīs, I refer the reader to Malcolm's History of Persia, vol. ii, Art. "Soofies."

The most celebrated of the ṣūfī teachers of Persia have been men as famed for knowledge as for devotion.

Of Ibrāhīm ibn Adham, they say:—

"That holy man turned day into night;
"Night into day by his constant and undivided devotion to God."

Among the ṣūfīs, the most celebrated are the poets.

The raptures of genius expatiating on an inexhaustible subject are deemed inspiration by those who believe that the soul can wander in the region of imagination, and unite with God.

---

* The original order is said to have been the ثباتيه (ṣabātiya), the (ancient) Sabians ——.

In sweetest strains, Jalālu-d-Dīn Rūmī (*b.* 1277, *d.* 1773) teacheth that all nature abounds with divine love such as to cause the loveliest plant to seek the loftiest object of desire.

Nūru-d-Dīn Abdu-r-Raḥmān-i-jāmī (*b.* 1414, *d.* 1492) breatheth ecstatic rapture in every line.

The Gulistān and the Būstān-i-Sa'dī* and the **Dīvān-i-Ḥāfiẓ** may be called the scriptures of the Persian ṣūfīs.

Ṣūfī tenets are involved in mystery; for every gradation, are mysteries never revealed.

Many of the most eminent ṣūfīs have been men of piety and of learning, whose self-denial attracted a fame they sought not; others have cloaked themselves in humility to attain greatness, and fled from observation only to attract it.

To fame and power, is no path however rugged, into which man will not enter.

Traces of ṣūfī-doctrine exist in every country; in the theories of ancient Greece; in the modern philosophies of Europe; in the dream of the ignorant and of the learned; in the shade of ease and in the hardship of the desert.

In place of the usages of religion, ṣūfīs adopt the wild doctrines of their teacher; and embark on a sea of doubt under a murshid whom they deem superior to all other men and worthy of confidence that is only adoration.

Some deny evil, saying:—

> "Good is all that proceedeth from God."
>
> They exclaim:—
>
> "The writer of our destiny is a fair Writer.
> "Never wrote He that which was bad."

All things in the world, they regard as the type and as the power of God. They see:—

> His beauty in the rose-cheek of lovely ones;
> His power in the impious daring of Fir'aun (Pharoah).

Saḥl ībn Abdu-l-lāh Shustarī saith:—

> "Revealed was the soul's secret when
> "Fir'aun, declared himself to be god."

Jalālu-d-Dīn (*b.*1207, *d.*1273) maketh 'Alī (the first of ṣūfīs) say when he was wounded by an assassin:—

> Lord of the land am I; yet with my body no concern have I.
> Me, thou hast not struck; only an instrument of God, thou art. On God, who shall avenge himself?
> Be not grieved; for to-morrow (the judgment day), thy mediator, shall I be.

---

* Sa'dī *b.* 1414, *d.* 1492.

Of Abdu-l-Ḳadir-i-Gilānī (*b.*1078, *d.*1166) Shaikh Muḥyu-d-Dīn 'Arabī (*b.* 1166, *d.* 1239) says:—

"I went to our house-top and saw all the pilgrims at 'Arafāt (near Makka).

Descending, I told my mother that I must devote myself to God; and that I wished to proceed to Baghdād to gain ma'rifat.

Weeping, my mother took eighty dīnārs; gave me half (my inheritance); made me swear never to tell a lie; and said:—

"Go my son: to God, I give thee, not till the judgment day, shall we meet."

At Hamadan, our Ḳāfila was plundered by sixty horsemen.

One asking me what I had; I replied:—

"Forty dīnārs are sewed up in my garment."

Disbelieving me, he laughed and left. Another asked me and received the same reply.

Whilst they were dividing the spoil, the Chief called me and said:—

"Boy, what property hast thou?"

I replied:—

"I have already told two of your men that I have forty dīnārs sewn in a garment."

He ordered the garment to be ripped; and found the money.

He said:—

"How camest thou so openly to declare what has, so carefully, been hidden?"

I replied:—

Because I will not be false to my mother, to whom I have promised never to conceal the truth.

Said the Chief:—

Boy, art thou at thy age so sensible of duty to thy mother, and am I at my age insensible of my duty to God?

Give me thy hand that, on it, I may swear repentance.

He did so. His followers were struck with the scene, and said:—

"Leader in guilt, thou hast been; in virtue, be the same."

They restored the spoil; and, on my hand, vowed repentance.

At this time, I was sixteen years of age.

---

To those who sought him, Uvais-i-Ḳarni said:—

"Seekest thou God? If thou dost, to me why comest thou? If thou dost not, with me, what business hast thou?"

Ḳāẓī Nūru-l-Lāth-i-Shustarī (*d.*1610) says that ṣūfīs are of two classes:—

(*a*) Mutakallim (advocate, observer) if they desire human knowledge; the usages of religion; and pursue them in the ordinary way.

(*b*) Ṣūfīs, if they practise austerity, and look to the inward purity of the soul.

After His prophets, God esteemeth none more than the ṣūfī; because his desire is (through divine grace) to raise himself from this earthly house to the heavenly; and to exchange his lowly condition for the condition of the angel.

The accomplished are :—

> the ḥukamā men of wisdom.
> „ 'ulamā „ knowledge.

These seek truth——the first by demonstration; the second by religion.

In this path to (God), are many dangers.

For false teachers and deceived seekers vainly pursue the desert vapour: and wearied return, the dupe of their own imagination.

The murshid-i-kāmil va kamāl (the perfect and excellent murshid) is rare. When he exists, to discover him is impossible.

Perfection, who shall discover, save he who is perfect?

The jewel's price, who shall tell, save the jeweller?

Hence, many miss the Path and fall into error. Deceived by appearances, they waste life in pursuit of defect, conceiving it to be perfection.

Neither austerity nor devotion can exclude shaiṭān who seeketh Zāhids in the garb of religion. The only ṯilism whereby the good can be distinguished from the bad is ma'rifat.

Said Muḥammad :—

> The irrational zāhid, God accepteth not;
> By pious fools, my back hath been broken.

From alarm at persecuting tyrants, ṣūfīs have often pretended to be of no particular faith.

Thus they confess not their religion; and to disclose the mystery thereof—is the deepest sin.

The murshid instructeth the murīd how to restore the inward man :—

| by purifying | the spirit. | by enlightening | the head. |
|---|---|---|---|
| „ cleansing | „ heart. | „ anointing | „ soul. |

Then the murshid avereth :—

> that the murīd's desire shall be accomplished; that his despicable qualities shall be changed into laudable qualities; that he shall understand the revelation, the stages and the grades of exaltation——till he reacheth the ineffable joy of beholding God.

If the murshid be not perfect and excellent, the murīd wasteth his time.

He will end by being an impostor, or by regarding all ṣūfīs alike and condemning them.

He will seek relief in infidelity, doubting all that he hath heard or read; and regarding as fable the accounts of holy men who have reached ḥaḳiḳat.

The murshid is sometimes :—

(*a*) the dupe of his own imagination.
(*b*) the wilful deluder of his own followers.

He desireth to abolish the form of religion ; alloweth no name to come between him and God, and yet desireth to come between all other men and God ; destroyeth names reverenced by men in order to substitute his own name.

Without the murshid, no murīd can advance ; his advance is in proportion to his faith* (in the murshid).

Ḥasan Ṣabāḥ † Shaikhu-l-Jabal (*b.* 1071, *d.* 1124) and his descendants were of the order of bāṭiniya. They filled Persia with murders ; and by their mysterious power, made monarchs tremble.

---

God is ever renewing all the matter and the form of the universe. Not a leaf sprouteth, not a sparrow falleth, not a thought occureth, without His impulsion.

Thus are muslims brought face to face with evil in a way that Europeans cannot realise.

God is the only real agent, though He sometimes fashioneth some (Iblīs, Ḳābil, Nimrūd, Fir'aun, Abū Jahl) to be His agents of wrath.

Equally with Mūsā̤, was Fir'aun, an agent of God's will ; and he bewailed the impulsion that made him oppose Mūsā̤.

The 'Ārif (the knower of ma'rifat) admiteth the ability to choose good. Not, like Iblīs, doth he cast his sins upon God ; but with Ādam, crieth :—

" O Lord, black our faces we have made."

The 'Ārif saith :—

God created all things, good and evil ; but evil, is non-existence, a departure from the Only Absolute existence. In relation to God, evil is naught.

If evil-passion exist not, how can there be control ? If affliction exist not, how can there be patience ?

The jail is the criminal's masjid making him cry to God.

The ṣūfī disregardeth outward forms and rites. God judgeth not as man judgeth ; at the heart, He looketh.

Jalālu-d-Dīn-i-Rūmī (vi. Prologue) saith :—

If with good and evil, a lover be befouled——these, regard not ; his aspiration, regard.

---

* The Murtaẓā̤ Shāhī (an order of ṣūfīs) make in clay an image of the murshid.

This, the murīd keeps to prevent him from wandering ; and to bring him into identity with the murshid.

† The Historian of the Crusades calls him " the old man of the mountain."

From his name, (Al Ḥasan) is derived our word " assassin."

See Asiatic Researches, vol. xi, p. 423 ; Malcolm's History of Persia, vol. i, p. 395 ; vol. ii, p 416.

The ṣūfī practiseth voluntary poverty, mortification, obedience, renunciation of the world; and the precepts of the gospel as to forsaking family, position, wealth, for religion sake.

All naught, he maketh save God: and giveth life to this non-existent universe by regarding it as permeated with God's presence.

Paradise, hell, all the dogmas of religion are allegories,—the spirit whereof he alone knows.

He longeth for death; for then he returneth to God whence he emanated, and in Him findeth annihilation.

On the unity of God, he meditateth to attain spiritual perfection; and unification with God.

This union, none can without faiẓu-l-lāh (God's grace) reach; but to those who fervently ask Him, He refuseth not aid.

The Ḳurān and the Ḥadīṣ represent:—

(*a*) God as having created the world once for all, and as now removed to the highest heaven, leaving His creatures, by their own free will, according to the light given by prophets, to work out their salvation.

(*b*) God as the being ever working in His creatures, the sun of all existence, the fulness of life, whereby all things move and exist—omnipresent, dwelling in, and communing with, each soul.

The ṣūfīs (men of heart; men looking behind the veil; inward men) developed the Greek mysticism popularised by—

| | | | |
|---|---|---|---|
| (*a*) Faryābī | *d.* 954. | (*c*) Ghazzālī | *d.* 1111. |
| (*b*) Abū Ālī Sīnā | „ 1037. | (*d*) Ibn Rashīd | „ 1199. |

and made:—

i. God to be the One, the Necessary Being, the only Reality, the Truth, the Infinite, the First Cause (source of all action, good and evil).

ii. The world of phenomena and of man—

Not being which like a mirror reflects being; and, by borrowing particles of being, rises to "contingent being" (which shares existence and non-existence).

In man, the spark of being is identical with the Infinite Being; but, while he is in "contingent being," he is weighed down and held apart from Being by "Not-being," whence evil proceedeth.

In this state, he requires laws and creeds to restrain him. Thus "Not-being" is when wanted something, and nothing when not wanted, and so do the ṣūfīs avoid the ill consequences of their theory.

The muslim doctrine of jabr (compulsion) driveth some to fanatical deeds; some to cry ḳismat; some to regard the action and the existence of the Universe as the manifestation of God's energy.

By divine illumination, man seeth the world, including man's self, to be an illusion, non-existent (and therefore evil).

He trieth to shake off this "Not-being," to efface himself, and to be united with the real Being, the Truth, that is, God.

The true course is to ignore self; to be passive that God may work. Then will God's light and grace enter the heart and draw man to Truth and unite him with the One.

---

The curl, the down, the mole, and the brow are the world now in jamāl (beauty), now in jalāl (terrible majesty).

The cheek and the curl are the types of mercy and of beauty; of vengeance and of majesty.

The mysteries of ecstatic vision cannot be interpreted by words, only by types and licenses in the mystic states of:—

(a) annihilation, effacement.
(b) intoxication.
(c) love's violence.

Only those who know these states comprehend the meaning of these words.

The curl enchaineth hearts; beareth souls to and fro; plundereth the kārvāns of reason; and never resteth.

With its perfume, Ādam's clay became leavened. Thus, the material world.

The down is the vestibule of almightiness, a verdant growth in the spirit-world, the well-spring of life, the hidden secret, the first plural emanation, that veileth the face of unity, the world of pure spirits that are nearest to God and the decoration of souls.

The mole is the point of unity, single yet embracing all phenomena. Fixed and stable, is the point of unity; but the heart is disquieted by emotions, illumined by epiphanies and darkened by the veil of plurality in the masjid, now in the inward and now in the outward, now in the hell of lust, now in the heaven of zauḳ.

It is the centre, whence is drawn the circle of two worlds; and whence is Ādam's heart and soul.

Unity (the mole) and the heart must be one. Which is the original, which the reflection?

Sometimes is the heart:—

| | | |
|---|---|---|
| sick | like His intoxicating eye. | a masjid of the inward and sometimes a masjid of the outward. |
| fluttering | „ curl. | |
| gleaming | „ face. | a hell of the inward and sometimes a heaven. |
| dark | „ mole. | |

The cheek is the theatre of divine bounty, the divine essence in respect of the manifestations of its names and qualities; the manifestation of the seven (beauteous) names (of God); and is as the seven verses (of the Fātiḥa). Know His face and down,—verily thou knowest plurality and unity.

The eye betokeneth frowns and coquetry, now holding aloof from its slave, now granting union. From it, proceed languishing intoxication, burning, plundering, and aching of heart; every corner thereof is a wine-shop.

Of His eye and lip, ask an embrace,—one saith nay; the other, yes.

The lip is the essence of being, the healing of the sick heart, the clothing of all souls. By His lip, souls are beside themselves, and compassion revealeth itself.

When, on His eye and on His lip, the world reflecteth, it giveth itself up to the worship of wine.

Beauty is Truth manifested and present; 'tis the beam of the light of spirits; 'tis the greatest of signs.*

Wine, the torch and beauty, are epiphanies of Truth.

Wine is the rapture that maketh the ṣūfī beside himself at the manifestation of the emanation of the Beloved.

By it, this one becometh the philosopher, the traditionist, the righteous one, and the lover (of God).

By it, that one swalloweth at one draught the cup, the wine-house, the sāḳī, and the wine-drinker; and yet open remaineth his mouth.

O ocean-heart! O mighty drinker! well done!

Drunken are :—

| | |
|---|---|
| reason. | the air. |
| the angels. | „ revolving earth. |
| „ soul. | „ reeling heaven. |

Better is the intoxicated than the self-righteous.

The wine of dying to self, drink; from thyself, thyself set free.

Wine is the transport and the light of the Ārif; the soul of that flashing light that in the consuming bush, Mūsā beheld.

The "veil of darkness" betokeneth dwelling in iniquity. Who is veiled knoweth his wickedness.

The "veil of light" betokeneth the practice of good deeds. Who is thus veiled, knoweth not his wickedness, being clouded by his self-righteousness.

Who are they that have lost their labour, and in life mistaken their aim?
They who think that what they do is right. (Ḳuran, xvii, 103.)

The tavern-haunter is one freed from self; one desolate in a desolate place (other than God, absent), headless, footless, neither the faithful nor the kāfir. One who, losing both head and foot, in every strain that he heareth from the minstrel, is seized with wajd from the hidden world.

Not of these words and sound, but of precious mystery, is every note of that mystic song.

The idol is the evidence of love and of unity. Idol-worshipping is making one; in it what is evil proceedeth from other than God.

The girdle is the emblem of obedience.

---

* The Ḳurān, liii, 18.

## Shuyūkhiyat (being a Shaikh).

VI. 5.

After the rank of being a prophet, no rank is higher than the being a deputy for a prophet, to call men, by the path of Muḥammad, to God.

The word shaikh signifieth being a khalīfa; hence its degree is excellent, as, in respect of the shaikhs of ṣūfīs, is in the ḥadīs stated.

The shaikh's purpose is to cleanse, from the rust of lust and of nature, the murīd's heart, so that in it, by attractions and inclinations, may be reflected the rays of the beauty of unity and the glory of eternity; so that, by beholding them, his eyes may be attracted; and so that, thus, divine love may rest in his sincere heart.

The rules of being a shaikh are fifteen.

1. The purifying of resolution and the searching for the cause.

First he should seek out of himself that the cause be not—

The desire of precedence.
" " being a shaikh.
" " being followed.

wherein are born the lusts of sons of Ādam; this he should do, though he may see his own lust at rest and the fires of nature extinguished.

When he seeth some of the seekers, with sincerity of desire, turn to him, and from him seek guidance, hastily he should not be their director, but should delay till, with penitence, true submission, and supplication to God, he discovereth the truth of the state and with certainty knoweth what God's purpose is to him in regard to their charge.

If he see that the charge of the crowd of the seekers is trial, he knoweth caution to be necessary, and is engaged in comprehending the hidden cause.

If he see that God's purpose is that he should instruct the seekers, he followeth God's order.

2. The knowledge of capacity.

The shaikh must regard the capacity of the murīd. If, in him, he see capacity for treading the path of those near to God, he inviteth him with skill, and by elucidating the states of him who is near to God.

If he see that he has not much capacity for the path of the pious, he inviteth him by admonishing, by inciting, by instructing, and by mentioning paradise and hell.

The shaikh urgeth the capable ones to deeds of the heart (murāḳiba, observance of mystery, distinguishing thoughts), and to pure devotion.

Thus, if he see the murīd's welfare in abandoning the world's chattels, or in holding to them, he ordereth as may be suitable to his state.

Who acquireth not knowledge of the different kinds of capacity, and discrimination as to the forms of understanding, hath no true power over the murīd.

3. Being pure (having no lot or part) in respect of the murīd's property.

The shaikh must show no greed for the property, or for the service, of the murīd. With a gratification, he should not make vain his instructing and directing, which are the best of alms (for God).

When, by divine information or by true knowledge, he knoweth that, for the general good, he should take the property, he may do so.

If the murīd desire at once to give up his property, the shaikh may accept; because, in return for it, he can give to the murīd that state (for which he is fit) which is the cause of tranquillity of heart.

If he knoweth that the murīd will look with regret at his property, he will allow him to spend a portion.

Once, one of Junīd's murīds wished to give up all his property. Junīd refused saying:—

> Keep what is sufficient and thereon subsist; the surplus, give. For, after the expending of all thy property, safe from the demands of thy desire, I shall not be.

4. Offering.

Delights of offering and of severing attachments are incumbent on the shaikh, so that, by observing their effects, the sincerity, and the conviction of the murīd may be greater; and the severing of attachments, easier; and the desire of celibacy, overpowering.

By offering, becometh sifted the murīd's suspicion as to the shaikh's state, and, as to the truth of his sway.

According to necessity, he should distribute the excess among the poor.

5. Concordance of deed with word in invitation.

When the shaikh wisheth to invite the murīd to a practice, or to an abandonment, it is necessary that, in his own state, this (practice or abandonment) should be evident, so that, without suspicion, the murīd may accept.

Upon persons, the mere word has no great effect.

According to the ḥadīs̤ the murīd should choose faḳr (poverty), which is the wealth of ṣūfī,ism, and the condition of ṭarīḳat (the path to God), although to him, poverty and riches are, as 'Umar hath said, one.

6. Compassion for the weak.

When, in the murīd, the shaikh seeth weakness of resolution; and knoweth that against lust and the abandoning of accustomed things, he hath no true resolution, he should display kindness.

To the limit of his power, he should abridge the austerities, so that the murīd may not shun him ; and so that, in time, and by intercourse, he may gain kinship with fuḳarā (faḳīrs).

Possibly, after resolution shall have been incited in him, he may gradually reach from the abyss of license (to disregard austerities) to the height of resolution.

Once one of the sons of favour (a rich man) joined the society of Aḥmad Ḳalānsī ; and severed himself from the world.

In him, Aḥmad found a weakness, whereupon, when a few dirhams were gained he used to purchase for him bread, round cake, roast meat, sweetmeat ; and to say :—

> " Out from the world's favour and from association therewith, this man has come; then fit it is to tread with him the path of compassion; and not to forbid him delights.

7. The purifying of speech.

Pure of the pollution of desire must be the shaikh's speech, so that its effect upon the murīd may be seen.

On the heart the effect of speech is like to seed : if the seed be bad, there is no fruit ; iniquity of speech is in entering into, and associating with, desire.

Into speech desire falleth :—

(*a*) either for attracting the hearts of hearers, which is unfit for the state of shaikhs.
(*b*) or from pride of himself on account of the beauty of his own speech, which (in the opinion of men of ḥaḳīḳat) is pure sin.

With the murīd the shaikh should winnow his speech from the pollution of desire ; should plant it in the heart's soil, and entrust it to God to be preserved from the bird of forgetfulness and from the power of shaiṭān.

On account of the pride of self, sincerity appeareth not save by observing the lights of God's excellence and the effects of His boundless favours,—in the splendour of which lights the glance of lust becometh dimmed ; and the darkness of pride, extinguished. Then in the buffeting of the waves of the ocean of perpetual bounty, he regardeth his own existence, much more his speech,—less than a drop.

8. Exalting the heart to God in the state of speech.

When the shaikh wisheth to speak to the murīd, he should turn his heart towards God, and from Him ask sense, that he may be the perfecter of time and the comprehender of the welfare of the hearer's state ; that his tongue may be the speaker of God ; and that his speech may be true in rendering benefit.

Thus they say :—

> In the hearing of his own speech he was equal to the other hearers.

Although sooner than the spectators on the shore, the diver in the sea collecteth pearl-shells and bringeth with himself the pearl, yet, as soon as he issueth from the sea and openeth the shell, he is only equal to the spectators on the shore.

9. Speaking ambiguously.

When in the murīd, the shaikh seeth something detestable ; and wisheth to admonish him thereto, so that he may strive to remove it, he should not speak fluently and conspicuously.

Nay, ambiguously he should cast the matter before the assembly, that to its object, its tenour may lead.

Thus if, in the murīd's soul, he should see :—

i. a pride of his own deeds and states.
ii. a claim to nearness (to God) and to perfection.
iii. a crookedness and a turning from the path of firmness.

He should relate to the assembly, in respect of it, an ḥadiṣ, or a tale, of shaikhs ; and briefly should hint at the abomination, so that those present may be profited.

In this way, counsel is nearest to courtesy and to ḥikmat.

10. Preserving the mysteries of the murid.

The shaikh should preserve the mysteries of the murīd, and not reveal his manifestations and miracles. By speaking to him in private, he should render them contemptible, saying :—

Although circumstances like these are the favour of God, yet, expecting and looking for them, is the cause of the murīd's path being closed.

In thanks for them, they should make return ; from them, take off their glance ; and, in observing the Benefactor (God) through observing His favour, be engaged.

Otherwise, in loss they remain.

11. Pardoning the murīd's blunder.

If, in the murīd, the shaikh should see a defect in abandoning a service, or in neglecting a rule,——it, he should forgive him ; and thereto by kindness, by courtesy, by indulgence, and by grace incite him.

12. Descending from (passing over) his own right.

Of the murīd, the shaikh should have no hope, although it is his right ; and to his right, the keeping of the murid is a most important rule. But the shaikh's expectation of it is not approved ; and his descending from his right is best.

Waḳī says :—

Once, in Egypt, with an assembly of fuḳarā, I was in a masjid, where Abu Bakr Wirāḳ stood before a pillar and prayed.

I said to myself, when the shaikh finisheth his prayer, I will salute him. When he had returned the salām of the prayer, he came and preceded me in salutation.

I said :—"Best it would have been if I had first stood in respect."

The shaikh said :—"I have never been bound with the expectation that any one should do me honouring."

13. The allowing of the murīd's rights.

In sickness and in health, the shai<u>kh</u> should not delay in allowing the rights of the companions.

14. The distributing of times in respect of <u>kh</u>ilvat (retirement) and of jilvat (rapid circular motions).

The shai<u>kh</u>'s time should not be plunged in intercourse with the people. His power of ḥāl, his perfection, his tamkīn, and his presence (with others) should not be the excuse.

With perfection of ḥāl, and of tamkīn, Muḥammad was not, all day, in men's society. For asking the aid of God's bounty, of mercy, he chose <u>kh</u>ilvat; for diffusing the mercy on the people, he chose society.

For the shai<u>kh</u> is necessary a special <u>kh</u>ilvat, wherein he may be employed :—

(*a*) in portions of devotion.
(*b*) in humbling himself and in supplicating God for his own sake and for others.
(*c*) in asking aid so that his <u>kh</u>ilvat may be secure from being employed with people.

By the opposition of man's composition, displaying assiduity to God is difficult; and languor in deeds is expected, and at such times, it is proper that he should pass his time in society and thereby dispel that languor.

Again, through shauḳ and ẓauḳ, he may incline to <u>kh</u>ilvat and to devotion; men may be benefited by his nature; and he may escape from languor.

15. The increasing of the works of supererogation (nawāfil).

The boiling of his ḥāl should not hinder him from repairing time with good deeds. For, with perfection of ḥāl, assiduous in respect to nawāfil, was Muḥammad :—

in the namāz-ī-tahajjud, prayer of midnight.
" " chāsht, prayer between sunrise and noon.
" " zawāl, prayer after noon.
" ruza,-i-taṭawwū, fasting during good deeds.
" other nawāfil.

At night so long used he to stand in prayer that his auspicious feet became swollen.

---

## The behaviour of the Murid to the Shai<u>kh</u>.

VI. 4.

For the murīd, in the society of the shai<u>kh</u>, the observance of manners (whereby love of hearts is attracted) is most important.

When he is possessed of manners, he taketh in love a place in the shai<u>kh</u>'s heart; and is agreeable to God's sight. Because, with mercy, favour, and care, God ever looketh at the hearts of His own friends (the darvīshes).

Then by dwelling in the shai<u>kh</u>'s heart, the constant blessings of God's mercy, and of His endless bounty, comprehend his existence; and the shai<u>kh</u>'s acceptance becometh his mark of the acceptance of God, of Muḥammad, and of all shai<u>kh</u>s.

Save by manners, one cannot gain the rights due to the shaikh's instruction.

The honouring of 'Ulamā and of shaikhs is a great right, the non-performance whereof is exceeding disobedience as is stated in the ḥadīṣ. "Whoever performeth not the shaikh's rights is defective in the performance of God's rights."

The shaikh, in the midst of the murīds, is as Muḥammad in the midst of his aṣḥāb (companions); for inviting the people to follow Muḥammad, he is in the Inn of the Khalīfa.

There are fifteen rules of conduct, which it is necessary the mūrīd should observe.

1. Perfect faith in the shaikh as regards his instructing, directing, and purifying mūrīds.

If he regard another more perfect, love's bond becometh weakened; and the shaikh's words affect him little.

For the means whereby the shaikh's words and actions take effect is—love.

As his love is greater, so is his readiness for the shaikh's instruction greater.

2. Perfect resolve in respect to attendance upon the shaikh.

To himself, he should say :—

> Save by attendance on the shaikh, no door can be opened. Then at his threshold I will either surrender my life, or reach my object.

Its mark is that, by the shaikh's driving and rejecting, he turneth not away.

Abū 'Uṣmān-i-Ḥairi went to Nīshāpūr with the intention of visiting Abū Ḥafaẓ Ḥadād.

When he beheld the light of his holiness, he was attracted : and asked permission to stay. Abū Ḥafaẓ drove him away, saying :—

> Not in our assembly, shouldest thou sit.

Abū 'Uṣmān retreated till he was hidden from sight : then he resolved to dig a pit at the house-door; to sit therein and therefrom not to come forth till Abū Ḥafaẓ should consent to receive him.

When Abū Ḥafaẓ beheld such proof of sincerity of desire, he called him, welcomed him, made him of the number of his special companions; married him to his daughter; and appointed him khalīfa.

On the death of the shaikh, thirty years after, he, Abū 'Uṣmān, sat as shaikh.

3. Being obedient to the shaikh's sway.

In respect to his soul and his wealth, the murīd should admit the shaikh's sway; and be obedient to his orders. For, save this, his object is not reached; nor his sincerity known.

4. The abandoning of opposition.

Neither outwardly nor inwardly, should the murīd oppose the shaikh's authority. When, on the shaikh's part, something becometh difficult to him ; and its truth is not revealed to him he should remember the tale of Mūsā and Khizr.

Despite his power of prophecy, his knowledge, and his great love, Mūsā refused obedience to Khizr's absolute commands; but when the mysteries and their hikmat were revealed, Mūsā returned to obedience.

5. The rejection of his own will.

The murīd should begin no matter of faith or of the world, wholly or partly, without reference to the shaikh's will.

Without the shaikh's permission, he should not :—

| | |
|---|---|
| eat, | take, |
| drink, | give, |
| sleep, | look. |

Without the shaikh's appointing, he should not begin :—

(*a*) fasting,
(*b*) breaking the fast
(*c*) many of the nawāfil such as—attaching one's self to precepts, to zikr, to meditation, and to murākiba.

---

One night, Muhammad passed by Abū Bakr's tent; and heard him reading with low voice the prayer of tahajjud.

Afterwards he passed by 'Umar's tent; and heard him reading with loud voice the prayer of the Kurān.

In the morning, he asked Abū Bakr :—
With low voice why readest thou the tahajjud !

Abū Bakr replied :—
Those who desire salvation, hear it.

He asked 'Umar.
With loud voice why readest thou?

'Umar replied :—
To drive away Shaitān.

Muhammad said :—
Read ye neither with low voice nor with loud voice. Nay, preserve ye the middle way.

This showeth that, with the existence of a shaikh (Muhammad), to be one who doeth aught alone is not proper.

6. The observing of the shaikh's thoughts.

To no matter, which is abhorrent to the shaikh's heart, should the murīd proceed; nor, having regard to the shaikh's excellence of character and of kindness, should he consider it a small matter.

7. Referring to the shaikh's knowledge in the explanation of dreams.

In the explanation of dreams, whether in sleepiness or in wakefulness, he should refer to the shaikh's knowledge.

For, possibly, the source of that dream may be an evil desire, whereto his knowledge reacheth not, and wherefrom injury may arise. He should present it to the shaikh, that with it, the shaikh may become acquainted.

8. Purity of custom in respect to the shaikh's speech.

The murīd should recognise the shaikh's tongue, as the link of God's speech; and should know for certain that he is the speaker of God not of lust. He should regard the shaikh's heart as a boisterous sea, filled with the pearl of 'ilm (knowledge), and with the jewel of ma'rifat, which, at times, from the furious blowing of the winds of favour of the Eternal, casts some of those jewels on the shore of the tongue.

Thus, he should ever be expectant and present that he be not excluded from the advantages arising from the shaikh's speech.

Between the shaikh's speech and his own state, he should seek the suitable way; and with himself commune.

At God's door, with the tongue of readiness, he should seek rectitude of state; according to his readiness, arriveth an address from the hidden.

With hypocrisy and the manifestation of his own 'ilm and ma'rifat, he should not come; for thus he putteth far from himself his desire and becometh deaf to the shaikh's speech.

9. Lowering the voice.

In the shaikh's society, the murīd should not raise his voice; for the doing so is the abandoning of good manners and the removing of the veil of dignity.

In the Ḳurān is reproved both the raising of the voice and the lowering of it beyond limit.

10. Forbidding nafs from ranging at large.

Neither by word nor by deed, should the murīd tread the path of mirth with the shaikh. By mirth, the veil of reverence becometh rent; and the way of grace, closed.

He should say :—

O my Sayyid ! O my Maulā !

At first, the ṣaḥāba (companions) used irreverently to say to Muḥammad :—

O Muḥammad ! or O Aḥmad !

For their reproof, descended a divine address ; and they afterwards said :—

O sent one of God (the salutation and the safety of God be on thee) !

In the shaikh's presence, he should not cast down his prayer-mat save at the time of prayer; should in samā' keep himself from moving and from za'ḳa (calling out) ; and should (so long as power of refraining and of containing himself shall be) keep himself from moving and from laughing.

11. Knowledge of times of speech.

When, on an important matter of faith or of the world, the murīd wisheth to speak to the shaikh,—he should first ascertain whether he hath leisure. Not hastily nor abruptly, should he approach the shaikh.

Before speaking, he should display penitence ; and, for grace of manner of speech, should (as the Ḳurān saith) seek aid from Muḥammad.

With much questioning, men importuned Muḥammad; and wearied him. Then descended a divine address whereby concord with hypocrites was severed.

12. Preserving the limit of his own respect.

In questioning the shaikh, he should guard his own respect ; and, from his own state, should not discover every state (of the shaikh's) that may be closed to him. On a matter, that is neither his maḳām nor his ḥāl, he should not speak.

Of the necessary matters of his own state, he should not ask much. The profitable word is that which they utter to the degree of the hearer's understanding; the profitable question, to the degree of the hearer's rank.

13. The concealing of the shaikh's mysteries.

Every state (of miracles, dreams, &c., &c.) which the shaikh keepeth concealed, and of which the murīd learneth—for its divulging, he should not seek permission.

Because in concealing it, the shaikh hath seen the profit of faith and of the world whereto his 'ilm reacheth not; and in revealing it, great calamity may be caused.

14. The revealing of his own mysteries to the shaikh.

From the shaikh, the murīd should not conceal his mysteries. Every miracle, and gift that God may have bestowed on him, he should plainly present to the shaikh's judgment.

15. Speaking of the shaikh to the degree of the hearer's understanding.

That matter wherein is un-intelligibility, and whereto the hearer's understanding reacheth not, the murīd should not utter.

From such speech, no profit ariseth; and possibly the hearer's faith in the shaikh may become languid.

If the murīd observe this collection of rules of manner, his object (from the acquisition of the splendours of God's mercy and from the descending of His boundless blessings) becometh, by means of the shaikh's society, revealed openly and secretly.

## The customs of the men of the Khānkāh (convent).

V. 5.

The men of the khānkāh form two parties—

- i the travellers.
- ii „ dwellers.

When ṣūfīs intend to alight at a khānkāh they try to reach it before the afternoon. If, for some reason, the afternoon cometh, they alight at the masjid or in some corner.

The next day, at sunrise, they proceed to the khānkāh and make :—

- (*a*) two rak'ats (of prayer) as salutation to the spot.
- (*b*) salām (peace-wishing).
- (*c*) haste to embracing and to hand-shaking those present.

The sunnat is that, to the dwellers they should offer some food or something as a present.

In speech, they make no presumption; so long as they ask not, they speak not.

For three days, for the business that they may have, beyond the visiting of the living and of the dead,—they go not from the khānkāh until the inward form, from the alteration caused by the accidents of travel, returneth, to its own ease, and they become ready for the interview with the shaikhs.

When from the khānkah, they wish to go out they prefer their request to the men of the khānkāh.

When three days have passed, if they resolve to stay, they seek service whereby they may stay.

If their time be engaged in devotion, no service is necessary.

The dwellers of the khānkāh meet the travellers with :—

- (*a*) tarḥīb (ye are welcome).
- (*b*) regard.
- (*c*) affection.
- (*d*) expansion of face (through joy).

The servant should offer light food, and be present fresh of face, sweet of speech.

If a traveller, unaccustomed to the customs of ṣūfīs, reach the khānḳāh, they should not look at him with contempt; nor should they prevent him from entering. For many of the holy and pious are ignorant of the customs of this assembly (of ṣūfīs).

If through contempt injury reach them, their heart may possibly be vexed; and its effects may injure faith and the world.

Kindliness to man is the best of manners; ill-naturedness is the result of ill nature.

If to the convent reach some one who hath no fitness therefor, him, after offering victuals, with kindness and fair words, they remove.

The dwellers of the khānḳāh form three parties:—

i. ahl-i-khidmat (men of service).
ii. „ ṣuḥbat ( „ „ society).
iii. „ khilvat ( „ „ khilvat).

The ahl-i-khidmat are "the beginners," who, out of love, come to the khānḳāh. They do them service, so that thereby they may become acceptable to the hearts of men of deeds and of stages, and may be regarded with the glance of mercy; may acquire fitness for kinship; and become a slipper out of the garment of alienation and of farness.

They gain capability of society and capacity for its advantages; and by the blessing of their society, words, deeds, and manner become bound by the bond of dignity. After that, they become worthy of khidmat.

To the old men, the passing of their time in khilvat is best.

To the youths, the house-assembly sitting in ṣuḥbat is better than khilvat, so that, with the bond of 'ilm, their lusts may (by the revealing of states, words, and deeds to those present) be bound.

Thus, has Abū Yaḳūb-i-Sūsī said.

The men of the khānḳāh have—a portion, devotion and a service; and aid each other respecting important matters of faith and of the world.

Fitness for "service" is when a person hath by outward resemblance, and inward and pure desire—acquired kinship with ṣūfīs.

Who hath not kinship with one of these two ways,—him, it is not proper to do "service"; or with him to associate except in compassion.

Because sometimes, through the exigency of human nature, issue from them things that appear ugly in the sight of people of desire and of love.

If from the khānḳāh is the allowance of their victuals; and the bequeather's condition is that they should expend the allowance on the purposes of the Lords of desire, and on the travellers of ṭarīḳat, that allowance is not lawful to the habituated, nor to that crowd that, from deeds of body, have not reached the stages of the heart.

If the khānḳāh have no bequest; and in it, be present one possessed of vision, he, according to the exigency of the time and their capacity, instructeth the murids.

If he consider it good to abandon kasb (acquisition) and to remain in beggary, he putteth them on tawakkul (reliance on God), and on the abandoning of the means (of livelihood).

If the men of the khānḳāh be a brotherhood, and no shaikh be present, they choose, as occasion demandeth, one of these three ways:

If they be of the crowd of the strong and of travellers, and resolute as to tawakkul (reliance on God), and as to patience, their sitting (in reliance) on the revealing (of God's aid) is worthy of their state.

Otherwise they should choose either kasb, or beggary, which they consider the better.

The men of the khānḳāh should, outwardly and inwardly, observe concord to each other; and should, at the time of eating, assemble at one table-cloth, so that outwardly they may not be separated; that the blessing of outward association may penetrate into the heart; that they may with each other pass life in love and purity; and may, in their heart, give no power to alloy and counterfeit (evil thoughts).

If from one to the heart of another, a foul deed should pass, they should instantly efface it; and with him not pass life in hypocrisy.

Every society, the foundation whereof is on hypocrisy and not on sincerity, giveth no result whatever.

When, outwardly to each other, they display reconciliation, and their heart is folded with hate,—hopeless is their good, and expected their destruction.

If an act of treachery appear, in it they should not persevere, but quickly for it make reparation by seeking pardon; and that pardon it is not right that the aggrieved one should withhold. For, in respect to this, promise (of blessing) hath arrived.

Outwardly and inwardly, they should strive to be in agreement with, and in equality to, each other; and to be in respect of all people free from impurity (of wrong).

Then to them may deferred paradise be hastened, and the mere promise of others be their realisation.

In the heart of the ṣūfī or of the faḳīr, how should there be the alloy and the counterfeit (of evil thought), the place of return whereof is the love of the world? By abandoning the world and turning from it, are they special and chosen.

After seeking pardon, the pardon-seeker should present victuals; just as doeth he who cometh from journeying.

Because the sinner, who, for sin, shall have come out from the circle of being present and of being collected (of the khānḳāh); and shall have entered on the journey of separation and of being hidden,—returneth not to this circle. To re-enter, it is first necessary that he should present victuals, which the ṣūfīs call gharāmat (fine).

When a person appeareth possessed of lust, with him they should strive to repel the darkness of lust by the luminosity of the heart.

The injurer and the injured both are in sin. Because if the injured one had heartily opposed the lust of the injurer, the darkness of lust would, through the luminosity of the heart, have departed.

The true ṣūfī is he who striveth in the purifying of his heart; and alloweth no pollution to abide in him.

As our allowance, may God grant us this state.

---

## On the rule of the safar (the journey).

VI. 9.

Doubtless, in subduing refractory lusts and in softening hard hearts, safar profiteth much.

The being separated from one's native land, from friends and familiar things, and the exercising of patience in calamities cause lust and nature to rest from pursuing their way; and take up from hearts the effect of hardness.

In subduing lusts, the effect of safar is not less than the effect of nawāfil, fasting and praying.

On dead skins, by tanning, the effects of purity, of softness, and of delicacy of texture appear; even so, by the tanning of safar, and by the departure of natural corruption and innate roughness, appear the purifying softness of devotion and change from obstinacy to faith.

Hence the master of sharī'at (Muḥammad) hath incited to safar, although to safar, is not limited the acquisition of the objects of the seekers of ḥaḳīḳat and of ṭarīḳat.

For there have been shaikhs who have, neither at the beginning nor at the end, made safar; but God's grace hath been their aid; and the noose of attraction hath drawn them from the lowest to the highest stage, and conveyed them to the stage of being a shaikh, the master of instruction.

Most shaikhs have made safar,—some in the beginning, for the sake of receiving profit; some at the end, for giving profit; and some both in the beginning and at the end, wherein they have regarded their own welfare of season and of ḥāl.

Ibrāhīm Khwāṣṣ used not to stay more than forty days in a city; because in this course, he regarded his welfare of ḥāl and of tawakkul.

With 'Īsā (Christ), the ṣūfīs are associated, because, during the whole course of His life, He was in safar; and for the safety of His faith, never stayed in a place.

---

Whoever maketh safar must observe twelve rules:—

1. The advancing of proper resolution, and the establishing of honoured purposes—

   (a) The acquiring of 'ilm (knowledge).

   (b) The meeting of shaikhs and of brothers.

   Because, on meeting men of ṣalāḥ and obtaining a glance from the Lords of prosperity, many advantages accrue to seekers of ṭarīḳat.

He may be worthy of a happiness-giver's glance; and therefrom he may take up advantages of faith and of the world.

In respect of the special ones, not far is this sense.

In the glance of some serpents, God hath established a special quality whereby he, on whom they glance, becometh destroyed. Wonder is it if, in the glance of His own special ones, God should have placed a virtue whereby they give the seeker on whom they glance life and happiness according to his capacity!

In the masjid of Khif at Minā, Shaikh Ziyā,u-d-Dīn Abū-n-Najībwas making the ṭawāf; at all he glanced; and in inquiring as to, and reflecting upon, their state made excess.

They said :—

What seekest thou?

He said :—

Slaves of God there are whose glance giveth happiness; their glance, I seek.

(*c*) The cutting asunder from familiar things and the swallowing the bitterness of separation from brothers and dear friends.

For patience, in separation from one's abode and friends, is worthy of many benefits.

(*d*) The revealing of the hidden treasure of the soul's state; and the expelling its decorations and claims.

Because many reprehensible qualities (which, being rested in their purpose, are concealed in lusts)—become, revealed, in safar, through farness from accustomed things.

Thus if at the khānkah (or at his abode), he see not (by reason of his rest with desire) a perturbation in his nafs, he thinketh that in him are existent, patience and rizā.

When, in safar, calamities become continuous; and from his soul, a passion or an abomination appeareth, he knoweth that he hath not these two qualities. Up, he riseth in search of them; and the claim of possessing them vanisheth.

(*e*) Solitude and abandoning the acceptance (of the people).

The breeze of the ḥāl of the master of ḥāl who dwelleth in a corner reacheth the soul of the true ones and of the seekers of that corner; and he becometh the ḳibla of prosperity and the master of the people's acceptance.

This state is, for travellers of ṭarīḳat, the source of trial; and, to those arrived at the stage, the mark of being chosen.

For travellers (who are afflicted with this calamity of trial) the journeying for solitude and for the abandoning of acceptance (of the people) is of the requisites (of safar).

Because the stage of acceptance (of the people) is the slipping place of travellers; here, do their feet slip; here, do they turn their face from God to the people—except the person, whom the favour of the Eternal aideth; and who avoideth that abode, and goeth elsewhere, so that, preserved from this calamity, he may remain.

(*f*) The reading of verses of singularity and unity of God from the books of the world and from souls; and reading the signs of ḳudrat (power) and of ḥikmat (God's mystery) and the wonders of created and destined things—so that thereby amplitude may appear to the power of thought; and proofs to the perfection of ḳudrat and of ḥikmat increase (in number).

2. Making safar with a friend.

In safar, calamities (which every one in solitude cannot bear) occur. Hence is necessary a friend who may aid.

Some of the strong, having power of endurance against afflictions, have in solitude made safar, yet to every one it is not easy.

3. Of the party (who make together safar) making one amīr, so that all shall obey him as in the Ḥadīṣ.

Greater is the capacity of power of that one who, in austerity, piety, liberality, and in compassion is greater.

It is related that Abū 'Abdu-l-lāh-i-Marūzī desired to make safar. His companionship, Abū 'Alī-i-Rabāṭī asked. Abū 'Abdu-l-lāh said :—

Only on the condition that thou be Amīr or I.

Abū 'Alī replied :—

Be thou Amīr.

Abū 'Abdu-l-lāh took up his road-provisions; and on his head placed his load.

One night, in the desert, it rained. All night Abu 'Abdu-l-lāh stood holding his blanket over Abū 'Alī to preserve him from the rain.

When Abū 'Alī said :—

Do not.

Abū Abdu-l-lāh used to say :—

"I am Amīr; obedience on thy part is necessary."

Whoever in power hath his glance over many followers; and hath the desire for rule or for the acquisition of lust's desires,——his is no portion in ṣūfī,ism.

4. The bidding farewell to brothers. He should, as Muḥammad ordered, bid farewell to the brothers (of the khānḳāh); and on the brothers, it is obligatory that they should pray for him.

For thus, when bidding farewell to travellers, did Muḥammad pray.

5. The bidding farewell to the stage (of sojourning).

When the traveller taketh up his chattels, he should perform two rak'ats of prayer; and with them bid farewell.

In the Ḥadīṣ is a tale by Anas bin Mālik that Muḥammad never alighted at a stage without performing, at the time of departure, two rak'ats of prayer, after which, he used to pray :—

O God, increase my piety; pardon my sins; turn me towards good——just as Thou wishest.

6. When he wisheth to ride his steed, camel, litter, or ship,——he should say :—

Praise be to God who made subdued to us this steed. In the name of God. God is great. I depend upon God; save with God, the great and powerful, is neither power nor command. Thou art the rider of all backs; and the aider of all matter.

7. From the stage, he should start early in the morning on the fifth day (Thursday), because Ka'b-i-Mālik relateth that, on that day, Muḥammad generally began his safar and despatched his troops.

8. When he cometh near to the stage, he should say :—

O God of the skies, of those that increase; of earth, of those that decrease: of Shaiṭān, of those that mislead; of the wind, of those that blow; of water, of those that flow! O God, I pray for the good of this stage and of its people; with Thee, I take shelter from the evil of this stage and of its people.

9. Salutation to the stage.

When he alighteth, he should, by way of salutation to the stage , offer two rak'at of prayer.

10. The arranging of the articles of safar.

With himself, he should keep the staff, the water-holder, and the girdle ; because their association with him is the sunnat. Abū Sa'īd-ī-Khazarī relateth that Muḥammad, going from Madīna to Makka, thus ordered.

11. When he reacheth a city whereat he wisheth to stop and from afar casteth on it his glance, he should make salutation to the living and to the dead ; should read some of the Ḳurān ; should send the blessing thereof as a present to them ; and should utter this prayer ;—

O God ! in it bestow upon us good rest and fair allowance.

12. Before entering the city, he should, if possible, bathe ; because when Muḥammad wished to enter Makka, he used first to bathe.

---

## Samā' (the song, the circular dance of darvishes).

V. 9.

Of the number of most laudable ṣūfī-mysteries, denied by outward 'ulamā, one is the assembly for :—

(a) the samā' (hearing) of the ghinā (song) and ilḥān (lilt).
(b) the summoning of the ḳawwāl (singer).

The reason of denial is that this custom is innovation, for in the time :—

| | |
|---|---|
| of Muḥammad | Of the 'ulamā |
| „ the ṣaḥāba | „ „ ancient shaikhs |
| „ „ tābi'īn | |

this was not the custom.

Some of the modern shaikhs have established the custom ; and, since it is not opposed to the sunnat, held it laudable.

Samā' is the comprehender of three benefits :—

1. To the soul and the heart of the companions of austerity and the Lords of strife (against sin),—weariness, sadness, ḳabẓ, and despair appear on account of many deeds. Then, for the repelling of this calamity, ' modern shaikhs have made a spiritual composition out of the samā ' of sweet sounds, harmonious melodies and verses desire-exciting ; and made them eager for it at the time of need.

2. Through the manifestation and the power of nafs, stoppings and veilings (of God's glory) occur to the holy traveller. Thus, the increase of ḥāl closeth ; and, through length of separation (from God), the violence of desire (for God) decreaseth.

Then, by hearing sweet lilts and ghazals (describing his ḥāl), that strange ḥāl (which moveth the claim of desire, and exciteth love's contest) appeareth to the hearer; the stoppings and the veilings arise and depart from before him ; and the door of increase openeth.

3. To men of the Path, whose state—from (slow) travelling to (swift) flight, from (laborious) travelling to (irresistible) attraction, from being a lover (of God) to being the beloved (of God)—shall not have ended, it is possible that, at the time of samā', the soul's ear may open and gain the rapture of the address of eternity without beginning, and of the "first covenant;" that with one shaking the bird of the soul may shake from itself the dust of existence and the clamminess of impurities; and may—from the pollution of the heart, of lust and of the crowd of existences—become free.

Then, with swift flight, the soul cometh into propinquity to God; the holy traveller's slow travelling changeth to swift flight; his laborious journey, to irresistible attraction; and his being a lover to his being the beloved (of God).

Then, in a moment, doth he travel, as without samā' he cannot travel in years.

---

The best of deeds (prayer) is for some the cause of prosperity; and for some of sorrow. Nevertheless, the abandoning of prayer is not lawful.

At this time in a way (which is the way of men of the time and of ṣūfīs) samā' is the essence of disaster; for many are the assemblies the foundation whereof is on the claim of lust and of sensual delights—not on the principles of sincerity, and on the desire of increase of ḥāl whereon hath verily been the way of this ṭarīḳ.

The cause of being present at an assembly of samā' is :—

(*a*) the claim to victuals that in that assembly are expected.
(*b*) the inclination to dancing, to sport, and to pastime.
(*c*) the delight of beholding things forbidden and abhorrent.
(*d*) the attraction of worldly kinds.
(*e*) the manifestation of wajd and ḥāl.
(*f*) the keeping brisk the market of being a shaikh; and the making current the chattels of self-adorning.

All this is the essence of disaster; and abhorrent to men of faith.

Every assembly the foundation whereof is on one of these desires,—from it becometh difficult the search for increase of :—

ḥāl.
inward purity.
tranquillity of heart.

This complaint was laid in the time of Junīd, which was the time of revealing of shaikhs and of ṣūfīs.

At the end of his life Junīd held not the assembly of samā' of the singer.

They said :—

Why holdest thou not samā'?

He said :—

With whom may I hold samā' ?

They said :—

For thy own soul, hear.

He said :—

From whom, may I hear ?

It is proper to make samā' with sympathising friends ; and to hear one who suffereth pain (of love for God), and who, for the sake solely of the next world, speaketh.

---

Doubtless the sweet voice is one of divine favours.

Thus by the camel-driver's song, the camel easily beareth heavy loads and joyfully travelleth many stages in a day.

Wahy saith :—

Once in the desert, I met an Arab tribe ; one of them took me to his tent.

Before the victuals appeared, I saw a black slave bound and several camels dead at the tent-door.

The slave said :—

" To-night thou art the guest ; and the guest my Lord holdeth dear. Hope is mine that thou wilt intercede for my release from these bonds.

When he had made ready the victuals, I said :—

I will not eat till thou releasest this slave.

He said :—

This slave hath ruined my property and my camels ; and cast me on the dust of poverty.

My income used to be from the profit of these camels. But this slave hath a voice exceeding sweet ; and he loaded the camels with heavy burdens ; and to the melody of Ḥudā urged them so that in one day they traversed three days' space. When they reached the last stage, they cast their loads and fell dead. Him, I will give to thee.

The next day I wished to hear the slave's voice ; my host accordingly ordered him to begin the camel-driver's melody.

Near, there was a bound camel.

When he heard the slave's voice, he revolved his head and snapped his tether ; and I became senseless and fell.

They asked Junīd :—

Why doth a person, who is resting with gravity and who suddenly heareth a sweet voice—fall into agitation and tumult.

He said :—

When, in the covenant of eternity without beginning and of mīṣāḳ, God said to the atoms of the progeny of the sons of Ādam—Am I not your God ? the sweetness of that address remained in the ear of their soul.

When they hear a sweet sound, the sweetness of that address cometh to mind ; and they delight thereat, and fall into tumult.

Thus also say Ẕu-n-Nūn'-i-Miṣrī and Samnūn Muḥib.

Bukā (lamentation) is of two kinds :—

(a) the bukā of joy.
(b) „ „ wajd.

For bukā is produced by fear, desire, joy, or wajd.

The bukā of joy is when, from exceeding joy, one weepeth—as when a son, or a beloved, long separated by seas, returneth.

The bukā of wajd is when a ray of the splendour of ḥaḳḳu-l-yaḳīn (the truth of certainty) flasheth, and the blow of ḳidam (eternity) cometh upon ḥudūs̤ (calamities), the rest of the existence of the wājid (the enraptured one) riseth up and disappeareth in the dashing together of ḳidam and ḥudūs̤.

This state is manifested in the form of drops of tears.

---

Whatever hath dominion over humanity, samā' strengtheneth.

For those engaged in love for God, samā' is the aider to perfection ; for those filled with lust, the cause of disaster.

Although wajd in samā' is the perfection of the ḥāl of "the first ones," it is the defect of "the last ones." Because wajd is the sign of resuming (after little losing) the state of witnessing. In samā', the wājid is the loser ; and the cause of the loss of the ḥāl of witnessing is the appearance of the qualities of wujūd (existence).

The qualities of wujūd are :—

(a) the darkness arising from lust, the veil of the vain.
(b) „ luminousness arising from the heart, „ „ verified.

The source of wajd in samā' is :—

(a) either purely sweet melodies, the delight whereof is shared between the soul and the heart of the verified ; and between the soul and the lust of the vain.
(b) or pure melodies (whereby the soul alone is delighted) wherein the listening heart maketh samā' in respect to the verified, and the nafs in respect to the vain.

For freedom from the veil of existence, the ḥāl of witnessing is constant and the samā' of addresses (of God) perpetual—to "the last ones."

The samā' of melody cannot agitate ; for agitation by assault is a strange state.

The ḥāl of witnessing and the samā' of addresses (of God) appear not strange to the man of constant witnessing and of perpetual samā', and therefore by them he is not agitated.

A companion of Sahl 'Abdu-l-lāh saith :—

Years in Sahl's society, I was ; and yet I never saw him changed by hearing—

the ẕikr
„ Ḳurān
„ other exercises

until, at the close of his life, they read to him this Ḳurānic verse.

"From you, sacrifice, He will not take to day."

Suddenly ḥāl turned to him ; and he so trembled that he nearly fell.

I asked the cause ; he said :—

Me, weakness hath befallen.

He became changed and agitated. Afterwards Ibn Sālim asked him of his state.

He said :—

"It was from weakness."

They said :—

If that were from weakness, what is power?

He said :—

Power is that when naught descendeth on a person but by the power of ḥāl, he suffereth it; and by it changeth not.

Once, Mūmshād-i-Dīnwarī passed a place where, in samā', was a crowd of "the first ones." When they saw him, they left off.

He said :—

Upon your state ye continue intent. If all the musical instruments were gathered in my ear, they would engage naught of my purpose and relieve naught of my pain.

Whoever hath the state of perpetual witnessing, his state in samā' is even as it was before samā'.

The heart that is ever present with God, and rejecteth samā',—understandeth from every sound that reacheth him, the address of God.

Then is his samā' not restricted to man's melodies even as Abū 'Us̤man-i-Maghribī hath said. The voice within himself is samā'; of the external ear is no need, even as Ḥassr hath said :—

Whose samā' is constant, ever present with the Hidden is he in heart; and ever void of lusts' tale is the ear of his heart.

He heareth sometimes the address of God; sometimes the praise of the atoms of existence; sometimes from the inward; and sometimes from the outward.

Once Shiblī heard one crying in the bāzār of Baghdād :—

Ten ' خيار (khiyar, cucumbers) for a dāng.

He cried out :—

When ten ' خيار (Khayyar, good men) are for a dāng, the state of the (worthless) wicked is what?

Once a man of heart (a ṣūfi) heard a proclaimer shouting :—

Sa'tarbari.

He fell senseless. When to sense he returned, they asked him the cause. He said :—

From God, I heard—asa'tarbarī.

Of the Amīru-l-Muminīn (Ālī) it is said that once he heard the sound of a conch. To his companions, he said :—

Know ye what this conch saith?

They said :—

Nay.

He said :—

It saith, praise be to God! O God! O God! verily living is the Eternal Master

'Abdu-r-Raḥman-i-Salīmī says :—

Once I went to Abū 'Us̤man-i-Maghribi. There, with an ox, they were drawing water from a well.

To me, Abū 'Us̤man said :—

Knowest thou what this ox saith?

I said :—

Nay.

He said :—

He saith—Allāh! Allāh!

Men of samā' are of three kinds :—

(a) The sons of truths. These in samā' hear the address of God to themselves.
(b) The men of needs. These by means of the meanings of couplets that in samā' they hear heartily address themselves to God; and, in whatever they ascribe to God, are in sincerity of purpose.
(c) The lonely fuḳarā. These have severed all worldly ties and calamities. In goodness of heart, is their samā'; and nearest to safety (in God) they are.

---

## The rules of Samā'.

V. 10.

The first rule of samā' is that, at an assembly of samā', they should keep foremost sincerity of resolution and seek out its cause :—

(a) If it be lustful desire, shun it.
(b) If the claim of sincerity, of desire, and of search for the increase of ḥāl and for comprehending the blessing (of God)—be united, free from lust's impurities, the grace of such an assembly (despite the absence of a shaikh, or men of samā' of the brothers of concord, and of sincere seekers) is great gain.

If it be not free from the impurities of lust,—it is necessary, in its purification, to bring forward subtleties of vision and graces of practice.

If the cause be first the claim of sincerity and afterwards lustful desire, it is necessary to repair the injury done by lust :—

(a) by sincerity of penitence.
(b) „ seeking aid (of God) against the wickedness of lust.
(c) „ putting forward prayer.

If the cause be first lustful desire and afterwards good resolution for reparation, —they credit the former desire, not the succeeding resolution; and shun such an assembly.

If samā' comprehend :—

i. prohibited things such as

(*a*) the morsel of tyrants,

(*b*) „ being near to women,

(*c*) „ presence of beardless youths,

ii. abhorred objects such as :—

(*a*) the presence of one who as a zāhid hath no affinity for this crowd; who delighteth not in samā',

(*b*) the possessor of rank of the Lords of the world to whom it is necessary to be respectful,

(*c*) the presence of one, who falsely revealeth wajd; and to those present, maketh time perturbed with false tawājud,

it is necessary for true seekers to shun such an assembly.

At an assembly of samā', he who is present should sit with respect and gravity; should keep restrained the parts of the body from excess of motion, especially in the presence of shai<u>kh</u>s; should not become agitated with a little of the splendours of wajd; should not affect intoxication with a little taste of the pure wine (of love for God); nor voluntarily express either the shahḳat (murmuring noise) or the za'ḳ (calling out).

If—let us flee to God for protection,—without the descending of wajd and of ḥāl, he manifesteth wajd and layeth claim to ḥāl,—it is verily the essence of hypocrisy and of sin, the foulest blameable act, and the most disgraceful of states.

In the time of Abū-l-Ḳāsim Naṣr Ābādī (who was a companion of Shiblī, and renowned in knowledge of the ḥadīṣ), the shai<u>kh</u> of <u>Kh</u>urāsān delighted in samā'.

One day between him and Abū 'Amr bin Najīd (who was a murīd of Abū 'Uṣman-ī-Ḥairī, and had seen Junīd) there chanced an assembly of concord.
Him, on account of his exceeding samā', Abū 'Amr reproached.

Naṣr Ābādī said:—

Thus it is, but an assembly, whereat one is a speaker in lawful song and the rest are silent—is better than an assembly whereat all are speakers in slander.

Abū 'Amr replied :—

O Abū-l-Ḳāsim ! alas, evil is motion in samā'; in it, is this and this.

The explanation of 'Amr's reply is this, that the error of samā' comprehendeth many errors :—

(*a*) Falsely slandering the Lord of the world (God). Because the revealing of wajd in samā' referreth to the mutawājid, to whom God hath bestowed a special gift.

(*b*) Deceiving some of those present in samā' by the manifestation of false ḥāl. Deceit is treachery; treachery is the source of repulsion.

(*c*) Breaking the confidence of followers of the men of rectitude. Thus is cut off from them the aid of holy men (ṣāliḥ) which is the essence of sin.

The way of true wājids is this :—

> So long as they gain not fully the ardour of samā', they move not in samā'; from them, motion issueth only when they cannot restrain it,—even as the palsied one cannot restrain himself from the motion of palsy.

Tawājud is this :—

> When, not in the true way of wajd and of ḥāl, but in the way of indulging the heart and bathing lust, a person displayeth a weighed motion with weighed cadences,—so that nafs (lust) becometh rested from the labour of deeds; and the heart from the labour of deliberation.

Thus, the heart vainly seeketh aid in search of God.

Although in the shar', dancing may be among the lawful pleasures, it is with the men of truths and the Lords of grandeur——vain.

Yet the vain thing which is aid to the search for God is the essence of devotion. This vain is verily a truth in the garb of the vain.

The mutawājid's resolution in tawājud is possibly a portion of wajd, so that (by its blessing) he gaineth a portion (of good) from his ḥāl.

Though this be permissible to "the first ones," it is unsuitable for the ḥāl and the office of shaikhs. Because their ḥāl is all, outwardly and inwardly, pure truth, wherein is no entrance to sport and pastime.

From them, especially in the presence of shaikhs, should not voluntarily issue the za'ḳ (calling out), but only at that time when the power of restraint is effaced. So the breather whose power of breathing cometh strait,—if he breathe not, his heart consumeth.

It is related that in Junīd's service, a youth used to display assiduity; and in samā' to make the za'ḳ. One day Junīd forbade him saying :—

> "If after this, thou restrain not thyself,—from us go far."
>
> After this, in samā' the youth restrained himself from za'ḳ. So, from the root of every hair flowed the sweat of restraint, till one day he expressed a za'ḳ, and at the same time his life.

The condition of za'ḳ is—

> The being hidden from things felt.

In the best ṭarīḳ, when not done through the overwhelming power of ḥāl and through the loss of the power of repression, unlawful are :—

(*a*) motion in samā'.
(*b*) the voluntary za'ḳ.
(*c*) ,, ,, rending of one's garment.

These are the pretensions to ḥāl without the truth of ḥāl, and the ruin of property.

In casting the khirḳa to the singer, there should be advanced an intention void of hypocrisy just as he may (in support of wajd and of exciting desire) wish to give ease to the singer.

The khirḳa (mantle) that passeth from the possessor of samā' to the singer is of two kinds,—

| | | |
|---|---|---|
| (*a*) | khirḳa-i- ṣaḥiḥa | the un-rent khirḳa. |
| (*b*) | ,, mumazzaka | ,, rent ,, |

The rule of the unrent khirḳa is as follows :—

(i) If the wājid's purpose in casting off the khirḳa and bestowing it be specially for the singer, in it, others have no concern.

(ii) If his purpose be not special, and a distinguished one, obedient to order, be present, he may give it to the singer, or to another. Over him, none hath authority, for his acts are from vision.

(iii) If those present at the samā' be all brothers, and there be no shaikh, they give the khirḳa to the singer; because the exciter of wajd (which is the cause of casting off the khirḳa) is his song.

Some say :—

(*a*) The khirḳa belongeth to the assembly; because the source of wajd is not only the singer's song but also the blessing of the assembly.

(*b*) If the singer be outside of the assembly, he is with all a sharer; otherwise he is portionless.

(*c*) If the singer be for hire, he is portionless; otherwise with the assembly he shareth.

(*d*) If some of the lovers (of God) present a gift, and with it, those present are satisfied,—every one may go after his khirḳa; and the gift they give to the singer.

(*e*) If in casting off the khirḳa some one shall have resolved not again to go after his khirḳa,—it, they give to the singer.

The rule of the rent khirḳa is—

When the possessor of samā', through the impetuosity of ḥāl and the capture of control, rendeth on his body the khirḳa,— it, they divide among those present at samā' whether of the same, or of diverse, kind (of brotherhood).

In dealing kindly with those of diverse kind, it is necessary that the assembly should hold a favourable opinion of them and of their casting off the khirḳa.

If, at the division, be present one who at the time of samā' was absent, to him they give a portion (of the khirḳa).

If of the cast-off khirḳas some be unrent and some rent, they rend (if the shaikh consider it fit) the unrent khirḳas and part them among those present.

The rending of the khirḳa and the parting of it among those present is an Ḥadīs̤ by Anas Ibn Mālik; but in it, they have made contrariety.

If by this ḥadīs̤, in respect of the samā' of (singing), of moving, of rending garments, and of parting them among those present,—the truth should be verified, it would to the ṣūfī be the best document.

---

## The Khirḳa (Darvish Mantle).

V. 2.

A custom of the ṣūfīs is the putting on of the khirḳa, which, at the beginning of their sway over the murīds, the shaikhs have considered laudable; but regarding which they have received no order from the sunnat except the ḥadīs̤ of Umm-i-Khā-lid.

It is related that once to Muḥammad they brought some raiment in the midst whereof was a small black blanket.

Taking it up, he said to the assembly :—

Who intendeth putting on this ?

All were silent. He said :—

I give it to Umm-i-Khālid.

They called Umm-i-Khālid; and Muḥammad covered her with it.

On that blanket, were marks (stripes) yellow and red; at them Muḥammad looked and said :—

O Umm-i-Khālid ! this is admirable (which is the ḥadīṣ).

In the arranging of the garment of the khirḳa, which is the ṣūfī-way, clinging to this ḥadīṣ,—is far.

Although from the sunnat is no clear command, since the khirḳa is surety for benefits and not an obstacle to the sunnat, it is laudable.

The following of the excellences of the Path is lawful; the excellences are :—

(*a*) The changing of custom and the turning from natural things and sensual delights.

For, as in eatables, potables, and spouses lust hath delight—in garments also, it delighteth.

The putting on of a garment, which hath become lust's custom, and in the particular form whereof it resteth—in it, doubtless lust delighteth.

Then is the change of garment, the change of custom which is the essence of worship, as in the Ḥadīṣ.

(*b*) The repelling of the society of contemporaries in sin and of shaiṭāns of mankind, who (by resemblance in form) incline to the other (good) society.

When a change of garment and an alteration of form appeareth in the murīd, his equals and associates depart from him.

For the khīrḳa is the shadow of the shaikh's love and frighteneth shaiṭān from the shadow of men of love as is in the Ḥadīṣ.

For the murīd, society of the good is necessary, that from them, he may take the colour of goodness.

Separation from the wicked is the condition of acceptance of the society of the good.

Even so the indigo-stained raiment taketh no colour till after the removing of the indigo.

(*c*) The revealing of the shaikh's sway in the murīd's heart—by reason of his sway outwardly, which is the mark of inward sway.

So long as the murīd's interior becometh not worthy of the shaikh's sway, and the murīd considereth him not perfect and one of consummate excellence—he becometh not outwardly obedient to the shaikh.

(*d*) The good news to the murīd is his acceptance by God. Because the putting on of the khirḳa is the mark of the shaikh's acceptance, which is the mark of God's acceptance.

By putting on the khirḳa by the shaikh possessed of love, the murīd knoweth that God hath accepted him; and his being united to the shaikh (by the bond of sincerity, of desire, and of acceptance) becometh a mirror wherein he seeth the beauty of his end.

The being united with shaikhs is the result of the acquaintance of his soul with the shaikh's soul which is the mark of kinship, as in the ḥadīs̤.
Even so the murīd's putting on of the khirḳa (by the shaikh possessed of understanding) signifieth the murīd's desire for the shaikh, and the shaikh's love for the murīd.
The exalted states (ḥāl) are the result of these two meanings (*c* and *d*) being wedded.

---

The khirḳa is of two kinds :—

(*a*) the khirḳa of desire.
(*b*) „ „ „ blessing.

The khirḳa of desire—

When the shaikh (with the penetration of the light of vision and with intelligence) looketh into the midst of the murīd's state, and beholdeth the sincerity of his desire for God, he indueth him with this khirḳa, so that he may become his giver of glad tidings; and that the eye of his heart may become luminous by the blowing of the breeze of God's guidance, whereof the khirḳa is the bearer.

So did Ya'ḳūb's eye, by the breeze of Yūsuf's shirt, see.

The khirḳa of blessing—

This khirḳa is presented to him who with the shaikhs hath a good report.

That one who, through good opinion and resolve for blessing by the khirḳa of shaikhs, desireth this khirḳa, and is a seeker of the conditions of men of desire and of putting off the garment of his own desire for the shaikh's desire,—him, as regards two matters, they order :—

(*a*) attendance to the orders of the sharī'at.
(*b*) the protection of the men of ṭarīḳat, by whose protection, he may gain kinship, and become worthy of the khirḳa of desire, which is forbidden save to the man of desire and to the Lords of sincerity of resolution.

To these two, some add the khirḳa of holiness :—

When the shaikh seeth in the murīd the effects of holiness and the marks of acquisition to the degree of excellence and instruction; and wisheth to appoint him his own khalīfa,—he clotheth him with the khil'at of holiness, and with the honour of his own favour, whereby may be effected the penetrating of his order and the obeying of the people.

---

## The choice of the coloured khirḳa.

V. 3.

The choice of the coloured khirḳa (for amending the defilements, and for evacuating man's heart of deeds and of contemplation) is (through solicitude for the care of the white garment and through being engaged in its cleansing) of the number of laudable deeds of shaikhs.

The sunnat is for the choosing of the white garment, and, in the opinion of ṣūfīs, this choosing is proved. But for those, whose times are immersed in devotion, the washing of the white garment occupieth too much time.

The coloured garment is best; because the excellence of nawāfil is greater than the excellence of garments.

Whenever the beginning of an excellence is the cause of abandoning the most excellent,—the abandoning of that excellence is excellence.

Blue colour is the choice of the ṣūfīs despite that black is better against defilements. The ṣūfī putteth on the garment with that colour suitable to his ḥāl.

Black is fit for him who is sunk in the darkness of lust, and whose times are surrounded with darkness.

Not thus is the ḥāl of the man of desire; because by the ray of the light of desire, the darkness of existence is trampled upon.

For them, the black garment is unfit, and since they have not wholly gained freedom from lust, the white garment is also unfit; for them is fit the blue garment, which is a mixture of light and darkness, of pureness and foulness.

In the flame of the candle are two portions—one pure light, the other pure darkness. Their place of union appeareth blue.

The white garment is fit for shaikhs that may have gained freedom from lust (nafs).

These aspects are only approximate.

---

The men of this Path are of three kinds:—

(*a*) mubtadiyān (the first ones) whose state is the abandoning of will to the shaikh; and with whom naught of garments, of goods and of other things is lawful save by the shaikh's desire.

(*b*) mutawassiṭān (the middle ones), whose state is the abandoning of will to God; and who have no will as to special raiment; as occasion demandeth they submit.

(*c*) muntahiyān (the end ones), who, by God's will, are absolute. What they choose is God's will.

When the true murīd entrusteth the rein of his will to the shaikh, perfect possessor of vision; and to him becometh submissive,—the shaikh withdraweth him from natural habits and sensual affections, and directeth him in all affairs of faith and of religion.

If he see that for a special garment the murīd thirsteth and desireth,—from it he bringeth him forth; and clotheth him with another garment.

If he see that his inclination is for splendid and soft raiment, he putteth on him the coarse grass khirḳa; if he see that his inclination is for the coarse grass khirḳa for the sake of hypocrisy and pretension, he clotheth him with soft silk raiment; if he see that he desireth a special colour or form,—it, he forbiddeth.

Even so in all his circumstances.

The choice of the colour and of the form of the murīd's garment dependeth upon the shaikh's vision; and that dependeth on the good counsel of the time.

Some shaikh's have not ordered the murīds change of raiment; their vision hath been intent upon concealing the ḥāl, and upon abandoning its manifestation.

Shaikhs are like to physicians; and of murīds many are the diseases, each one of a kind that shaikhs have known, and that they have applied the remedy to.

Their directions are on counsel and on rectitude; and the foundation of the path of salvation and prosperity.

## Khilvat (retirement).

V. 6.

Keeping khilvat (retirement) in the way of the ṣūfīs is an innovation. In Muḥammad's time, the sunnat was naught save ṣuḥbat (society); and its excellence excelleth other excellences.

Thus, by ṣuḥbat they have described the ṣaḥāba and by no other description; and outside the society of Muḥammad, their description is naught, because their souls were, by the grandeur of prophecy, described with rest, and, by the light of integrity encompassed with purity; hearts, were void of love for the world and solaced by the vision of the beauty of certainty, and filled with love for God, with affection, with purity, and with fidelity.

When the sun of prophecy became hidden, the souls of the companions came gradually into motion; opposition became manifest; and in time reached a place where ṣuḥbat (society) became overwhelmed, and khilvat (retirement), pleasant and beloved.

For the safety of faith, the seekers of God sought the ṣauma' a (convent) and khilvat, as Junīd hath said.

Though in the time of the sending of the sunnat, was no khilvat, yet before that time, Muḥammad, through exceeding love for God, and sincerity of desire—held esteemed khilvat; used to go to the caves of Ḥarā; and there used to pass nights in ẓikr and in devotion.

In the choice of khilvat, the tradition is firmly held by the ṣūfīs; but the appointing of forty days is from a tradition from Muḥammad and from God's word.

With Mūsạ̄, God promised to speak; and appointed a place of meeting and a stated time.

God said:—"Keep fast thirty days and nights." Ten days more, He afterwards added.

During that time Mūsạ̄ consumed neither food nor drink; he was engaged in worshipping God; and for talking with Him became prepared.

Since, for propinquity to God and for talk with Him, Mūsạ̄ had need of khilvat, —so have others.

Even so in the case of Muḥammad—

his being cut off from ṣuḥbat.
„ retiring (to talk) with God.
„ separating himself from the people.
„ reducing his daily food.
„ constant ẓikr in desire's path in the beginning of divine impressions.

are further proofs.

Thus for the seekers of God, acceptable is the obligation (of khilvat) and indeed, wājib (necessary).

The source whence the sharī'at fixed the appointed time (forty days) is obscure; and knowledge of it difficult save by the prophets, by the special ones, and by the holy ones.

In the 'Awārifu-l-Ma'ārif the Shaikhu-l-Islām saith :—

> "When God wished to appoint Ādam to His own khilāfat, and to make him architect of this world after he had, by his existence, made paradise prosperous,—He gave to him a composition of elements of earth, fit for this world; and for forty mornings made them ferment.
>
> Every morning signifieth the existence of a quality that becometh the cause of his attachment to this world; and every attachment became his veil against beholding the glory of ḳidam (eternity).
>
> Every veil is the cause of farness from the hidden world; every farness, the cause of nearness to the material world till that time when the veil becometh heaped up, and this world's fitness, complete in Ādam.

In the establishing of forty mornings with sincerity (which is the condition of khilvat) its ḥikmat (philosophy) is :—

> For every morning (of khilvat), a veil should lift and a nearness (to God) appear, so that in forty mornings, the forty-fold veil should lift, and refined human nature, from farness to the native land of nearness to God (the summation of beauty and of glory; the essence of 'ilm, and of ma'rifat) return; and for it, the vision of the grandeur of eternity without beginning should be verified and painted; the sight of its resolution, from inclination to the world's impurity, be preserved; and the fountain of ḥikmat go running from its heart and on its tongue.

The mark of khilvat is —

> The preservation of the condition of that revelation of ḥikmat.

The revelation of ḥikmat is in—

> The proof of the lifting of the veil and the doubtless manifestations.

Khilvat is like unto a smith's forge whereon by the fire of austerity, lust becometh fused, pure of nature's pollution, delicate, and gleaming like unto a mirror; and without (beyond, through) it, appeareth the form of the hidden; and is a collection of contrarieties of nafs (lust) and accustomed austerities :—

> Little eating.
> ,, talking.
> Shunning the society of man.
> Perseverance in ẕikr.
> Denying thoughts.
> Constant murāḳiba (fearful contemplation).

The meaning of رياضت (austerity) is the abandoning of desire and of the requisites of effort.

## The Conditions of Khilvat.

V. 7.

In the opinion of the ṣūfīs, khilvat is not restricted to forty days. The being severed from the people and the being engaged with God is a desired matter, the duration whereof is for life.

The advantage of appointing forty days is that, on the completing of this period, the manifestation begins to appear.

If to a person who to life's end keepeth his time engaged in devotion to God, and in freedom from the people, that manifestation appeareth,—beyond it, is no greater favour.

If this bounty of God be not his, it is necessary for him at certain periods to practise khilvat.

At least once a year, he should sit in khilvat, so that when, for forty days and nights, he shall have accustomed his nafs—

to the preservation of times; to the observance of readings (of the Ḳurān) and of rules,

he may be expectant that the order will not be extended to his former mixing with people; that, in God's protection, his khilvat may be; and that his khilvat may be the aider of the structure of the times of glory.

Only in the preservation of its conditions, appeareth the advantage of khilvat.

Who resolveth upon khilvat must purify his intention from the pollution of desire for the objects of this world; and of prayers for (his welfare in) the next world.

According to intention is the reward of deeds. As intention is better than the deed, more full is its reward.

No object is better than propinquity to God; whatever is exterior to Him is called the indigo of ḥudūṣ (calamity), and is directed by the disgrace of fanā (effacement).

In the heart's purification, inclination to the polluted is the essence of pollution; propinquity thereto, especially impure.

Who hath desire for that exterior to God, great and glorious of both worlds, is polluted; from that pollution, purification is necessary for approach to the holy God, and for fitness of prayer to Him.

His intention should be restricted to propinquity to God by practising worship; and far from desire:—

for rank, for hypocrisy, for the revelation of miracles, and for the explanation of the verses of power (the Ḳurān).

If to that crowd—whose desire from khilvat and austerity is the revelation of miracles and not propinquity to God,—something of that desired be revealed, it is the essence of deceit, and the cause of farness, of folly, and of pride.

In the purifying of the interior, in the cleansing of the heart, in affecting nafs,—freedom from occupations, reduction of food, and continuity of ẕikr have perfect effect.

When by khilvat, his interior becometh luminous and the outward form of some un-attainable knowledge appeareth; and true thoughts appear to him and over his nafs gain sway,—the seeker of miracles thinketh that that is the lofty and far object of khilvat; and by the exalting of wicked shaiṭān becometh proud; and contemptuously glanceth at others—(let us flee to God for refuge).

Possibly out from his heart, he bindeth up the chattels of the sharī'at and of prophecy; considereth not the abandoning of laws, of orders, and of the lawful and unlawful—so by the path of retrogression, he becometh cast out from the highway of the shar' and from the path of Islām.

If, to one who is in intention pure, the manifestation of miracles falleth, it becometh the cause of the power of certainty and of the confirmation of resolve.

The condition of sincerity being observed, it is necessary that, out from the bond of debt,

> by cancelling tryranny; by making right (apologising for) calumny; by removing enmity hate, malice,—

he should come; and pure to all make his heart.

If, in his property, there be something whereto his heart clingeth,—it, from his property he should expel.

If he be possessed of property in respect to family he performeth (so that outwardly and inwardly he may be free and pure) complete washing; exerciseth care as to the cleansing of raiment and of the prayer-mat; and chooseth for his khilvat a place where, from occupations, he may be free.

When he reacheth the door of khilvat, he saith :—

> O God! by the right ingress, let me enter; by the right egress, let me pass out. By Thy grace, me make a conquering king.

When to the prayer-mat he wisheth to go, he first advanceth the right leg and saith :—

> In the name of God; by the grace of God; praise be to God, and peace and blessing be on the prophet of God!
> O God! my sins pardon; open me the door of mercy.

Then, with the desire of the presence of God, he performeth two rak'ats of prayer with khushū'; and with khuẓū' (humility of the heart and of the limbs).

In the first rak'at, after the fātiḥa, he saith :—

O God of ours! on Thee is our reliance; in Thee, be our refuge; in Thee, our shelter.

Then, with sincerity and humility, he asketh pardon for all his sins. To God, he displayeth in his heart penitence for turning to that exterior to Him.

Before the ḳibla he sitteth; and as long as he can, is in "tashahhud." *

With himself he reflecteth that God is present, also the Prophet of God, so that he may be bound with the bond of reverence, and is ever wishing within that he may, outwardly and inwardly, offer himself in devotion and in praise, and in the raiment of concordance with divine decrees.

Thus, may he become the meeting-place of divine breathings, ready for the descending of boundless bounty.

---

In khilvat, after the purifying of resolution, penitence, and continuity of employment with God, he must observe seven conditions :—

i. Constant ablution.

When he seeth in himself lassitude, he should renew ablution, so that in his interior the light of outward purity may be brightened, and be the aider of the heart's-luminosities.

ii. Constant fasting.

Ever should he be in fast, so that the blessing of the sunnat may comprehend his times.

iii. Little eating.

At breakfast, the quantity of food should be not more than a riṭl. If he restrict as to bread and salt, 'tis well.

If to relish (that is in the place of food) he stretcheth his hand, to its extent, he should reduce the bread. If he begin with a riṭl, he should in the last tenth (of the period of forty days) reduce to half a riṭl. If he be strong and begin with half a riṭl he should reduce to quarter of a riṭl.

The companions of khilvat are of three kinds :—

the strong ones.
,, middle ,,
,, weak ,,

The weak break their fast every night; the middle every two nights; and the strong every three nights.

He may devour all on the first, or on the last, night; or some on the first night and some on the last night.

---

* I profess that there is no God but God; I acknowledge Muḥammad to be the apostle of God.

The last division is the best, so that he may have power—

(*a*) for devotion.
(*b*) „ standing up for the midnight prayers.

In reducing the clayey parts—the source of pollution, of darkness, of coarseness—scantiness of food is wholly effective.

iv. Little sleep.

So long as he is able he should not sleep. If sleep be overpowering, he should repel it by renewing ablution, or by reading the Ḳurān. If it cannot be repelled and involuntarily sleep seizeth him, he should (when he returneth from sleep) renew ablution and be engaged in prayer.

Every sleep that is of necessity is the essence of devotion when thereby is attainable the repelling of lassitude of the senses and of nafs (which are the cause of weariness of the soul of devotion and of the delight of worship).

By sleep, the purity of the senses and the expansion of the interior (which are the cause of wajd of the soul) return to him. Then, are his times immersed in devotion.

In putting lust to death and in keeping the heart alive,—ever keeping awake is profitable by loosening the humours of the body, by weakening the points of forgetfulness, of sins, of ignorance, and of carelessness.

v. Little talking.

He should ever guard his tongue from talking with people.

The sage practiseth silence though no calamity he expecteth.

Whether the speech be beautiful or ugly, it is not void of calamity. For so long as to perfect purification it shall not have reached, nafs hath in the revealing of beautiful speech a delight, wherefrom is expected the revealing of the qualities of pride and the thickening of the veil. Doubtless, ugly speech is followed by punishment.

Save by silence, not attainable is the path of safety.

In the tale of Maryam and of 'Īsā̤, God maketh Maryam's silence the fore-runner of 'Īsā̤'s speech. Even so the Ī'sā̤ of the heart cometh into speech when the Maryam of nafs is silent of talk.

vi. The negation of thoughts.

By ẕikr and by the occupation of the heart in contemplation of the divine aspect, he should repel the crowd of thoughts.

Excellent though the penetration of some thoughts is, discrimination of thoughts occurreth not to beginners. Then, the being engaged in thought is for him the way of the ḥadīs̤u-n-nafs; and to him is formidable.

The meaning of ḥadīs̤u-n-nafs is this:—The nafs of man, by its connection with the rūḥ (soul) of speech, is innate in the qualities of speech; and is ever expectant of the opportunity of converse with the heart which is its beloved.

Whenever nafs seeth the heart inclined to itself, and findeth its ears void of other sayings, immediately with the heart, it cometh into speech ; and to it, by way of remembrance, confirmeth past matters of things spoken, heard, seen, tasted, touched; or giveth future news of hope ; and keepeth engaged the ear of the heart with hearing its own speech rather than with hearing the speech of the soul and of God,—so that the heart may ever be before it, and averse to aught save nafs.

When the possessor of khilvat persevereth in the heart as to negation of thoughts, and as to the confirmation of tauḥīd,—the source of ḥadīṣu-n-nafs becometh effaced ; nafs, silent ; the ear of the heart, void of its saying, and ready for the hearing of divinc words.

vii. The perpetuality of deeds.

Outwardly and inwardly, he should keep himself arrayed in the garb of devotion. Every moment in a work which at that time is most important and best, he should be engaged. Thus who is "a first one" should limit himself to divine precepts, and to the sunnat of prayer; and at other times to ẕikr.

Out of all the aẕkār (ẕikrs) the shaikhs have chosen :—

Lā ilāha illa llāh (no god but God).

because its form is formed of negation and of affirmation, so that at the time of the flowing of this speech on his tongue, the ẕākir is present (alive to God) and preserveth conformity between the heart and the tongue.

As to negation, he regardeth the existence of ḥādīṣ wholly with the glance of fanā ; as to affirmation, the existence of ḳadīm with the eye of baḳā.

By repeating this creed (Lā ilāha, &c., &c.) the form of tauḥīdr eposeth in his heart; its root is established in his heart, its branches are extended to the soul.

At this time, ẕikr becometh the necessary quality of the heart ; its aid is continuous. To it, at times of lassitude, the ẕikr of the tongue of languor findeth no path ; after that, it reacheth a place where ẕikr becometh enjewelled in the heart.

The ẕākir in ẕikr ; the ẕikr in the heart ; the heart in maẕkūr (the origin of ẕikr, God) become effaced.

---

At this stage, if the form of the phrase of tauḥīd (which is the meaning of ẕikr) become effaced from the outward face of the heart, to the inward face of the heart its truth is joined. The meaning of this is ḥāl.

Ẕikr, ẕākir and maẕkūr are one.

But for the "middle one" assiduity in the reciting of the Ḳurān after the performance of divine precepts is best.

Verily that speciality (that to "the first one" from assiduity in ẕikr appeareth) becometh acquired from reading the Ḳurān with other specialities as——

the glory of the qualities (of God), the various spiritual truths, the subtleties of understanding and the truths of knowledge,——by readings of various Ḳurānic verses.

To "the last one," to whom the light of ẓikr may have become his innate quality,—excellent, is the reading (of the Ḳurān) ; and perfect, the act of prayer (ṣalāt).

Because this form of prayer is a devotion completely comprehending, wherein are comprehended :—

ẓikr.
tilāwat reading.
khushū' humility (of the limbs).
khuẓū' „ ( „ heart).

As long as nafs is in obedience,—in it, is concordance with the heart.

The aid of the soul of propinquity, the proclaiming, the delight of society, and the need of forms of prayer become joined to the prayer-mat.

In it, perseverance is best.

If on account of it, an abhorrence should appear in nafs, the descending from praying to reading is best ; for reading in comparison with praying is easy.

If reading end in weariness, the descending from it to ẓikr is best.

For perseverance in respect to ẓikr merely, and the repeating of light phrase is easier to nafs than the preservation of words weighty and of varied signification.

If languor fall upon the ẓikr of the tongue,—best is assiduity in ẓikr of the heart —which they call murāḳaba (fearful contemplation), that is, considering the manifestations of God—in respect to his own state.

If as to murāḳaba languor chance, he may rest awhile his limbs and senses ; and in sleep give ease.

Thus from nafs, fatigue may depart ; and, again with pleasure, he may advance to deeds.

Verily it is unfit that, with detestation and compulsion, he should engage nafs in a work (whereby it may be vexed and the power whereof it hardly hath).

The possessor of khilwat should devote all his time to these readings, so that the path of hidden events may be disclosed.

---

## The dreams of the men of Khilvat.

V. 8.

In the midst of ẓikr, it sometimes happens to men of khilvat that, from things felt (this world) they become concealed (in unconsciousness); and that to them become revealed, as to the sleeper truths of hidden matters. It, the ṣūfīs call wāḳi'a (dream).

Sometimes this (revelation of truths) appeareth in the state of being present (in consciousness) without being absent (in unconsciousness).

Often the wāḳi'a is like to nawm; of wāḳi'a and manāmāt some are true and some false.

In most waḳāi' and manāmāt, nafs is partner with the rūḥ (soul); and in some absolute (alone). Truth is the quality of rūḥ, and falsehood of nafs.

Mukāshafa is never false; it signifieth oneness of soul by contemplating mysteries in the state of freedom from the gloomy thoughts of the body.

---

Wāḳi'a and mānām are divided into three parts:—

1. Free revelation (kashf).

Thus, with the eye of the free soul, by the imagination, a person, in sleep (khwab) or in wāḳi'a (dream) contemplateth the state of things which is yet in the hidden.

After that, even as he may have seen, it happeneth in the material world. But to the beholder it hath, on account of its concealment from outward sense, the order of the hidden.

If in khwāb (sleep), a person seeth that a certain spot containeth hidden treasure; and on searching findeth it,—it is kashf-i-mujarrad (pure revelation).

If this meaning fall to the understanding:—

(*a*) by way of manifestation, it is "the vision of the soul."
(*b*) by invisible messengers, „ "the ear „ „

Once in Baghdād was a darvīsh, who took the path of reliance on God; and closed the path of question. One day great need befell him; and he wished to beg.

Becoming penitent, he said:—

Much time in reliance on God, I have passed; that reliance, shall I now reject?

That night, in khwāb, he beheld a vision:—

An invisible messenger said:—In a certain place is deposited a blue rent khirḳa wherein are folded gold filings. Take it; and expend upon thy need.

When out from sleep he came, he found it to be even so.

This khwāb, they call true ruyā, a (dream) which is a part of prophecy.

For, in the beginning of prophecy, every khwāb (dream) that Muhammad beheld came true.

In this kind (of dream), is no falsehood; for, to the wise, after proof given by the traditions of the prophets, the sense in this revelation is a proof.

After separation from the body, the soul knoweth even of the small things heard and seen of this world.

The soul's knowledge is not restricted to small matters in respect to the outward and the inward senses. Nay, from the use of the outward senses, gain occurreth. By it, in the free state from the body, it discovereth the form of things felt. From using the vision, in it becometh painted the eye; from using the hearing, the ear.

2. Imaginary revelations from kinds of naum and wāḳi'a.

In khwāb or in wāḳi'a, the soul beholdeth some of the things hidden ; and in it, through connection with the soul, nafs displayeth partnership.

On the soul, by the power of imagination, nafs putteth the garment of a form fit for things felt; and thus beholdeth it.

In wāḳi'a, the murīd-warrior seeth that he is in contest with the lion, and wild beasts; with serpents and scorpions; and with kuffār.

The true shaikh knoweth that nafs is with him in strife; and its meaning he seeth to be:—

(*a*) in the form of wild beasts, violence.
(*b*) „ „ serpents and scorpions, enmity.
(*c*) „ „ kuffār, disobedience and separation (from God's mercy).

If he see that he travelleth deserts and wastes, passeth over rivers and seas, ascendeth in the air, or passeth over the fire—the shaikh knoweth that he travelleth the stages of lust; and beholdeth him in the form of the elements (the four natures).

If he see that from the qualities of a

| | |
|---|---|
| clayey, | airy, |
| watery, | fiery, |

nature, something passeth, the imaginary power giveth it glory to the dreamer's eye in the fancy-garment of travelling:—

| | |
|---|---|
| over wastes, | in the air, |
| „ seas, | over fire, |

The natures are:—

CLAYEY—

| | |
|---|---|
| parsimony, | iniquity, |
| slothfulness, | darkness, |
| ignorance, | foulness; |

WATERY—

| | |
|---|---|
| haste to society, | forgetfulness, |
| union with wicked lusts, | inclination to sleep'; |
| acceptance of change and of effect of society, | |

AIRY—

| | |
|---|---|
| inclination to lust, | haste to change from state to state; |
| great grief, | |

FIERY—

| | |
|---|---|
| anger, | desire for rank, |
| pride, | exaltation. |

The last stage of the stages of nafs, over which he passeth is this.

If it be revealed to him, he seeth :—

(*a*) the soul's truth in the form of the sun.
(*b*) ,, heart's ,, ,, ,, moon.
(*c*) ,, ,, qualities ,, ,, constellation.

Every truth that is revealed to him, he seeth in a suitable fancy-garment. Hence, this is called :—kashf-i-mukhayyal (fancied revelation).

In this, is possibility of falsehood but not of pure falsehood; for it is not void of the soul's understanding.

If, in the state of the soul's understanding, sensual thoughts join not with the soulish* understanding; and the imaginary power clothe not the soul with the fancy-garment,—that wāḳi'a, or khwāb, is all true.

If some of the sensual thoughts join with the soulish* understanding; and the imaginary power clothe all with the fancy-garment,—some are true, some false.

The dream interpreter freeth the soulish truths of understanding from the impurity of sensual thoughts; and interpreteth.

3. Pure fancy, when sensual thoughts have superiority over the heart, whereby the rūḥ (soul) is veiled from considering the hidden world.

In the state of naum and wāḳi'a, those thoughts become more powerful. Each one, the imaginary power clotheth with the fancy-garment; the form of those thoughts is seen by the eyes of the imaginary power; and its deceit becometh clear.

Thus, that one who ever hath the thought of finding treasure, and who in khwāb seeth that he hath found it; or the austere one, who claimeth the people's acceptance of him, and seeth in wāḳi'a that he is their adored,—the shaikh knoweth that this manifestation is only the result of lust's desire, which on its beholder hath become depicted.

If he calleth it vain desire; or—

(*a*) in khwāb, azghāṣ-i-aḥlām, confused un-interpretable dream.
(*b*) in wāḳi'a, false dream.

In these, the truth never appeareth; because nafs possessed of doubt is void of partnership with rūḥ (soul), the composer of those thoughts. From nafs, truth is far.

The conditions of true wāḳi'a (dream) are :—

(*i*) the being immersed in ẕikr, and being hidden from things felt.
(*ii*) the existence of sincerity and freedom of desire from the observance of others.

Possibly, free fancy, in respect to the sincere man, becometh "fancied revelation"; and, by reason of being immersed in ẕikr and in God's presence, the rūḥ (soul) of revelation becometh transmitted into the form of the fancy of nafs.

Then becometh true wāḳi'a, and capable of interpretation.

---

* Rūḥānī, soulish.

In all states, wāḳi'a with naum is similitude,—except when free fancy (khayāl-i-mujarrad) in khwāb is not proved. In wāḳi'a, free fancy may be proved.

---

It is evident that in wāḳi'a and manām, truth occurreth and also falsehood. In other manifestations, truth is impossible ; because there is naught save "free revelation (kashf-i-mujarrad) ."

Free revelation is :—

(*a*) in mukāshafa in the state of wakefulness.
(*b*) in khwāb or in wāḳi'a, in the state of being hidden from things felt.

In mukāshafa, the soul's understanding is attached to what is :—

(*a*) either in the hidden world.
(*b*) or „ material „

In the first case, its appearance in the material world,

(*a*) is impossible such as :—

| | |
|---|---|
| paradise, | the preserved tablet, |
| hell, | „ pen of creation. |
| God's throne and seat, | |

(*b*) is possible in the natural form as—possible events, necessary of acquirement, the form whereof shall not, in the hidden world, have yet been manifested.

(*c*) is possible in an accidental form as—
angels.
souls free from the body.

To Muḥammad, Jibrā,il used to appear in the human form, sometimes as a divine inspiration and sometimes as a desert-dweller, as in the Ḥadīṣ of 'Umar :—

Once a desert-dweller with white raiment and very black hair saluted Muḥammad, and sat close to him, knee to knee. Of Islām, of faith and of bounty he asked Muḥammad and heard his reply.
When he disappeared, Muḥammad said to the companions :—
Know ye who this asker is ?

They said :—

God knoweth and His prophet.

He said :—

It was Jibrā,il who came from God to teach you the dogmas of faith.

In this form, 'Umar and the other companions beheld him.

Then it became known that the form was not the result of imaginary power otherwise every one, according to contrariety of state, would have seen it in a different form as the semblance of free soul—

(*a*) in separation from the body
(*b*) „ attachment to „ „

The semblance of angels and of free souls in the human form is an accidental form. The manifestation of their natural (spiritual) state is, save in the hidden world, impossible.

In every way that they desire, they make semblance of the human form, as is stated in the ḥadīs̤ and in the verified speech of holy shaikhs.

In the second case, we have the following instances :—

(*a*) Muḥammad's beholding the masjid of Jerusalem, when he returned from the mi'rāj* (ascent to the highest heaven).

The infidels denied this tale and said :—If truly thou speakest, say how many columns there are in that remote masjid (of Jerusalem)?

In ḥāl, it became revealed; from his gaze the world uprose; he counted its columns; and gave the information.

(*b*) They asked Muḥammad to give some news of a ḳāfila near unto Shām.

The veil being lifted, Muḥammad saw that the ḳāfila had reached to a distance of one stage from Makka.

He said:—

Early in the morning, the ḳāfila will arrive. Even so it did.

(*c*) Once at Madīna, 'Umar Khaṯṯāb was on the Mimbar reading the khuṯba after he had sent Sāriya with an army to Nihāẕar.

Suddenly, in the midst of the khuṯba, he went into mukāshafa and saw that, against him, the enemy had made an ambush.

He cried out :—

O Sāriya! (go) to the mountain.

Sāriya heard; went to the mountain; and gained the victory.

The Shaikhu-l-Islām—Shaikh Shahābu-d-Dīn 'Umar bin Muḥammad-i-Sahrwardī —telleth many a tale like unto these.

---

The true murīd is he whose khilvat is not weakened by the desire for semblances of these revelations and miracles, and whose spirit is not restricted to their acquisition.

For to the rahābīn (Christian monks) who are not on the highway of the sharī'at and of the sunnat of Islām, this kind of revelation is not withheld.

This kashf (revelation) is naught save deceit; for, in its wajd, the rahābīn are daily prouder and further from the path of salvation.

If in the path of the true and the sincere, this kashf fall, it is a miracle; for it is the cause of strengthening of certainty, and of increase of devotion.

---

* See the Ḳurān P. D. xvii, i, 95; Clarke's translation of the Sikandar Nāma-i-Niẕāmī, canto 4.

## On 'ilm (knowledge).

II. 1.

'Ilm is a light from the candle of prophecy in the heart of the faithful slave whereby he gaineth the path—

(*a*) to God.
(*b*) ,, the work of God.
(*c*) ,, ,, order ,,

'Ilm is the special description of man ; from it, is excluded the understanding of his sense, and 'aḳl (reason).

'Aḳl is a natural light, whereby becometh distinguished good from evil.

The 'aḳl that distinguisheth between the good and evil :—

(*a*) of this world is an 'aḳl that belongeth to the kāfir as well as to the faithful.
(*b*) of the next world is an 'aḳl that belongeth only to the faithful.

'Ilm is special to the faithful ; 'ilm and 'aḳl are necessary for each other.

The eye of 'aḳl (of the next world) is luminous with the light of guidance ; and anointed with the kuḥl of the sharī'at. In its essence, it is one ; but it has two forms.

(*a*) One in respect of the Creator. Its meaning is the 'aḳl of guidance, special to the faithful.
(*b*) One in respect of the created. Its meaning is the 'aḳl of livelihood.

For people of faith and for seekers of God and of the next world, "the 'aḳl of livelihood" is obedient to "the 'aḳl of guidance."

Whenever these two 'aḳls agree, they credit "the 'aḳl of livelihood;" and according to exigency act : whenever they disagree, they discredit it, and to it pay no attention.

Thus, to the seekers of God, the man of this world ascribe weak 'aḳl. He knoweth not that outside their 'aḳl is another 'aḳl.

'Ilm is of three kinds :—

i. 'ilm-i-tauḥid, knowledge of the unity of God.
ii. 'ilm-i-ma'rifat, ,, ,, ,, work ,, ,,

| | |
|---|---|
| in respect of annihilation. | in respect of dispersing. |
| ,, creation. | ,, assembling. |
| ,, propinquity (to God). | ,, reward. |
| ,, distance (from God). | ,, punishment. |
| ,, making alive. | ,, other things. |
| ,, putting to death. | |

iv. 'ilm of the orders of the sharī'at of orders and of prohibitions.

Each one of these three paths hath a separate traveller. The traveller of :—

(*a*) the first path is the "sage of God." In his 'ilm, are, without opposition, included the other two 'ilms.

(*b*) the second path is the "sage of the next world." In his 'ilm, is, without opposition, included the 'ilm of the sharī'at.

(*c*) the third path is the "sage of this world." Of the other two 'ilms, no knowledge is his. If he had possessed it, he would have brought it into use. For the decline of good deeds is the result of defect of faith. If he had had his heart with God; and belief in the next world, he would not have passed below the doing of good deeds.

The sages of God have, with reason and conviction, faith in the unity of God; in the next world; and in the work of God.

Obedient to the orders of Islām, are :—

the first ones (near to God).
„ ṣūfis.

The sages of the next world, despite their belief in the next world, have a share (as much as is needed) of the knowledge of Islām; and employ it. They are :—

(*a*) the abrār (the pious).
(*b*) „ companions of the right hand.

The sages of this world have no share at all except the outward knowledge of Islām, which they have gained by being taught. What they have learned, they use not. Through defect of faith, they are not secure from passing into deeds, prohibited and detested. They are :—

(*a*) the companions of the left hand.
(*b*) „ wicked ones of men.
(*c*) „ sages of sin, upon whom have descended threat upon threat of God's wrath.

In the account of the mi'rāj* (the night-ascent to the highest heaven), it is said of Muḥammad :—

> I passed by a crowd, whose lips they had cut with fiery scissors. I asked saying :—Who are ye? They cried : - We are those who ordered for goodness, and prohibited from badness; and yet to badness we ourselves proceeded. (Ḥadīs̤.)

Better than the sage of God and of the next world, is none; worse than the sage of this world, none. (Ḥadīs̤.)

Than 'ilm, when they seek it for God's sake, naught is more profitable; when for the world's sake, naught greater loss.

'Ilm is like to victuals that essentially have, as regards the healthy, whose temperament is firm and quarters of the body free from humours, the power of nutrition;

---

* See p. 53 (foot note).

and that are as regards the sick, whose temperament is declining and quarters of the body filled with humours, the source of disease.

In its own nafs, 'ilm is a useful food, the cause of the expanding of nafs and of the heart, on the condition,—

that the follower is not infirm of desire, and of temperament; nor in love for the world; nor a turner from God.

When the temperament of the heart turneth in love to the world; and the parts of existence become filled with low humours, 'ilm becometh the cause of increase of desire, of pride, of haughtiness, of hate, and of the rest.

For the destruction of this great deceit, there is naught—

(*a*) save when that 'ilm, which is the guide of salvation, becometh the cause of destruction.
(*b*) save when that sage by whom the captives of the leader of desire gain freedom, becometh foot-bound in the snare of desire.

In nafs profitable 'ilm—

increaseth piety.
„ humility.
inflameth the fire of love and desire.
increaseth non-existence.

It is the aid of life; its severance from the heart is putting to death. Thus have spoken Fatḥ-i-Mūṣilī and Amīru-l-Mumūnīn, Ălī.

In nafs, noxious 'ilm increaseth—

pride.
haughtiness.
presumption.
desire for the world.

Profit from 'ilm appeareth to that one, who displayeth the service of resolution, not the following of license as Abū Yazīd-i-Bisṭāmī hath said.

In the midst of men the existence of the sage of God is God's best favour; his being hidden, the absence of God's favour, and the source of the darkness of kufr and of error.

---

## On ma'rifat (deep knowledge).

III. 1.

Ma'rifat signifieth the recognizing of the abridged 'ulūm (knowledge) in detail:—

'ilm-i-naḥw:—
is the knowing how each agent (of word or of meaning) acteth.

ma'rifat-i-naḥw:—
is the recognising of every agent in detail, at the time of reading, without either delay or consideration and its use in its place.

ta'rif-i-naḥw:—
is the recognising of the agent by thought.
To be careless of this (despite the 'ilm-i-naḥw) is a blunder.

The ma'rifat of God is dependent upon and bound up with the ma'rifat of the nafs. Ma'rifat of God signifieth :—

The recognising of the nature and the qualities of God in the form of detailed circumstances, of accidents, of calamities, after that it shall (in the way of abridgment) have become known that He is the True Existence and the Absolute Agent.

The possessor of the 'ilm-i-tauḥīd seeth in the form (of details, of dreams, and of state) :—

| | | |
|---|---|---|
| of loss | the causer of loss | who is God. |
| „ profit | „ profit | „ |
| „ prohibition | „ prohibition | „ |
| „ gift | „ gift | „ |
| „ contraction | „ contraction | „ |
| „ expansion | „ expansion | „ |

And recognizeth them without delay ; him, they call Ārif.

If at first he be careless of ma'rifat, and soon present (alive to it) becometh ; and in the form of different powers, recognizeth the Absolute Agent,—him, they call Muta'arrif.

If he be wholly careless, and (despite his 'ilm) recognizeth not God in form, in means, in links ; and to means assigneth the effects of deeds—him, they call—

sāhī, negligent, or g͟hāfil careless.
lāhī, playful.
mushrik, secret believer in partnership with God.

For instance, if he explaineth tauḥīd (the unity of God) and in its sea immerseth himself—and another, in the way of denial, refuseth him, saying :—

Not the essence of ḥāl is this speech ; 'tis the result of thought and of consideration.

he grieveth and becometh enangered.

He knoweth not that his grieving is a proof of the truth of the denier's speech ; otherwise he would have recognized the Absolute Agent in the form of this denial ; and against the denier would not have gathered anger.

In ma'rifat of nafs, every unapproved quality (which is known by abridged 'ilm) at the time when at the very beginning in nafs, it appeareth, he recogniseth and as to it exerciseth caution,—him, they call 'ārif : otherwise muta'arrif or g͟hāfil.

If in detail the abridged 'ilm he knoweth not,—him, they call g͟hāfil (careless). To him, this 'ilm is a source of loss.

If by 'ilm, he knoweth that pride is a blameable quality in nafs ; and when in nafs this appeareth, he fleeth into the screen of humbling himself—so that, recognising this quality in himself, his nafs may not again be with outward pride.

This, they call the ma'rifat of nafs.

The portion of—

(*a*) the 'ārif, is riẓā (agreement) with God's decrees.
(*b*) „ muta'arrif, patience in respect of God.
(*c*) „ ghāfil, detestation and perturbation.

The ma'rifat of God hath degrees:—

i. every effect that he gaineth, he knoweth to be from the Absolute Agent (God).
ii. „ „ that appeareth from the Absolute Agent, he knoweth to be result of a certain quality of His.
iii. in the glory of every quality, he recogniseth God's purpose.
iv. the quality of the 'ilm of God, he recogniseth in his own ma'rifat; and expelleth himself from the circle of 'ilm, of ma'rifat, and of existence.

Greater the degrees of propinquity (to God),—more apparent, the effects of God's grandeur.

By ignorance,* 'ilm is generally acquired; the ma'rifat of subtlety becometh greater; astonishment on astonishment increaseth; and from the 'ārif ariseth the cry—Increase in me astonishment at Thee.

This is all the 'ilm of ma'rifat, not ma'rifat; because ma'rifat is a matter of rapture the explanation whereof is defective, but its preface is 'ilm.

Then without 'ilm, ma'rifat is impossible; 'ilm without ma'rifat, disaster.

'Ilm and ma'rifat have some forms.

i. 'ilm-i-ma'rifat.
ii. ma'rifat-i-'ilm.
iii. 'ilm-i-ma'rifat-i-ma'rifat.

The last form is the perfection of form.

---

## On Ḥāl (mystic state) and Maḳām (stage).

IV. 1.

In the opinion of ṣūfīs, ḥāl signifieth a hidden event that, from the upper world, sometimes descendeth upon the heart of the holy traveller and goeth and cometh, until the divine attraction draweth him from the lowest to the loftiest stage.

Maḳām signifieth a degree of the Path that cometh in the way of the holy traveller's foot; becometh the place of his staying; and declineth not.

Ḥāl (which relateth to the zenith) cometh not in the traveller's sway; in its sway, is the traveller.

Maḳām (which relateth to the nādir) is the place of the traveller's sway.

---

* Till one knoweth one's ignorance, 'ilm (knowledge) cannot be acquired.

The ṣūfīs have said:—

The ḥāl is a gift (mauhab); the maḳām an acquisition (kasb).

Void of the entrance of ḥāl, is no maḳām; separate from union with maḳām, is no ḥāl.

As to ḥāl and maḳām, the source of contention of holy shaikhs is that some call this ḥāl; and some maḳām. For all maḳāms are at the beginning ḥāl, and at the end maḳām, as:—

| | |
|---|---|
| tauba, | penitence. |
| muḥāsiba, | calling one's self to account. |
| murāḳaba,* | fearful contemplation. |

Each one is at the beginning a ḥāl in change and in decline; and when by propinquity to kasb (acquisition), it becometh maḳām, all the ḥāl are lightened by makāsib (acquisitions) and all the maḳām by mawāhib (gifts).

In ḥāl, the gifts are outward, the acquisitions inward: in maḳām, the acquisitions are outward, the gifts inward.

The shaikhs of Khurāsān have said:—

Ḥāl is the heritage of deeds.

Hence the word of 'Alī ibn-i-Abī Ṭālib:—

The path of union with ḥāl (which through superiority relateth to the heavens) ask not of me.

The maḳāms are:—

| | |
|---|---|
| tauba, penitence, | ṣabr, patience, |
| zuhd, austerity, | and others. |

These are the means of the descent of ḥāl.

Some shaikhs urge:—

(a) that ḥāl is that which findeth neither resting nor confining. Like lightning it appeareth, and effaced becometh. If it be left, it becometh the ḥadīṣu-n-nafs.

(b) that so long as it is not left, it is not ḥāl. Because resting demandeth permanency; that which like lightning flasheth and expireth is not truly ḥāl.

This is the religious order of Shaikh Shahābu-d-Dīn-i-Sahrwardī.

It is said that if ḥāl be left, it is not the source of ḥadīṣu-n-nafs. Its source is a weak ḥāl, which, at the time of glittering, strong nafs seizeth; to nafs, strong ḥāl never becometh accustomed.

Every event that like lightning glittereth, and in ḥāl expireth,—
they call in ṣūfī-idiom:—

| | | | |
|---|---|---|---|
| lā, iḥ | evident | ṭariḳ | exploding. |
| lāmiḥ | glittering | bādih | apparent. |
| ṭāli' | arising | | |

---

* See p. 69.

Its manifestation is followed by concealment. Thus hath said Abū 'Uṣmān Ḥairī.

This hinteth at perpetual riẓā (contentment), and doubtless riẓā is of all ḥāls then perpetual ḥāl is unnecessary for ḥadīṣu-n-nafs.

Is the amending of a maḳām (which is his foot-place) before ascending to a higher stage, possible or not?

Junīd hath said:—

> Possible it is before the first ḥāl is finished for a slave to advance to a higher ḥāl. Thence he gaineth information of the first ḥāl and amendeth it.

'Abdu-l-lāh Anṣārī hath said:—

> Impossible is the amending of any maḳām till from a higher maḳām the holy traveller looketh into the lower maḳām, of it gaineth information, and it amendeth.

Shaikh Shahābu-d-Dīn-i-Sahrwardī hath said:—

> Impossible is advance to a higher maḳām before amending the maḳām (which is his foot-place). But before advancing, there descendeth from the higher maḳām, a ḥāl whereby his maḳām becometh true. Hence his advance from maḳām to maḳām is by God's sway and of His gift—not of his own acquisition.
>
> So long as from the low to the lofty, advance approacheth not; from the lofty to the low, no ḥāl descendeth.

In the Ḥadīṣ, is the imputing of the slave's approach to God; and of God's approach to the slave.

---

## On Tauḥid (unity of God), and Zat (existence of God).

I. 2.

The 'Ulamā of ṣūfī,ism who through being detached from affairs, have gained union with the wine of 'ilm; the step of whose souls and hearts hath become firm; the eye of whose vision by the light of beauty of eternity without beginning hath become anointed,—know, see and find by the path of 'ilm-i-yaḳīn, established proof, of kashf (revelation), of seeing, of ẓauḳ (delight), and of wajd (ecstasy).

Witness, do they bear that no person nor thing is worthy of being worshipped save the one God, the God of unity, the Eternal, pure (void) of parent, of offspring, of aid; pure (void) of resemblance, of equal, of wazīr and of counsellor.

Neither in opposition to His order, is an opposition; nor in the government of His realm, an enemy.

Ever is described His ancient existence by unity; and known by singularity.

Expelled from His holiness and purity, are the qualities of accidents,—

> of form, similitude, union, separation, association, descent, issue, entrance, change, decline, alteration, and translation.

From the understanding of the reading of men's thoughts, the perfection of His beauty and the beauty of His perfection (un-connected with the beauty of His singularity)—free; from the trouble of the clothing of ẓikrs, the grandeur of His eternity—free.

In description of Him, narrow is the power of the warriors of the plain of eloquence; in praise of Him, lame is the foot of the chiefs of the plain of ma'rifat.

Than the offering of the senses, than the discussion of conjecture, loftier is the column of understanding Him; of the passing of imaginings and the happening of understandings, void is the honour-plain of His ma'rifat.

In the beginning of His ma'rifat, is no guide save astonishment and perturbation to the pure ones of Lordship, who are at the limit of reason; in the splendour of the light of His grandeur is no path save blindness and ignorance to the vision of the possessors of Sight.

If thou say:—
He hath created His abode,—where?

The answer is:—
(In the place of)—He.

If thou say:—
(Visible) to the eye, brought He time,—when?

The answer is:—
(At the time of)—He.

If thou say:—
Resemblance and sufficiency made He—how?

The answer is:—
(By means of)—He.

No limit hath He. Within this limit, are comprehended—eternity without beginning and eternity without end; folded in the fold of His plain, are existence and dwelling (the universe); in His beginning, all beginnings—the end; in His ending, all endings, the beginning; in His outwardness, the outward manifestation of things, the inward; in His inwardness, the inward parts of worlds, the outward; in His eternity without beginning, the collection of eternities without beginning only an accident (ḥādiṣ); in His eternity without end, all eternities without end, only an event (muḥdaṣ).

From whatever is contained in reason, in understanding, in the senses, in conjecture,—exempted and free is the nature of the Lord.

For these all were muḥdaṣāt (accidents); save understanding muḥdaṣ (accident), muḥdaṣ can do naught.

The argument of His existence is His existence; the proof of His witnessing is His witnessing.

Naught save the beauty of eternity without beginning is the bearer of the beauty of eternity without beginning. In this stage the limit of understanding is weakness.

To the substance of the understanding of Wāḥid (unity of God), save Wāḥid—no muwaḥḥid (professor of unity) can reach.

Where his understanding is ended, there is the limit of *his* understanding not of Wāḥid (God).

Who considereth Wāḥīd comprehended in his knowledge, is verily deceived and presumptuous.

Tauḥīd is the negation of separation; and the affirmation at the limit of collection.

In the beginning of the tauḥīd of ḥāl (mention whereof will presently be made), this description is necessary.

But, possibly, at its end, one in separation may be immersed in collection; and in collection, the spectator (with the eye of collection) of separation—as each collection, or separation, is not a forbidder of the other. In this is the perfection of tauḥīd.

Tauḥīd hath degrees:—

| | | | | |
|---|---|---|---|---|
| i. | tauḥīd-i-īmāni, the tauḥīd of faith. | | | |
| ii. | ,, | 'ilmī | ,, | knowledge. |
| iii. | ,, | ḥālī | ,, | ḥāl. |
| iv. | ,, | ilāhī | ,, | Godship. |

Tauḥīd-i-īmānī is:—

When (according to the urgency of the order of Ḳurānic verse and of the Ḥadiṣ) the slave verifieth to his heart, and confesseth with the tongue, as to the singularity of the description of Godship and to the unity of rights of the adored Lord.

This tauḥīd is the mukhbir (news-bringer) and the belief of sincerity is the khabar (news). Profit from outward 'ilm and holding thereto is freedom from open partnership; turning in the thread (entering the circle) of Islām giveth profit.

Through necessity, with muslims, ṣūfīs believe in this tauḥīd; but, in other degrees, are separate.

Tauḥīd is:—

An 'ilm of benefit from the heart of 'ilm which they call the 'ilm-i-yaḳīn (the knowledge of certainty).

This 'ilm-i-yaḳīn is such that, in the beginning of the path of ṣūfi,ism, the slave knoweth, from the desire of yaḳīn (certainty), that the true existence and absolute Penetrator is none save the Lord of the world.

In His ẓāt (nature) and qualities, effaced and naught he (by 'ilm) regardeth his own ẓāt and qualities.

The splendour of every nature, he recogniseth from the light of Absolute Existence; and every ray, from the light of the quality of the Absolute (God).

When he gaineth:—

| | |
|---|---|
| an 'ilm. | a hearing. |
| a ḳudrat. | ,, seeing. |
| ,, desire. | |

he knoweth them to be the effects of:—

| | |
|---|---|
| an 'ilm of God. | a hearing of God. |
| a ḳudrat ,, | ,, seeing ,, |
| ,, desire ,, | |

Thus for all qualities and deeds.

This degree is of the first degrees of tauḥīd of the man of speciality and of ṣūfī,-ism; its preface is joined to the column of tauḥīd-i-'āmm; and the semblance of this degree, those short of sight call tauḥīd-i-'ilmī, but verily it is the tauḥīd-i-rasmī, mutilated of the rank of credit.

This tauḥīd-i-rasmī is such as a person, with desire of intelligence and of understanding, might through reading and hearing, conjecture as the meaning of tauḥīd. In his mind, a rasm (impression) of the form of 'ilm-i-tauḥīd becometh painted; thence, in the midst of argument,—since, in him is no effect from the ḥāl-i-tauḥīd—he uttereth brainless words.

Tauḥīd-i-'ilmī, although it is a low degree of the tauḥīd-i-ḥālī, wherefrom fellow-traveller with it is a temperament:

"Its temperament is one of tasnīm, a fountain wherefrom those near to God drink,"

is the description of the wine of this tauḥīd.

Hence, its possessor is often in ẓauk and joy; because, by the effects of the temperament of ḥāl, some of the darkness of his impressions becometh lifted. As in some changes, he worketh according to the demand of his own 'ilm, and bindeth up, in the midst, the existence of causes which are the links of the deeds of God; but, in many a ḥāl, by reason of the residue of the darkness of existence, he becometh veiled from the demand of his own 'ilm.

In this tauḥīd, some of the hidden shirk (the giving companions to God) departeth.

Tauḥīd-i-ḥālī is when the ḥāl of tauḥīd becometh the necessary description of the nature of the muw,aḥḥid (professor of unity).

Save a little residue in the superiority of the rising of the light of tauḥīd, all the darknesses of impressions of His existence vanish, and, in the light of his ḥāl, veiled and included (like to the being rolled together the light of the constellations and the light of the sun) becometh the light of 'ilm-i-tauḥīd.

In the stage of existence, in viewing the beauty of the existence of Wāḥid (unity), the muw,aḥḥid becometh so immersed in jam' " (union) that, in the vision of his witnessing, naught cometh save the nature of the qualities of Wāḥid—so much so that he regardeth tauḥīd the quality of Wāḥid not his own quality. This (act of) regarding (of his) he regardeth His quality.

In this way, his existence falleth like a drop in the power of the dashing waves of the ocean of tauḥīd ; and in jam' (union) becometh immersed.

The source of :—

(*a*) tauḥid-i-ḥālī is the light of manifestation.
(*b*) „ „ 'ilmī „ „ murāḳaba (fearful contemplation).

By tauḥīd-i-ḥālī, (like to the light of the sun in whose superiority of manifestation, most parts of darkness rise up and disappear from earth's surface) become repulsed many of the impressions of humanity.

By tauḥīd-ī-ḥālī most of the hidden shirk (giving companions to God) ariseth (to disappear); and from the truth of pure tauḥīd (wherein all at once the effects and the impressions of existence vanish) to the special muw, aḥḥids in the ḥāl of life sometimes the flash like unto flashing lightning becometh bright, and immediately is extinguished.

The residue of other circumstances aideth; in this state, the residue of hidden shirk becometh wholly repulsed; outside this degree of tauḥīd, is possible no other degree.

By tauḥīd-i-'ilmī (like to the light of the moon in whose manifestation, parts of darkness become repulsed and some are left), become up-lifted (to disappear) some of the impressions of humanity.

The cause of existence of some of the residue of impressions in tauḥīd-i-ḥālī is this :—

On the muw,aḥḥid's part not possible is the issuing of the arranging of deeds and the purifying of words; for this reason in the ḥāl of his life, the right of tauḥid (as is necessary) becometh not discharged.

Tauḥīd-i-ilāhī is :—

That whereby in the eternity without beginning of eternities without beginning by His own nafs, not by the tauḥīd of another,—God is ever described with singularity and qualified with praise.

Now, in praise of eternity without beginning He is wāḥid and one ; and thus, to the eternity without end of the eternities without end, is.

So that to-day it became known that in His own existence, the existence of the beauty of things vanish.

For the veiled ones, is the promise of beholding this ḥāl (of God) till to-morrow (the judgment-day). But for the Lords of vision and for the companions of beholding (who have obtained freedom from the restricted places of time and of abode), this promise is cash indeed (immediate).

The honour of His singularity and the wrath of His unity gave not power in His existence, to other existence.

The right of tauḥīd is this: this is the tauḥīd that is free from the reproach of defect.

By reason of defect of existence, the tauḥīd of angels and of man is defective.

Thus, Shai<u>kh</u> Abū 'Abdu-l-lāh Anṣārī hath said.

---

## The Affairs of the next world.

I. 10.

The preface to pure 'ilm is true faith.

So long as increase of faith descendeth not into the stages of the hearts of will, the ḳāfila of 'ilmu-l-yaḳīn (the knowledge of certainty) taketh not down its chattels of staying in the heart; the treading of the path by verification and by seeking the traces of the prophets, is impossible save by the foot of faith and of submission and by the guide of love and of reverence; and the effort in desire of advance, without preserving one's self from sin by the rope of God and by the sunnat of prophecy, is error and disaster.

If, with the foot of defective reason and understanding, a person wisheth to advance from the abyss of ignorance to the summit of ilm, although he may put forward great effort, he seeth himself in the end, at the first place, momently descending into degrees of loss.

For when the path with lofty degrees becometh closed, and yet the motive of desire is left,—nafs turneth to decline and rolleth about in the seventh hell to the lowest of the low.

As to the hidden world and the circumstances of the next world (as by the Ḳurān-i-Majīd, and by the Ḥadīṣ of prophecy have arrived), it is incumbent on every one to have faith—

In the torment of the grave, in the questioning of munkir and nākir, in the assembling and dispersing, in the account and the balance, in the bridge and ṣirāt, in paradise and hell, in the issuing of nations (through the intercession of the prophet) from fire.*

and, not with weak reason and fine understanding, to begin for one's self upon its interpretation; and not to wander about the sufficiency and the wherefore.

Because in respect to 'ilm-i-īmānī (the knowledge of faith), the limit is not the degree of human understanding. In it, even the prophets have not exercised power.

What from revelation they have seen, in it with certainty, they have had faith the faith, which (from the prophets) to the hearts of nations (according to their purity) hath reached.

Reason hath a limit beyond which when it passeth, into error it falleth.

---

* See Wherry's Ḳurān (Index):—Nākir and munkir, the bridge, hell, paradise, intercession.

The limit of the five senses is :—

When things felt by them are apparent and existing as :—

| | |
|---|---|
| things seen. | things tasted. |
| „ heard. | „ touched. |
| „ smelt. | |

When out of these something issueth and the understander is in his senses, true is the understanding of it :—

When he perceiveth something not existing (as things comprehended by the distraught),—not true is the understanding of it.

The limit of khiyāl (fancy) is :—

When, after effacement, it regardeth things comprehended of the outward senses. When it passeth its limit and trieth to comprehend things not perceived,—the fancy is error.

A person heareth the name of one whom he hath never seen; he evoketh a form purely imaginary. When the hidden becometh present, the imaginary form may, or may not, be concordant with his (real) form.

The limit of wahm (imagination) is—

When out of a form of things perceived he gaineth in part a sense of things not perceived; as a sheep from seeing the wolf comprehendeth the sense of enmity not perceived.

When he transgresseth, and imagineth things sensible and spiritual, he falleth into error.

Thus he cannot imagine rūḥ (the soul) merely from the form of the body as to :—

| | |
|---|---|
| its entering. | its separation. |
| „ issuing. | „ nearness. |
| „ union. | „ farness. |

He cannot find the limit of the world of bodies.

When beyond it he beginneth imagining, he falleth into error.

The limit of 'aḳl (reason) is :—

the understanding of the world of ḥikmat; no path into the world of ḳudrat is its.

The world of ḥikmat signifies :—

The existence of cause. For to a cause, the absolute Wise One hath bound every existing thing in the world of dominion and of witnessing (the world material); and by means of that cause, hath caused to pass the sunnat (the creation of that existence)—not in this sense that, without that cause, existence is impossible in God's power. For the arrangement of the world of ḥikmat, God hath joined existence to cause. Guardian over the world of ḥikmat, they have made reason; to it not true (is) a power in the world of ḳudrat (the creating of something without the means of a cause).

Whenever out of the world of ḳudrat, he heareth something, he saith it is not reasonable; or ordereth as to its alteration.

He knoweth not that—not inexcused is what is un-reasonable.

Not reasonable is the existence of the child. Without the seed of the father, the acceptance of it by the mother, its settlement in the womb, and the passing of the appointed time in the world of ḥikmat—it existeth not.

But, in the world of ḳudrat, it is possible and doth occur. As the existence :—

of Ādam.
„ Ḥavvā.
„ 'Isā̤.

When to the world of ḳudrat, reason findeth no path, and desireth sway in it,—it falleth into error.

To explanation, he hasteth saying, the meaning is such and such.

Verily the imputation of ignorance he accepteth not; and knoweth not whence is the source of error. If in his own limit (the world of ḥikmat) he had stood, into this error he would not have fallen; evident it would have been that from the garment of ḥikmat one cannot find the world of ḳudrat save by faith.

Possibly if words like these reach the ear of hypocrites, they will in the way of jest laugh at the speaker's reason; and name it delirium.

No knowledge have the helpless ones. At them, the man of vision and the Lords of explanation look with pity; and, at the lowness of their reason and at the poverty of their understanding, laugh. Like a captive, they are in the world of ḥikmat veiled from the world of ḳudrat.

Like this is the confining of the embryo in the narrow place of the womb.

If, by chance, to it a person were to say :—

> Outside the narrow place of the womb is another world, a great space, a great breadth, a sky, a land, a sun, a moon, and other things.

Never would the imagining and the reasoning of it appear true save by faith.

Even so the dwellers of the narrow world of ḥikmat cannot save by faith gain the circumstances of the world of ḳudrat until man's soul from the narrow place of the womb of the world of ḥikmat cometh to the space of the world of g͟haib and of ḳudrat; or by the death of nature and of will which they call "the second birth,"* even as 'Isā hath written.

Before faith, whatever they have accepted, only by the eye, they see; so long as the veil of humanity is not uplifted, only the eye revolveth.

To-day save by the power of inward taste (which meaneth faith), one cannot find the ẕauḳ (delight) of the limit of (this given by) the prophets.

There is a crowd in whom that power is not created; and whose directing is impossible; and a crowd in whom this power is created.

But, by the power of sickness of desire, they have been ruined; and in their palate, the food of truths, like the 'ilm of faith, appeareth bitter.

On all men of faith, it is incumbent to aid God :—

> by raising the faith of Muṣṭafā̤ Muḥammad); by destroying the vain; by repelling the deceit of men of error; and by prohibiting the power of shaiṭāns, man-in-form.

The sharī'at of Muḥammad and his creed is the straight path and trodden highway; the seal (last) of the sent ones (prophets), trusted one of the Lord of both worlds with so many thousands of troops of nations (holy ones, pure ones, martyred ones)

---

John iii, 3.

hath gone on that highway and swept it of thorn, of rubbish, of doubt; and of suspicion; hath established knowledge of it and of its stages; hath left behind a trace of every pace; hath established an alighting place at every stage; hath for the repelling of the robbers of the path sent the guide of resolution as fellow-traveller.

If a strange surveyor claimeth that the path is not straight, and inviteth the people to another path,—his word should not be regarded; and for its repelling, the aid of the true faith is of the number of ordinances and of requisites.

The men of deceit and of error are a crowd who outwardly wear the robe of Islām; and towards Islām inwardly keep concealed kufr and hate; outwardly mix with the men of Islām; show themselves to the people as verified 'ulamā and confirmed ḥukamā; instruct in the eternity of this world and in the denial of the resurrection; regard the 'ulamā and the shai<u>kh</u>s of Islām as the enemy; and (because by the light of their 'ilm, their own hiding and dark places become discovered) render contemptuous their form.

The God-like 'ulamā are the stars of the sky of sharī'at; it, they ever keep preserved from the sway of shaiṯāns of men. Their luminous breath like to the penetrating meteor pelteth those (the shaiṯāns of men) concealing and carrying off the mysteries of the sharī'at; keepeth them on every side perturbed and restless; and repelleth from the people their deceitful wickedness.

Wherever these men of deceit gain sway, they make the people shun the 'ulamā; begin in the souls of those ready, satanic sway, and (by iniquity of faith, and by the cutting off of the link of Islām from the order of man) the ruining of their faith; turn the pure simple heart from the purity of nature; conceal themselves behind the shield of Islām; make sure the arrow of treachery and of loss at the butt of faith and of religion; and secretly, with courteous glance, call man to destruction.

They are the enemies of faith, the brothers of shaiṯān; ignorant of rules, the causer of injuries.

Before the Lord of both worlds, no devotion hath such a lofty degree as the repelling of this crowd and the uplifting of the foundations of their deceit and hypocrisy.

---

The men of submission (to repel these men of deceit and error) are:—

(*a*) men of ḵudrat (power).
(*b*) „ 'ilm (knowledge).

The men of ḵudrat act:—

by way of slaughter and of rapine; of chastisement and punishment; of denial and of banishment.

The men of 'ilm act:—

by manifesting deceit, hypocrisy and heresy.

Who, on one of these two ways, hath power, is by it ordered; by accepting it, rewarded; and by abandoning it, requited.

## 'Ilm-i-Ḳiyam (knowledge of God's standing as the slave's observer).

II. 5.

In the opinion of the ṣūfīs, 'ilm-i-ḳiyām signifieth :—

A special 'ilm, wherein, in all movings and restings, outward and inward, the slave seeth God standing over him and observing him.

This sense is from the Ḳurān.

Hence, the slave keepeth himself adorned, outwardly and inwardly, with the garment of rules agreeing with the orders of God, and separated from the garment of opposition (to Him).

This is a precious 'ilm which, in ṣūfī,īstic idiom, they call :—

'ilm-i-muraḳaba.*

Who maketh it his inward habit, becometh delighted with all exalted maḳāms and precious ḥāls ; the reverence and the fear of God become his teacher in all affairs as Muḥammad hath said.

Sahl Abdu-l-lāh Tastarī mostly ordered his murīds by this 'ilm of precept ; and said :†—

Void of four things, be ye not.

i. 'ilm-i-ḳiyām, that ye may—, in every ḥāl, witnesser and observer of you,—see God.
ii. the service of devotion, that ye may ever keep yourselves established in confirmity with devotion to Him.
iii. constantly ask God for the aid of His grace in respect of these two things, (i, ii).
iv. persevere in these three things till death ; for, in these four things, are the good of this, and the next, world ; and happiness inwardly and outwardly.

'Ilm-i-ḳiyām is the ẕikr of the heart at the time of motion limbs and resolution of the heart in respect to :—

(*a*) ḳiyām, on himself.
(*b*) shuhūd-i-ḥaḳḳ, „

So that in conformity with that ordered, the motion and the resolution may be.

This they call :—

(*a*) ẕikr-i-farīẕa, the ẕikr of God's ordinance.
(*b*) „ „ zabān, „ the tongue.
(*c*) „ „ faẕīlat, „ excellence.

Thus, they say :—

Yesterday is dead ; to-morrow is not born ; to-day is in the agonies of death.

Who is engaged in the ẕikr of the past and of the future is in destruction.

---

* See pp. 59, 64, 86, 114.

† To the end, is 'Abdu-l-lāh's discourse.

The safety and the salvation of the people is in their being engaged in the ordinance of the time ('ilm-i-ḳiyām), with the practice of the pleasurable deed. Because, in this ḥāl, theirs can be :—

| | |
|---|---|
| breathing. | rest. |
| doing anything. | favour. |

Than other 'ilms, this 'ilm is :—

more dear
„ strange
„ profitable.

Yours the service of that in surety whereof are included perpetual country and constant favour.

Who perpetually seeketh this fortune without preface, maketh severance of connections ; without shunning the society of strangers, patience as to the opposition of nafs appeareth not.

---

## 'Ilm-i-ḥal (knowledge of the mystic state).

II. 6.

Of the special ṣūfī,istic 'ilms, one is :—
'ilm-i-ḥāl.

which consisteth—

in regarding the heart and considering the mystery of that state (which is between the slave and the Lord) by equalling the increase and the loss ; by levelling powerfulness and feebleness by the touch-stone of proof, so that by observing truths and by preserving rule he may establish ḥāl.

For, there is a rule for every ḥāl in respect to its own nafs, according to :—

(*a*) the time.
(*b*) „ makām.

Thus from the ḥāl of riẓā, in respect to its nafs, is a rule,—the rest of nafs.

As to the calamities arising from God's order, according to the time when calamity :—

(*a*) increaseth is a rule,—the performance of thanks so long as the increase of the ḥāl of riẓā and the folding of nafs in the folds of despair are not confirmed until the quality of independence and of pride becometh not evident.
(*b*) ceaseth is a rule—asking God for help so that He may open the door of advance and of increase ; may preserve nafs from motion ; and (for desire of increase) may into the slave's heart, bring a desire shauḳ-exciting, and a shauḳ, affliction-mixing.

For the increase of the ḥāl of riẓā is another order and rule in the stage—

(*a*) of concordance (with the orders of God),—riẓā and joy.
(*b*) of opposition,—denial and grief.

In each of these two stages, contrary to the rule of increase, is a rule for the decrease of the ḥāl of riẓa.

> Who regardeth the form of his own state between him and the Lord, according to its rule, according to every time and stage, is preserved; and, to the maturity of perfection and to the stage of men (devoted to God), reacheth.
>
> Who is careless of it is not secure of the robbers of the Path. This is an employment wherein if his life be expended, not discharged is its due.

The holy travellers of this Path are separate according to difference of power of capacity and of weakness thereof.

Some, in their nafs, know this difference of circumstances (joy and sorrow) and thereby discriminate between their increase and decrease.

Momently, in respect of a former moment they discover the difference of their ḥāl.

Some discover this change at times; some in hours; some in days.

Sahl Ȧbdu-l-lāh-i-Tastarī hath said:—

> Safety, the slave gaineth not, save when he is learned in his ḥāl and forgetteth it not; and, by it, is obedient to God.

They asked saying:—

> What is the 'ilm-i-ḥāl?

He said:—

> Whose state with God is the abandoning of will and the negation of desire, ever regardeth this ḥāl according to exigency; and ever abandoneth design; whenever in himself, he findeth inclination to a plan, he denieth it; what knoweth he but that it is the repeller of his ḥāl.

Sahl hath by the abandoning of will made the speciality of the 'ilm-i-ḥāl; because loftier than it, is no ḥāl.

---

## 'Ilm-i-yaḳīn (knowledge of certainty).

II. 9.

'Ilm-i-yaḳīn (the knowledge of certainty) signifieth—

> The revelation of the light of ḥaḳiḳat in the state of concealment of humanity by the evidence of wajd (ecstasy) and of ẓauḳ (delight), not by the guidance of ȧḳl (reason) and ḥadiṣ (report).

They call this light:—

(*a*) beyond the veil,—the light of faith.
(*b*) through „ „ yaḳīn.

Verily, not more than one light—the light of faith,—is there when it becometh the heart's agent.

Without the veil of humanity, it is the light of yaḳīn. As long as a residue of existence is, ever the cloud of the qualities of humanity go rising from the soul of humanity; and covereth the sun of ḥaḳīḳat (truth).

Sometimes, it becometh scattered; and by way of wajd, the heart from the flashing of the light gaineth ẓauḳ, as the cold-stricken one, on whom suddenly shineth, the sun's light from its splendour and warmth gaineth ẓauḳ (delight).

Regard the sun as the ḥaḳīḳat-i-ḥaḳā,iḳ (the truth of truths) ; its light, like the flashing of ḥaḳīḳat, shining from outside the veil of the light of safety, manifested through the veil of the light of yaḳīn ; and the cold-stricken one, like that one veiled with the qualities of humanity in the light of faith.

Then is the light of faith ever firm ; the light of yaḳīn, sometimes flashing and bright, as in the ḥadīṣ.

Yaḳīn hath three degrees. Thus, as to the sun's existence, a person is void of doubt:—

i. by seeking guidance from beholding the sun's splendour and understanding its heat.
This is 'ilm-i-yaḳīn.

ii. by beholding the sun's body.
This is 'ainu-l-yaḳīn.

iii. by the dispersing of the eye's light in the sun's light.
This is ḥaḳḳu-l-yaḳīn.

Then—

(*a*) in 'ilmu-l-yaḳīn, it is known, verified and evident.
(*b*) „ 'ainu-l-yaḳīn, it is manifest and witnessed.
(*c*) „ ḥaḳḳu-l-yaḳīn, a double way ariseth in consequence of—

| | |
|---|---|
| the witnesser. | the looker on. |
| „ witnessed. | „ looked „ |

Thus, the seer becometh the eye ; the eye, the seer.

In the ḥāl of the residue of the composition, this sense (like lightning that cometh into flash and immediately expireth), appeareth not more than a moment to the perfect and to those joined with God.

If an hour it be left, the thread of composition looseneth ; and the way of existence ariseth (and departeth).

Of yaḳīn—

(*a*) the root is 'ilmu-l-yaḳīn.
(*b*) „ branches are 'ainu-l-yaḳīn and ḥaḳḳu-l-yaḳīn.

Faith hath many degrees, whereof one is yaḳīn.

Yaḳīn giveth the heart freedom from the perturbation of doubt : it, the shar' hath called faith as in the ḥadīṣ.

What by way of adducing reasonable proof becometh known is far from 'ilm-i-yaḳīn ; because :—

(*a*) that (the adducing of reasonable proof) is the 'ilm of adducing proof.
(*b*) this (yaḳīn) „ „ ḥāl.

Not all at once, save by the rising of the sun of ḥaḳīḳat, becometh the darkness of doubt removed.

## Nafs (essence).

III. 2.

Nafs hath two meanings :—

(*a*) nafs-i-shay (the nafs of a thing) which is the ẕat (essence) and the ḥaḳīḳat (truth) of a thing. Thus they say :—

" By its own nafs, a certain thing is standing."

(*b*) nafs-i-nātiḳa-i-insānī (the human rational nafs) which is the abstract of the graces of the body, which they call—the human natural soul, and a luminosity (which is bestowed on it from the lofty human soul) by which luminosity the body becometh the place of revelation of iniquity and of piety, as the Ḳurān hath said.

The ma'rifat of nafs is in all qualities difficult, for nafs hath the nature of the chameleon.

Momently appeareth a different colour; hourly cometh forth another form. It is the Hārūt of the Bābil of existence; momently, another vanishing picture on water nafs expresseth, and beginneth another sorcery.

Hints as ṭo the ma'rifat of nafs are (found) in the links and conditions of the ma'rifat of God.

The recognising of nafs in all its qualities, and the reaching to a knowledge of it is not the power of any created thing. Even so difficult, is the reaching to the substance of the ma'rifat of God; and even so, to the ma'rifat of nafs, as Ȧlī hath said.

The names of nafs are :—

nafs-i-ammāra, imperious nafs (concupiscence).
" " lawwāma, reproaching "
" " muṭma,inna, restful "

They call nafs :—

(*a*) nafs-i-ammāra
At the beginning, as long as under its sway, is existence.

(*b*) nafs-i-lawwāma.
In the middle when obedient to the heart's sway it becometh, while is left yet some residue of the nafs of obstinacy whereon it ever reproacheth itself.

(*c*) nafs-i-muṭma,inna.
At the end, when extirpated from it, become the veins of contention and of abhorrence; when from contention with the heart it gaineth rest, and becometh obedient to order; when to riẓā becometh changed its abhorrence.

In the beginning, when nafs is yet firm in the dwelling of nature, it ever wisheth to draw to its own low dwelling the rūḥ (soul) and the heart from the lofty region; and ever giveth to itself in their sight the splendour of a new decoration. As a broker, shaiṭān adorneth the worthless majesty of nafs; and restless for it maketh souls and hearts, so that he may make low the exalted soul, and polluted the purified heart.

Thus have said :—

Sahl Ȧbdul-l-lāh.
Abū Yazīd.
Junīd.

The crowd who consider rational nafs and heart to be one, do so because at the end, they find nafs described with the description of rest and contentment (the specialities of the heart).

The suspicion is that between the heart and rational nafs is no difference.

Nafs-i-muṭma,inna is indeed another nafs. They know not that it is verily nafs-i-muṭma,inna, which is stripped of the garment of vagrancy, and clad in the honour-robe of rest and of riẓā; and which hath taken the heart's colour.

Whenever, nafs-i-ammāra taketh the heart's colour, the heart also taketh the soul's colour (and pursueth good deeds).

---

## On some of the qualities of nafs.

III. 3.

The source of the blameable qualities in man is nafs: the source of the laudable qualities is rūḥ (the soul).

The blameable qualities of nafs are ten :—

1. hawā (desire).

Nafs desireth to advance as to its desires; to place in its bosom the desires of nature; to bind on its waist the girdle of its consent with desire and to hold God in partnership, as saith the Kalām-ī-Majīd.

This quality departeth not save by austerity and by love for God.

2. nifāḳ (hypocrisy).

In many outward states, nafs is not concordant with its interior; not one before it, is man's being absent or his being present.

In man's presence, nafs praiseth and displayeth sincerity; in his absence,—just the contrary.

This quality departeth not save by the existence of sincerity.

3. riyā (hypocrisy).

Ever in its bond, is nafs that, in man's sight, it may keep itself adorned with laudable qualities (though in God's sight through hypocrisy they are blameable) :—

| | |
|---|---|
| abundance of property and boasting thereof. | violence. |
| pride. | independence. |

Whatever is reprehensible before the people, nafs shunneth and concealeth,—though in God's sight it be laudable:—

| | |
|---|---|
| faḳr (poverty)<br>submission<br>humility | Laudable in God's sight; reprehensible in the people's. |

This departeth not save by knowledge of the paltry worth of the people as Junid and Abu Bakr Warāḳ have said.

Nafs is a hypocrite like unto fire that revealeth the good quality (light), and concealeth the bad quality (consuming).

Although nafs revealeth the beautiful and concealeth the ugly,—it is not concealed save to those of defective vision.

It is like unto an old woman detestable of appearance, who adorneth herself with sumptuous apparel of varied colour and with henna. Only to boys, doth that decoration appear to be good ; to the wise, abhorrence increaseth.

4. The claim to Godship, and obstinacy against God. Nafs ever desireth that people should praise it ; should obey its orders ; should love it above all ; should of it be fearful and display the bond of dependence upon its mercy.

Thus against these orders, God cautioneth His own slaves.

These qualities depart not save by the glory of the qualities of God.

5. Pride and self-beholding.

Nafs ever looketh at its own beauteous qualities ; regardeth with contentment the form of its own ḥāl. The paltry benefaction that from it occurreth to another, it exalteth ; for years forgetteth it not ; and regardeth him as being immersed in obligation.

If to nafs, great benefaction cometh, it regardeth it as paltry and almost forgetteth it.

This is of the number of deadly sins as Muḥammad hath said, and as is entered in the ḥadīṣ.

This departeth not save through self-contempt.

6. Avarice and parsimony.

Whatever chattels of goods and of desire it gathereth, it letteth not go save through pride, or through fear of poverty (in the future).

When this quality is strong in nafs, from it springeth envy ; for envy is the breeding of miserliness for the property of others.

If it see another with special favour, it seeketh his decline ; when it gathereth power, hate appeareth.

Him, who with itself gaineth equality in affluence ; whom it seeth distinguished for an excellence, whom it regardeth as the cause of a favour being refused,—his destruction, nafs ever desireth.

This departeth not save under the power of the light of yaḳīn.

7. Greediness and asking for more.

Nafs is ever in prolonged delights, and restricteth not itself. Never becometh full the stomach of its need.

It is like the moth that with the candle's light contenteth not itself; by understanding the injury of its heat it becometh not warned; and casteth itself on the body of the fire so that it becometh consumed.

As nafs suffereth calamity, so its greed for delight becometh greater.

This departeth not save by wara' (austerity) and by taḳvạ̄ (piety).

8. Levity and light-headedness.

Nafs resteth on nothing. When thoughts of lust and of desire arrive, it putteth not in the first place steadiness or delay; it immediately desireth to enact it; therefore in their (proper) place evident become not rest and motion. For its desire, it displayeth celerity.

The sages have likened it to the spherical globe which they place in a court, plain and smooth. It is ever in motion.

This departeth not save by patience.

9. Haste to fatigue.

To nafs, fatigue of things quickly appeareth; and to it showeth the false idea that its being up-plucked from the present state and its being employed in a following state—will be its rest.

It knoweth not that the guidance of ideas like to these will never convey it to its idea. Mostly, the form of occurrence is contrary to its purpose.

If it gain success, then everything that was pleasing becometh abhorrent to it.

From this calamity it is impossible to escape save by the establishing of the ordered thanks (to God).

10. Negligence.

As towards desires is haste, so towards devotion and good deeds is slothfulness. This disease departeth not save by great austerity and rigorous effort, which fighteth nature by coldness and dryness; and maketh it acceptable of order and gentle and smooth like tanned skins.

To each of these qualities of nafs, physicians of nafs (prophets and holy men, their followers) have applied a remedy.

---

These ten qualities are the mother of qualities, wherefrom many other qualities are derived.

The roots and the branches of lustful qualities are all sprung from the root of the creation of nafs. That is the four natures:—

| | |
|---|---|
| heat. | wetness. |
| cold. | dryness. |

## Ma'rifat-i-rūḥ (deep knowledge of the soul).

III. 5.

The ma'rifat of the soul and the majesty of its understanding is lofty and inaccessible. Not attainable, is its acquisition with the noose of reason. It is a sīmurgh that hath its nest on the Ḳaf (Caucasus) of majesty; and as the prey of understanding entereth not the dwelling of writing.

It is a jewel that hath risen from the abyss of the ocean of grandeur; not possible, is the writing of its qualities by the scale of conjecture.

The Lords of revelation and the Masters of hearts (who are prefects of the mysteries of the hidden, and who have become free from the following of desire and from the servitude of nafs) have grudged explanation save by hint.

The most honoured existence, and the nearest evidence to God,—is the great soul* which to Himself God hath joined.

Great Ādam, the first khalīfa, the interpreter of God, the key of existence, the reed of invention and the paradise of souls,—all signify the qualities of rūḥ (the soul); and the first prey that fell into the net of existence was the soul.

The will of the ancient one assigned it to His own khilāfat in the world of creation; entrusted to it the keys of the treasuries of mysteries; dismissed it for sway in the world; opened to it a great river from the sea of life,—so that ever from it, it might seek aid of the bounty of life; might add to the parts of the universe; might convey the form of divine words from the establishment-place of collection (the Holy Existence) to the place of separation, (the world) might give, with the essence of abridgment, dignity in the essence of division. To it, God gave two glances of divine blessing:—

(*a*) One for beholding the majesty of ḳudrat.
(*b*) The other „ „ beauty of ḥikmat.

The first glance signifieth natural reason; its result is love for God.

The second glance signifieth reason, common and low; its result is wholly nafs.

Every bounty, the aid whereof the soul of ncrease seeketh from the essence of collection (God),—worthy of it, universal nafs becometh.

By reason of active deed, of passive deed and of power, of weakness,† the attribute of male and of female appeareth; in the soul of increase and universal nafs,—the custom of love-making became confirmed by the link of temperament; by means of marriage, the races of worlds became existing; and by the hand of the midwife of Fate appeared in the apparent world.

Then all created beings are the outcome of nafs and of rūḥ (the soul).

---

* See the Ḳurān, P. D.; XVII, 87.

† The male qualities are:—the active deed and power.
„ female „ „ —the passive deed and weakness.

Nafs is the result of rūḥ; rūḥ, of order. Because by His own self, without any cause (whereto the order is the hint) God created the soul; and by means of rūḥ, (whereof creation is the hint) the crowd of created beings.

Since it is necessary that every khalīfa should be the comprehender of varied qualities, He clothed the God-like grace and the endless bounty of the soul, in the khilāfat of creation, with the honour-robe of all names, and with the qualities of His own beauty and grandeur; and made it honoured in the chief seat of creation.

When the circle of causing to create reached accomplishment, in the mirror of the existence of dusty Ādam, the soul became reflected; and in it, all the names and God-like qualities illuminated.

Spread abroad in lofty places, became the rumour of Ādam's khilāfat; and on the mandate of his khilāfat came this royal seal; on the standard of his blessing, became revealed this Ķurānīc verse:—"To Ādam, all names He made known."*

In the grasp of his sway, they placed the gate of subduing and the eye of decreeing.

For his adoration, they ordered the angels; for that tranquillity (collectedness) was not the angels'.

Some of the angels are in the stage:—

(*a*) of jamāl (beauty) only; they are the angels of kindness and of mercy.
(*b*) „ jalāl (grandeur) „ „ „ wrath, of mercy, and of vengeance.

By all names, Ādam knew God; but the angels only by that name, which was their stage.

The existence in the material world:—

(*a*) of Ādam became the stage of the form of rūḥ in the hidden world.
(*b*) of Ḥavvā (Eve) „ „ „ nafs „ „

Havvā's birth from Ādam is like unto the birth of nafs from rūḥ (the soul); and the effects of the marriage of nafs and rūḥ, and the attraction of male and of female, became assigned to Ādam and Ḥavvā.

Like to their issuing from rūḥ and nafs, came into existence the atoms of progeny (which were a deposit in Ādam's back-bone) by the union of Ādam and Ḥavvā.

The existence of Ādam and Ḥavvā became the exemplar of the existence of rūḥ and nafs.

In every person of mankind, another exemplar becometh—by the union of rūḥ (in part) and of nafs (in part) transcribed from the exemplar of Ādam and Ḥavvā.

Became produced the birth:—

(*a*) of the heart from the two (soul and nafs).
(*b*) of the form of the male of the sons of Ādam from the form of the universal soul.
(*c*) „ „ „ female from the form of universal nafs.

---

* The Ķurān, II, 31.

In the form of the female, no prophet hath been sent. Because by reason of sway in the souls of men; and by its effects in creation, prophecy hath the attribute of the male; and the means of revealing the mystery of prophecy is the soul suitable to the form (of man).

---

## Jam' (collected) and tafraḳa (dispersed).

IV. 2.

In the idiom of the ṣūfīs :—

jam' signifies :—

(*a*) the repelling of structures (creation).
(*b*) „ dropping „ additions (worldly advantages).
(*c*) „ withdrawing shuhūd-i-ḥaḳḳ from creation.

tafraḳa signifies—

the accepting of structures (creation).
„ confirming of devotion and of God-ship.
„ separating of God from creation.

Jam' without tafraḳa is impiousness; tafraḳa without jam' is uselessness; jam' with tafraḳa is the very truth, for it hath the order of jam' joined to souls, and of tafraḳa to forms.

As long as the soul and the body are linked, the union of jam' and tafraḳa is of the requisites of existence.

The true Ȧrif is ever joined :—

(*a*) to rūḥ (which is the dwelling of mushāhida) in the essence of jam.'
(*b*) to the body (which is the instrument of strife) in the maḳām of tafraḳa.

Thus have Junīd and Wāsiṭi written.

This state, the ṣūfīs call jam'u-l-jam'.

In devotion, who looketh :—

(*a*) at his own acquisition, is in tafraḳa.
(*b*) „ God's grace, is in jam'.
(*c*) „ neither himself nor at his own deeds, is in jam'u-l-jam' (wholly effaced).

Thus Abū Ȧlī Daḳḳāḳ and Junīd have said.

Jam' signifies :—

the veiling and the concealment of the people in the superiority of ẓuhūr va shuhūd-i-ḥaḳḳ (revelation and manifestation of God).

tafraḳa signifies :—

the veiling, and the concealment of God in the shuhūd-i-wujūd-i-k͟halḳ (manifestation of the existence of creation).

---

## Tajallī (epiphany) and Istitār (being hid).

IV. 3.

Tajallī signifieth :—

the manifestation of the sun of the ḥaḳīḳat of God out from the clouds of humanity,

Istitār signifieth :—

the cloud of the light of ḥaḳīḳat in the revelation of the qualities of humanity.

Tajallī is of three kinds.

1. Tajallī-i-ẕāt.

Its mark (if of the holy traveller's existence something hath remained) is the fanā (effacement) of ẕāt, and the annihilation of qualities in the glories of their lights. They call it "falling into a swoon," as was the state of Mūsā, whom (by beholding tajallī) they took out of himself and effaced.

When from God, he sought the appearance of ẕāt,* he had not yet after fanā reached baḳā; in conformity with the guidance "let me see," at the time of the tajallī of the light of ẕāt* on the Ṯūr of the nafs of his existence,—the residue (which is the seeker of manifestation) of the qualities of his existence became effaced.

If from the residue of his existence, fanā be wholly separated; and after the fanā of existence, its truth be joined to absolute baḳā (God),—he seeth, by the light of the eternal, the ẕāt of the eternal.

This is an honour-robe that they specially gave to Muḥammad; and is a draught that they caused him to taste.

From desire for this cup, they cause to drop a draught into the jaw of the soul of the special ones of his followers.

This sense demandeth the exaltation of the walī (saint) above the nabī (prophet).

For the walī gaineth this rank not of himself,—nay by the perfection of his following the prophet.

2. Tajallī-i-ṣifāt.

If the Ancient Existence display tajallī:—

(*a*) with jalāl, he is (on account of His glory, ḳudrat, and force) in khushū' and khuẓū' (humility of heart and of limbs).

(*b*) with jamāl, he is (on account of His mercy, grace and blessing) joyous and loving.

The ẕāt of the Eternal changeth not; but according to exigency of will, contrariety of capacity, are evident sometimes outwardly jalāl (grandeur) and inwardly jamāl (beauty); and sometimes the contrary thereto.

3. Tajallī-i-af'āl.

This signifies;—

The averting of one's glance from the deeds of other people; from them, the severing of additions of good and of evil, of profit, and of loss; the moderating of their praise and blame; of their acceptance and rejection (of one).

For the bare manifestation of divine deeds dismisseth to themselves the people from the addition of deeds.

---

* This is the ẕat of God.

To the holy traveller in the stages of travelling come in order:—

i. tajallī-i-af'āl.
ii. „ ṣifāt.
iii. „ ẕāt.

Deeds are the effects of qualities; and, enfolded in ẕāt, are qualities.

For the people, deeds are nearer than qualities; and qualities, nearer than ẕāt.

They call:—

(*a*) the shuhūd-i-tajallī-i-af'āl (the manifestation of the glory of deeds), the muḥāẓira (the being present).

(*b*) „ shuhūd-i-tajallī-i-ṣifāt ( „ „ „ qualities), the mukāshifa (the manifestation).

(*c*) „ shuhūd-i-tajallī-i-ẕāt ( „ „ „ ẕāt), the mushāhida (the beholding).

They call:—

muḥāẓira, the ḥāl of hearts.
mukāshifa, „ mysteries.
mushāhida, „ souls.

Cometh truly mushāhida from a person, who is standing in the existence of the witnessed (God), not in his own. For the power of the glory of the light of eternity (God) is not of accidents (ḥādiṣ).

So long as in the witnessed, the shāhid (witnesser) is not effaced; and in it becometh not left, His mushāhida one cannot make.

After beholding the effects of the flame of separation, and the violence of desire on Majnūn's state, a party of the tribe of Majnūn interceded with the tribe of Lailạ̄, they said:—

"What would it be if, a moment, Majnūn's eye become illumined and anointed "with the sight of Lailạ̄'s beauty?"

The tribe of Lailạ̄ said:—

"To this extent is no harm. But Majnūn himself hath not the power of beholding Lailạ̄."

At last, they brought Majnūn; and uplifted a corner of Lailạ̄'s tent.

Immediately his glance fell on the fold of Lailạ̄'s skirt,—senseless he fell.

In short:—

The glory of God is the cause of the people being veiled; His being veiled is the cause of manifestation (of glory) of the people.

When God becometh glorified :—

(a) in His own deeds,—in them, the deeds of the people become veiled.
(b) in His ẕāt,— in it, the ẕāt, the qualities, and deeds of the people become veiled.

For the welfare of the world of ḥikmat and for enlarging the effects of mercy on His own special ones,—the Absolute Wise one (God) leaveth the residue of the qualities of lusts (which are the source of being veiled), so that, for them and for others, there may be mercy.

For them (the special ones),—

that by the occupations of lusts, they may remain persevering; and by permanency may acquire nearness (to God).

For others (the people in general),—

that annihilated in the essence of fanā, and immersed in the sea of jama' they may not become; and that to others their existence may become a source of profit.

Some of the 'Ulamā (who are ṣūfīs) have said :—

The istighfar of Muḥammad is the demand for this veil in order that he may not be immersed in the sea of shuhūd; and that, by him through the link of humanity, men may be benefited.

---

## Wajd (rapture) and Wujūd (existence).

IV. 4.

Wajd (wajdān) signifieth :—

(a) an event that from God arriveth, and turneth the heart from its own form to—great grief, or to great joy.
(b) a state wherein all the (mortal) qualities of the wājid become cut off; and his nature becometh painted with joy.

The wājid (possessor of wajd) signifieth :—

One who hath not yet come forth from the veil of sensual qualities; and is, by his own existence, veiled from God's existence.

Sometimes in the veil of his existence, appeareth an opening whence a ray from the light of God's existence shineth and helpeth him. After that the veil becometh folded; and maujūd (existence), lost.

Wajd is intermediate between the preceding disappearing and the following disappearing (of maujūd).

Wujūd signifieth :—

(a) that in the superiority of the light of the shuhūd of maujūd (the existence of God), wujūd and wājid become lost and naught.
(b) the quality of muḥdaṡ (accident).
(c) ,, existence of the quality of Ḳadīm (the Ancient One, God).

As Zu-n-Nūn hath said.

When, out from his own existence, the possessor of wajd is not effaced,—he is wājid; and standing in him, is wajd.

When out from his own existence, the possessor of wujūd is wholly effaced; and in the existence of maujūd is left standing—he is the ẕāt of maujūd (the existence of the existence of God) not the ẕāt of wājid (or the ẕāt of the slave).

Wājid signifieth :—

One who is the disappearer of his existence.

Thus, hath Shiblī said.

Who, by the appearance of his own wajd, becometh veiled from the seeing of the wajd of the maujūd (the existence of God),—in him joy cometh.

Who, by seeing the wajd of maujūd (the existence of God), becometh deprived of the appearance of his own wajd,—from him descendeth the possibility of joy.

Thus, hath Junīd said.

Wajd is the preface to wujūd.

In victory over the fortress of human wujūd (existence) every wajd is like to a manjaniḳ (catapult) established by the attraction of the divine world, so that, when the fortress of wujūd (existence) is subdued,—it becometh the wajd of wujūd.

The end of wajd is the beginning of wujūd. That is—

The wujūd of wajd is the cause of the wājid's being deprived of existence, which is the condition of the wujūd of maujūd (the existence of the existence of God).

Thus have said :—

(*a*) Abū-l-Ḥusain-i-Nūrī.
(*b*) Shiblī.

The taking away of the addition of wajd to self is the essence of accepting tauḥīd; and its addition to self is the essence of denying (tauḥīd).

Thus hath Bāyizīd said.

As wajd is the preface to wujūd, so tawājud (wajd-making,) is the preface to wajd.

Tawājud signifies :—

The asking for, and the attracting of wajd, by way of—

(*a*) taẕakkur (repeating),
(*b*) tafakkur (reflecting).
(*c*) sincere resemblance to the man of wajd (in motion and in rest).

Although apparently tawājud is preparation; preparation is the opposite to sincerity, yet since the resolution of the mutawājid, in this form of tawājud, is wholly inclination for acceptance of the aid of divine bounty; and (is) true offering for snuffing up divine odours,—it is not contrary to sincerity.

Thus, the sharī'at hath permitted and ordered.

The description of the man—

(*a*) of the beginning is tawājud.
(*b*) „ path „ wajd.
(*c*) „ acquisition „ wujūd.

## On Waḳt (period) and Nafas (moment).

IV. 6.

To waḳt, ṣūfīs assign three meanings.

Waḳt may mean :—

a quality such as ḳabẓ (contraction), basṭ (expansion), sorrow or joy,—that prevaileth over the slave.

From exceeding superiority of ḥāl, the possessor of this waḳt cannot understand another ḥāl.

So the possessor of the ḥāl of ḳabẓ, with the superiority of the ḥāl, is so impressed and filled that he findeth an impression neither from the passed basṭ, nor from the coming basṭ. All his time, he seeth the waḳt-i-ḥāl ; over the ḥāl of others, according to his own ḥāl, is his own sway which thus becometh the source of error.

Every ḥāl concordant with his own ḥāl, he decreeth as to its truth ; otherwise, as to its falsity.

In this explanation, the sense of waḳt is general,—both for the holy traveller, and for him who is not.

Waḳt may mean :—

A ḥāl that, by assault, appeareth from the ghaibat (the hidden) ; taketh by the superiority of its sway the holy traveller from his own ḥāl ; and maketh him submissive to its own order.

Special to the holy traveller, is this waḳt and is a hint to the saying—

"Son of his time is the ṣūfī."

When they say "by the decree of waḳt," they mean :—

That, by God's will, out of his own will, he is seized and veiled.

In respect of the order of "other than God,"—who showeth contentment, cometh into strife (with God) ; and by its influence, is subdued.

Hence they have said—

"Waḳt is the slaying sword."

The sword hath two qualities,—one soft and smooth ; the other the keen, cutting edge. Who displayeth to it softness and rubbeth it with gentleness—findeth from it softness ; who displayeth to it roughness suffereth the wound of its violence.

Even so waḳt hath two qualities—gentleness and wrathfulness.

Agreement and concordance with it who maketh, enjoyeth its grace ; repulsion and opposition to it, who maketh, becometh overpowered by its violence.

By the passing of God's purpose, waḳt, is over all purposes and states the prevailer ; and, according to its own decree, fashioneth them—like the sword, the severer.

Waḳt may mean —

The present time, which is middle, between the past and the future.

They say :—

"Master of waḳt is such a one."

That is :—

Being engaged in the performance of recitations of the present time, solicitude for a thing (which at that time may be important and best) keepeth him engaged from mention of the past, and from thinking of the future. Thus, his time, he loseth not.

In this waḳt, decline is not passed save in connection with holy travellers, to whom, by reason of the talwīn of ḥāl, this waḳt is sometimes existent and sometimes lost; and who, into the volume of credit, bring not the account of their own life save at the time when waḳt is existent.

For those joined to God and for the companions of tamkin, this waḳt is constant; and to it the path of decline is closed.

Thus, hath Shiblī said.

The possessor of this waḳt is issuer from beneath the sway of ḥāl.

In the second sense, waḳt is not powerful in him. Nay, he is powerful in waḳt in the sense that he keepeth all waḳt engaged in important affairs.

Some ṣūfīs call the possessor of waḳt :—

The father of waḳt, not the son of waḳt.

---

Nafas signifieth :—

The succession of ḥāl of mushahida (manifestation), whereto is joined the life of hearts of men of love, which is like unto the succession of breaths, whereto is conditioned the permanency of the life of bodies.

If for a moment from the path of the heart, the succession of fresh breath be cut off,—from the volume of natural heat, it becometh inflamed; if for a moment, from the essence of the desirous heart, the succession of shuhūd,—from the violence of its thirst and rage, it consumeth with desire.

The difference between waḳt (in the second sense) and nafas is this :—

Waḳt is a ḥāl in the place of languor and of stoppage; and an event in the pursuit, and in the observing, of mushahida (manifestation) and of ghaibat (concealment).

Nafas is a ḥāl ever free from languor and stoppage. Hence they have said:

Waḳt for the beginner, for the finisher, nafas.

---

## Shuhūd (being present) and Ghaibat (being absent).

IV. 7.

Shuhūd signifieth :—

Being present. With whatever the heart is present, shāhid (witness) of it, it is; and that thing is mashhūd (witnessed) by it (the heart).

If the heart be present with God, it is shāhid (witness) of God: if the heart be present with the people, it is shāhid of the people.

The way of ṣūfīs is :—

to call the mashhūd (witnessed) shāhid (witnesser); because with whatever the heart is present, that thing also is present with the heart.

For the sake of the unity of God and the plurality of the people, they mean :—

(*a*) by shāhid (singular) God.

(*b*) „ shawāhid (plural) the people.

(*c*) „ shuhūd (singular) being present with God; for ever is their heart shāhid (witness) of, and ḥāẓir (present) with, God.

Men of shuhūd are two parties :—

(*a*) the companions, of muraḳaba (fearful contemplation).

(*b*) „ lords of mushāhida (manifestation).

Ghaibat is a description opposed to shuhūd :—

(i) the blameable ghaibat, opposed to shuhūd-i-ḥaḳḳ.

(ii) „ laudable ghaibat, opposed to shuhūd-i-khalḳ which (through the superiority of the shuhūd-i-ḥaḳḳ) is of two kinds :—

(*a*) the ghaibat of beginners; the ghaibat of things felt.

(*b*) „ ghaibat of the middle ones; the ghaibat of his own existence; this is the limit of ghaibat and the beginning of fanā (effacement).

The stage of "the last ones" is outside the ḥāl of ghaibat. For ghaibat is the ḥāl of that one, who hath not freed himself from the narrow place of existence; nor reached the amplitude of Absolute Existence (God); nor gained the limit as to ghaibat (the being hidden) and as to shahādat (the being present).

Men of blameable ghaibat are hidden from the shuhūd-i-ḥaḳḳ by the shāhid of the people: men of laudable ghaibat are hidden from the shuhūd-i-khalḳ by the shāhid of God.

To the man of perfection, they conceal neither the shuhūd of God from the people; nor the shuhūd of the people from God.

The observing of rules and the following of shuhūd and of laudable ghaibat is for holy travellers and for men of talwīn.

For those joined to God and for the established ones at rest is no ḥāl save constant shuhūd-i-ḥaḳḳ. For them is no ghaibat, laudable or blameable.

---

At the beginning of the superiority of ḥāl, and at the time of manifestation of the good news of the morning of revelation, Shiblī went before Junīd; and present, was Junīd's lawful spouse.

She wished to go behind the screen. Junīd said :—

Shiblī is ghāib (hidden); be thou in thy place.

Even as Junīd was speaking to her, Shiblī wept.

To his wife, Junīd said :—

Now thou shouldest be concealed, for to sense Shiblī hath come.

The state of beginners is :—

Ghaibat from the people in shuhūd of the beloved ; from out of it, "the last ones" have passed.

The tale of Zulaikha (Potiphar's wife), who, in love for Yūsuf, had the degree of tamkīn ; and in shuhūd of him became not ghā,ib from the senses as her companions and reprovers ( yet beginners in love for Yūsuf and in the shuhūd of his beauty), who, by the force of the ḥāl of shuhūd for him, were ghā,ib from the senses ; and were unaware of the cutting of their own hand (through the passion of love for him).

---

## Tajrīd (outward separation) and Tafrid (inward solitude).

IV. 8.

Tajrīd signifieth :—

Outwardly abandoning the desires of this world ; and inwardly rejecting the compensation of the next world and of this world.

The true mujarrad :—

is one, who as to tajarrud* (tajrīd) from the world is not the seeker of compensation ; nay the cause of tajarrud is propinquity to God.

Who outwardly abandoneth request of the world ; and for it expecteth compensation, in this fleeting world, or in the next world,—freed from the world, verily hath not become ; and is in the place of exchanging and trafficking.

In all his devotions, by worship only his gaze is on the performance of his rights to God, not on compensation nor on other desire.

Tafrīd signifieth :—

the rejecting the increase of deeds of himself, and the concealing their appearance by regarding on himself God's favour and bounty.

Tajrīd is the abandoning of the expectation of compensations.

Because when he knoweth the grace of tajrīd and of devotion (to be) God's favour —not his own deed nor his own acquisition,—for it, he expecteth not compensation. Nay, immersed in God's favour, he seeth his own existence.

Tajrīd in form is not necessary to tajrīd ; for possibly, in abandoning, he may be expectant of a compensation. So tafrīd is not necessary to tajrīd ; for possibly, in abandoning hope of compensation, he seeth himself in the acquisition of entrance (to God).

---

## Maḥv (obliteration) and Is̤bāt (confirmation).

IV. 9.

In the opinion of the ṣūfīs, maḥv signifieth :—

the obliterating of the slave's existence.

Is̤bāt signifieth :—

the confirming (after maḥv) of the slave's existence.

Related to the will of the Eternal. are maḥv and isbāt.

---

* See p. 93.

Maḥv hath three degrees :—

(1) the lowest degree—the maḥv of blameable qualities and of dark deeds.
(2) the middle degree—the maḥv of blameable and of laudable qualities.
(3) the highest degree—the maḥv of ẕāt.

In opposition to every maḥv is an is̤bāt.

Near to each other, is the meaning of—

| | |
|---|---|
| fanā (effacement). | maḥv (obliteration). |
| baḳā (permanency). | is̤bāt (confirmation). |

The difference between maḥv and fanā ; between baḳā and is̤bāt, one cannot comprehend save by the aid of the kind Friend, and of gracious faith.

After the fanā of ẕāt,—

(*a*) baḳā appeareth not.
(*b*) is̤bāt is not necessary.

Thus the is̤bāt of agreeable qualities and of beautiful deeds is not necessary after the maḥv of misdeeds of natures and of the sins of deeds of the companions of purifying and of the Lords of glorying.

The fanā of deeds and of qualities becometh not wholly acquired save after the fanā of ẕāt ; but their maḥv is not restricted to the maḥv of ẕāt.

Maḥv and is̤bāt are generally (derived) from fanā and baḳā ; because they practise not fanā and baḳā, save in the maḥv of humanity and in the is̤bāt of Godship.

In the sense of maḥv, they use :—

sahk (grinding), the effacing the essence of qualities.
maḥk (abolishing), „ „ „ ẕāt.
t̤ams (effacing), „ „ effects of qualities and of ẕāt.

---

## Talwīn (change) and Tamkīn (rest).

IV. 10.

Tamkīn signifieth :—

perpetuity of manifestation of ḥaḳīḳat by reason of the tranquillity of the heart in the place of nearness (to God).

Talwīn signifieth :—

the subjugating of the heart between manifestation and veiling by observing times, and by the pursuit of the ghaibat* of nafs, and its manifestation.

Possessor of talwīn, they call not :—

him, who shall not have passed beyond the qualities of nafs, nor reached to the world of the qualities of the heart, for talwīn is through the succession of varied states.

Possessor of ḥāl, they call not :—

him, who is bound in the qualities of nafs.

Then talwīn is possible for the Lords of hearts, who may not have traversed the world of qualities (of God), nor reached to (knowledge of) ẕāt ; because they are innumerable qualities.

---

* See p. 85.

Talwīn is possible where numbering is possible.

The Lords of revelation of ẕāt have passed the limit of talwīn and reached to the stage of tamkīn; because in ẕāt by reason of His unity change appeareth not.

Escape from talwīn is for that one whose heart ascendeth from the stage of the heart to the stage of the soul; cometh forth from beneath the sway of the numbering of qualities; and becometh a dweller in the open space of propinquity to Ẕāt (God's existence).

When, from the stage of the heart to the stage of the soul, the heart arriveth,—from the stage of nafs to the stage of the heart, nafs emigrateth.

Talwīn (which before was the heart's) becometh in this stage the accident of nafs through—

| | |
|---|---|
| ḳabẓ (contraction) | sorrow and joy. |
| basṭ (expansion) | fear and hope. |

Nafs becometh the khalīfa of the heart of the possessor of talwīn.

By reason of the light of manifestation and the certainty of the existence of this talwīn not being veiled,—this talwīn is verily not the reviled tamkīn.

So long as the custom of humanity is left, impossible is it that out of nature change should be wholly obliterated; but change excludeth not the possessor of tamkīn from the stage of resting.

## The Aurād (prayer-exercises) and the Kalimā-i-shāhādat (the creed).

VII. 2.

On his tongue, the slave should urge the two shahādats (witnessings) saying :—

I declare no god but God; I declare Muḥammad, His slave and prophet.

For the verifying of his own heart, he should witness to this confession.

The confession of shahādat is special; because, in respect to his own nafs, every confession is shahādat; the shahādat is not confession.

As every confessor is taken as to the confessed, so the confessor (of faith) is taken as to his own faith and questioned to the limits of the shar' as to his service.

The shahādat of confession is not the place of suspicion. Although confession is of the crowd of (mere) words, yet it is a most honoured column of deeds.

Because the meaning of :—

(*a*) 'amal (deed) is the use of the limbs upon the orders of the sharī'at.

(*b*) iḳrār (confession) is the use of the tongue in the creed of faith whereto most men are subjected.

The tongue is the interpreter and the witness of the heart, whose mystery it relateth; and to whose faith, it witnesseth.

The other limbs are interpreters and witnesses of the heart, whose mystery they relate; of whose ḥāl they give evidence.

This shahādat, they perform by the tongue of deed (not by the tongue of the mouth).

Thus the tongue hath inwardly a word, outwardly a deed; all the columns have inwardly a word and outwardly a deed.

The limb that men use in the requisites of the shar', it, with the tongue of ḥāl, witnesseth to the existence of faith in their heart.

Iḳrār and 'amal, each, is a witness to the existence of faith, not a part thereof.

Faith is verification by the heart; confession, by the tongue; action by the limbs.

This signifieth—

Not that the essence of faith is confession, or deed; for faith alone is the verification of the heart. Confession and deed both are the marks, though it is possible that the witnessing of these two may be false:

as, in the case of hypocrites, in whom are strong confession and deed, while faith languid is.

But, because the base of rules is on outward things, the order in respect to the faith of one (for whom witnessing is made) is dependent upon the shahādat of these two witnesses; and to it opposition declineth.

After the witnessing (shahādat) of witnesses the order in respect to one (against whom, witnessing is made) is incumbent upon the ḳāẓī, although the witnessing be suspicious.

Once Bilāl cast down in battle one of the infidels who presented the shahādat.

To it, Bilāl paid no consideration; and separated his head from his body.

When he related this to Muḥammad, he was reproved.

He replied:—

O prophet! his confession was from fear, not from faith.

Muḥammad said:—

How splitedest thou his heart? How knowest thou that in his heart was no faith?

---

## Zuhd (austerity).

IX. 3.

Zuhd signifieth:—

(*a*) the heart's turning away from the pleasure of the world's goods; and shunning its desires.

(*b*) the third stage of tauba (penitence) and of wara' (piety).

The holy traveller on the path to God at first forbiddeth his own nafs with the elephant-goad of sincere penitence from falling into difficulties as to sins; to it, maketh straight the power of delights; and maketh, with the polisher of piety, his heart pure of the rust of greed, so that therein may appear the verity of this, and of the next, world.

Therein, he seeth this world ugly and transitory, and therefrom turneth; the next world, beautiful, and thereto inclineth.

The abandoning and the being alone is :—

(*a*) for "the last ones," not the necessity of the truth of zuhd.
(*b*) „ "the first ones," of the requisites of zuhd.

In praise of zuhd, for the distinguishing of pretenders from the sincere, most of the words of shai<u>kh</u>s comprehend the necessity for abandoning property and delights.

There are three zuhds :—

i. the zuhd of the common in the first rank.
ii. „ „ „ „ special in the second rank is zuhd in zuhd. It signifieth—
Change of delight from the acquisition of zuhd which is the prop—of delight; of the will of the slave; and of his nafs being filled with delights of the next world.
By the fanā (effacement) of his own desire in the will of God, this sense cometh true.
iii. the zuhd of the special of the special ones in the third rank, which is zuhd with God.
It is peculiar to the prophets and to other holy men; and is in the world after the fanā of his own will by God's will.

Zuhd is the result of ḥikmat and of the birth of knowledge.

In the application of zuhd, pleasure in the world is the result of ignorance, and the birth of the heart's blindness as in the ḥadīs.

For the shunning of the fleeting world and for delight in the lasting world,—the zāhid hath laid on a sure foundation (God's will) the foundation of his own work.

Thus, have Lukmān and Shiblī said; and so is it in the Ḥadīṣ.

Benefit by ḥaḳīḳat is not the denial of the stage of zuhd, of its excellence, and of exaltation of the rules of effort; but—through the humbling of zuhd in the glance of zāhids,—the purpose of ḥaḳīḳat is the repelling of pride.

---

## Faḳr (poverty).

IX. 4.

At the stage of faḳr (which meaneth taking possession of no chattels) the holy traveller of the path of ḥaḳīḳat arriveth not, till he hath passed through the stage of zuhd (austerity).

For one who hath desire for the world although he hath no property, the name of faḳr is illusory.

Faḳr hath a name, a custom and a truth.

Its name is taking possession of no chattels despite desire; its custom is taking possession of no chattels, despite zuhd; its truth is the impossibility of taking chattels.

Since the man of ḥaḳīḳat seeth by its means all things in the sway of the master of lands (God), he regardeth not lawful the consigning of property to others.

The faḳr :—

(*a*) of men of ḥaḳīḳat is a natural quality which,—despite having, or not having, chattels—becometh not changed. If, in their power, be the whole world, free from taking it they regard themselves.

(*b*) of spectators who have found only an impression of the truth of faḳr; in whose hearts its meaning hath not become enjewelled—is an accidental quality. By the accession of chattels they become changed, and of them regard themselves possessed.

For the sake of being numbered, for excellence of faḳr, and for desire of the good of the next world, they shun wealth more than the man of wealth shunneth faḳr.

On the excellence of faḳr over wealth, and of wealth over faḳr, the man of meaning hath urged speech.

**Faḳr—**

(*a*) is with "the first and the middle ones" more excellent than wealth.

(*b*) " " "the end ones" equal to wealth.

Because wealth cannot deny them the sense of faḳr and its truth, as Ȧbdu-l-lah bin Jallād hath said. Although to him faḳr and wealth are one, the quality of gift leaveth not in him the impression of the form of wealth, as Nūrī hath said.

Who is independent of God, how may he grasp aught? Save in God, the quality of the faḳīr is naught.

There are several crowds of fuḳarā :—

(*a*) Those who regard as no property the world and its chattels. If it be in their power, they give it away; for it, in this and in the next world, they have no desire.

(*b*) Those who regard not their own deeds and devotion, although from them they issue—them their own property they know not; and in return for it expect no reward.

(*c*) Those who with these two qualities regard not as their own their own ḥāl and maḳām. All, they regard the favour of God.

(*d*) Those who regard not as their own their own ẕāt and existence, nor even their own self. Their,—ẕāt is none, nor quality, nor ḥāl, nor maḳām, nor deed. No trace have they in the two worlds.

Need is the quality of the needy one, and in his nature standeth. Here is neither confirmed nature nor quality. This is the meaning of faḳr, which some of the ṣūfīs have not.

The possessor of this faḳr in both worlds, none recogniseth save God, because the Lord of the world is jealous. So concealed from the glance of strangers keepeth He His special ones that, concealed from their own sight, they are.

This faḳr is the stage of the ṣūfīs and of "the last ones,"—not of holy travellers.

Because after passing the stages, in every stage (for the joined one), the pace is (according to his state) sometimes beyond the foot of the traveller.

Like tauba (penitence), which is the first stage of the stages of holy travellers, it is his foot-place which (after traversing all the stages and the maḳāms) becometh attained.

## Tajarrud (celibacy) and ta,ahhul (marriage).

VI. 8.

The tales of the prophet in respect of tajarrud and of ta,ahhul are contradictory.

The source of this opposition is the contrariety of states and of lusts of some who are captive to exceeding passion.

Marriage is necessary :—

(*a*) for those, from whom are expected,—weakness of piety, poorness of patience (as to abandoning desire); the falling into contrarieties (of state); and the committing of adultery.

(*b*) for those whose nafs hath turned away from following desires; hath obtained rest from excess of desire; hath, from contention with the heart, become torn up, and to the heart's suggestion become obedient.

Tajarrud* and tafarrud are excellent :—

for those who are in the flower of desire; whose nafs, in the seat of desire, is vain; and who are in the midst of travelling.

To a darvīsh, they said :—

Why desirest thou not a wife?

He said :—

A wife is fit for man; the stage of man, I have not reached. Wherefore should I desire a wife?

Thus to another they spake. He replied :—

Of the divorcing of nafs, my need is greater than of marriage. When I divorce nafs, it will be lawful to desire a wife.

To Basharḥāris̤, they said :—

Of thee, men say so and so.

He said :—

What say they?

They said :—

They say that thou hast abandoned the sunnat of marriage.

He said :—

Tell them that since I am engaged in enjoined observances, in the sunnat I engage not.

For the travellers of ḥaḳīḳat, it is known that, at the beginning of journeying, there is no help :—

of severing attachments, of avoiding delay, of holding to resolution; and of shunning the license of nature.

Marriage is the cause :—

of binding the heart to the chattels of livelihood, of descending from the height of resolution to the abyss of license: and of inclining towards the world, after austerity and faithfulness of desire (for God).

---

* See p. 87.

Freedom from wives and offspring aideth :—

to tranquillity of heart, to purity of time, to the delight of ease, to freedom for devotion, and to loftiness.

As long as in respect to celibacy, and to strife against nafs,* he hath power, it is necessary for the celibate traveller to esteem as booty—license of time, tranquillity of heart, so that he become not dull through solicitude for the wife.

Submission to the heart's orders becometh easy to him who beareth the celibate life :—

till nafs becometh worthy of kindness; its vein of contention torn up, and to it stubbornness, forbidden.

Then to him God giveth a pure wife who shall be his aider in faith and in the chattels of livelihood in a way that shall be the tranquillity of the heart, and his preservation from the calamities of nafs.

Shaikh 'Abdu-l-Ḳādir-i-Jabalī said :—

A long while I had thought of marriage but, to it for fear of time's distress I advanced not; between impulsion and repulsion, I hesitated; at last when I had displayed perfect patience,—God gave me four concordant wives, each of whom voluntarily bestowed on me her property.

In the preferring of marriage to celibacy, the firm 'ulama have the 'ilm-i-sa'at (the knowledge of expansion), whereby they know :—

(*a*) when, in respect of the observance of limits of "rights," they may satisfy nafs;

(*b*) " " taking "delight," they may give it the power of expansion.

Ḥuḳūḳ ("rights†") signify :—

The requisites of nafs, whereby are preserved the prop of the body and the preservation of life, and without which permanency of nafs is hindered.

Ḥuẓūẓ ("delights") signify :—

Whatever (of desire) is in excess (of rights).

The firm 'ulamā and the great ones of ṣūfī,ism know that nafs is unworthy of kindness, or of the gift of delights so long as—

it resteth not from stirring, striving in wickedness, stubbornness; and is not reproved against contentions with the heart.

When under the sway of orders, nafs becometh quiet and the veins of its attachment to the heart are torn out, there appear integrity and concordance between it and the heart, and it becometh worthy of delights and of kindness.

Then the "delights" of nafs become its "rights;" its pain becometh its remedy.

The "delights" of a nafs like this become its "rights;" because the taking of delights becometh not the cause of stubbornness. By every delight, is its rank (in propinquity and devotion) greater.

When by taking delight, nafs gaineth delight,—there reacheth to the heart a great delight (the cause of increase of its rest).

---

* See p. 73.

† "The rights" are that, once every four nights, he should visit each wife.

Even so by his neighbour's joy, becometh glad the kind neighbour. When the heart putteth on the rest-robe, it clotheth nafs with the ease-garment.

When the increase of the ḥāl of each (the heart and nafs) is the cause of increase of ḥāl of the other, then the delight of marriage for a nafs like this is excellent.

Sufyān bin 'Ainiya saith:—

> (Better) than the whole world, is the increase (in number) of the woman (wives).

For the Amīru-l-Muminīn (the wisest, most pious, most austere of the companions), had four wives and seventeen mistresses.

Such is the state of "the end ones," thereto the idea of the state of the man of "the beginning," or of the "middle," reacheth not.

Many are the pretenders and the deceived ones, who, by doubt of this stage, become proud; lay down in the plain of license their own nafs free from incumbrance; and travel in the desert of destruction.

The rule of the celibate traveller is—

> So long as to this stage he arriveth not, in the heart, he advanceth no excess as to marriage, and no thought thereof, until, in the heart, the imaginary power showeth no sway. When a thought of it appeareth, he denieth it by penitence to God and by seeking His aid.

If it (nafs) be not repelled, he persevereth awhile in fasting.

If it gather strength, thereto he maketh no haste without the preferring of earnest prayer and of much knowledge.

Weeping and groaning, he returneth to God; with submission and weeping, placeth his head in the dust; and uttereth this prayer:—

> O God! this thought tormenteth me to commit this sin. Thy forgiveness for it, I ask; before Thee, I repent; me, forgive and my repentance accept. Verily Thou art the Merciful, and great Accepter of repentance.

If it depart not, he goeth to the shaikhs (living and dead) and to the brothers, and seeketh aid; and desireth them to refer these matters to God.

If after this, his heart is established, the brothers rely (according to excellent opinion) on God's will; and to them it becometh evident that they should aid him.

The rule of ta,ahhul is—

> In choosing the wife, regard her faith, not the world.

As far as is lawful (ma'rūf) he should live with her; should observe her "rights," therein showing no negligence; and for the preservation of the shar' should order her —as Ibn 'Abbās saith.

---

In marriage, he should preserve himself from three calamities:—

1. Inordinate lying with the spouse, which is the calamity of nafs. Therefrom appear three injuries:—

   (*a*) decline in deeds and in readings (of the Kurān), wherefrom defects in ḥāl necessarily come.

(*b*) the inflaming the fires of praised nature, and the wolves of dead nafs. For, when with a nafs, nafs hath commerce, each (nafs), by ḳinship becometh the aider of the other. In each (nafs), a delight cccurreth and the fire of nature kindleth.

*c*) the superiority of nafs after being subdued. For through its own obedience and will, nafs never lowereth its head to the heart's devotion.

When, by the aid of divine attraction the heart gathereth power; and beneath its sway, nafs seeth itself like a powerless amir–in the hand of a powerful amir then, from itself, nafs effaceth the greed of wishing to be followed and by necessity and compulsion becometh submissive to the heart. The kindness, which in this state it gaineth from the heart, nafs seeth is the result of the heart's kindness and of its own submission and of its being subdued,—not the result of the heart's (vain) desiring to be followed.

When in passion, nafs exceedeth moderation, and from the heart hath no reproof, it thinketh that this negligence is through the heart's weakness and its own power; and in the heart's wishing to follow and in its own power (of being followed) reneweth vain desire.

2. Solicitude as to daily victuals, which is the calamity of the heart—

This is the result of doubt]; doubt is the calamity of yaḳīn (certainty); yaḳīn is the light of vision; vision is the eye of the heart.

The sign of the light of yaḳīn in the slave's heart and its not being veiled by the darkness of doubt is this—that, cn God's surety and His pledge, the slave relieth; as to the acquisition of daily victuals (apportioned from the beginning of life to known death) wherein appeareth neither excess nor defect,—is void of doubt; and knoweth that the heart's sway (in solicitude for daily food) is the weakness of yaḳīn; and the want of reliance on God's pledge.

Reliance on any one by one's own deliberation is the result of want of reliance on God's power.

3. Attachment of the heart to the beauty of the spouse, which is the calamity of the soul.

It is for him the prohibitor of sincerity of divine love; and, as regards the violence of shauḳ (desire) for God, and the torment of zauḳ (delight), and the delight of love,—maketh him dull.

To the extent that he becometh attached to the net of beauty, verily changeable, effaceable, and ḥādiṣ (accidental),—he becometh deprived of viewing the beauty (of God), whole, eternal, permanent, and lasting.

---

The repelling of these (and other) calamities becometh attainable if, at the time of lying with the spouse, two glances are his:—

1. one glance outwardly, in the way of desire, and cf being engaged with the spouse.
2. the other glance inwardly at God, from Him seeking aid for the repelling of calamity and in Him being engaged.

A crowd of deceived ones keep glancing at the visible (outward) beauty of the friend; and say:—

In this spectacle-place, behold we the beauty of God!

This claim is the essence of falsehood, and of slander.

When from the lawful glance, resulteth the folly of the soul (rūḥ) and its opposition to the payment of the established portion of love to God—behold from the unlawful glance what (greater) calamities spring.

The source of error of this crowd is:—

When, in that (unlawful) glance, they rest from passion's assault, they hink that the source of this is delight, not passion.

This idea is false; for if it had not been the residue of nafs, the pleasure of the glance in a form (which is the stirrer of passion) would not have been special.

When in them this desire hath become slight, from its slightness, they gain not that passion.

When that (unlawful) glance is repeated; and in it, the imagination gaineth sway—possibly it becometh gross and outwardly its effect appeareth.

Hence, for the quieting of love's assault, physicians order conjunction even with one, other than the beloved.

Who, in this way, claimeth the truth of ḥāl,—him, they should hear naught of, and regard as a mere pretender.

## Tawakkul (trusting to God).

IX. 9.

Tawakkul signifieth :—

Trusting one's affairs to the Absolute Agent (God); confiding in the suretyship of the surety of daily victuals.

After rijā (hope), is this stage; because the matter (of trusting and of confiding) is that one's who first shall understand His mercy.

Tawakkul is—

the result of the truth of faith, by good deliberation and by fate.

This is faith in the rank of yaḳīn (certainty), the possessor whereof knoweth that all affairs are predestined and distributed by fate (taḳdīr), perfect of will, just of distribution, wherein, as to increase or decrease, is no change.

Its sign is—

that, to the grasp of fate (taḳdīr), he entrusteth the rein of deliberation; and from his own power is up-plucked.

Even as have said :—

Zū-n-Nūn.
Sarīy.
Junid.

Ḥamadūn-i-Ḳaṣṣār.
Sahl 'Abdu-l-Lāh.

Every stage hath a beginning and a prosperity suitable to its face; and an end and a calamity suitable to the back of the head—except the stage of tawakkul, which is all beginning or prosperity, and which never terminateth in end and calamity, which signifieth :—

the tawakkul-i-'ināyatī (the tawakkul of favour) trust to the beauty of the will of the Ancient One (God); not the tawakkul-ki-ifāyat (the tawakkul of sufficiency) which is an enterer that never returneth from tawakkul-i-'ināyatī.

The true mutawakkil (truster)—

is that one, in whose sight is no existence save the existence of the Causer-of-causes. His tawakkul becometh not changed by the existence, or by the non-existence, of causes.

This is the tawakkul of that one who shall have reached the stage of tauḥid (the unity of God). Till he reacheth this stage the mutawakkil, in amending his own maḳām, is in need of abandoning causes; because, in his tawakkul, the belief of the existence of causes is blameable.

Therefore, in repelling causes, he ever striveth.

In the amending of this maḳām by abandoning causes, the state of Ibrāhīm Khwāṣṣ is well known.

In one place, he never sojourned more than forty days; and used to take great precaution to conceal his state from the people, so that their knowledge as to his tawakkul should not become a cause of the causes of his daily victuals. Generally, in deserts and solitudes, alone, void of food and of information,—he travelled.

That crowd, in whose tawakkul the existence of causes is blameable,—the existence of causes is the veil of their state, so that on them falleth not the glance of strangers; and beneath the towered dome of causes, they are concealed from the glance of others.

The people think that they are possessed of causes; with the Causer-of-causes they are, in khilwat of union, engaged in being benefited with the delight of holding talk at night, and with the zauḳ of appearances and of presences (divine).

As to the force of the ḥāl of the mutawakkil, the master of the sharī'at (Muḥammad) hath decided.

In tawakkul, who is possessor of yaḳīn (certainty) and of tamkīn, his head shivereth and trembleth not at any disaster.

An assembly asked Junīd :—

If, in search of daily victuals, we make no effort, how will it be?

He said :—

If ye know that the Provider of daily victuals hath forgotten you, strive in search of victuals.

They said :—

Then, will we sit in the house; and practise tawakkul.

He said :—

By your own tawakkul, tempt not God; for, save disappointment, naught will ye have.

They said :—

What thought shall we take?

He said :—

Abandon thought.

Thus it is in the gospel.*

---

* The passage is :—

چه حیلعت کنیم what virtue (force, art) shall we practise.

## Riẓā (Contentment).

IX. 10.

Riẓā signifieth :—

the lifting up (and removing) of the abhorrence of ḳaẓā and ḳadr (fate and destiny) ; and the sweetening of the bitterness of their orders.

After traversing the stages of tawakkul (trusting to God), is the stage of riẓā.

For despite the yaḳin (certainty) of the past division (by fate) and the confidence in the Distributor, it followeth not that abhorrence should not exist, nor that the bitterness of orders should appear sweet.

Thus hath it appeared in some of the recorded prayers of Muḥammad.

With this difference, because he besought "the first certainty," whereby it becometh known that to none arriveth save what in eternity without beginning they (fate and destiny) have decreed.

To it (the first certainty), prayer, for riẓā was added, so that it became known that over ḳismat (destiny) riẓā is not appointed by ḳismat.

The maḳām of riẓā is the end of the maḳām of holy travellers. The being joined to its exalted dignity and to its inaccessible pinnacle is not the power of every hastener. In this maḳām, to whomsoever they gave a footing, him, in haste, they conveyed to Paradise.

For, in riẓā and in yaḳin, they have established rūḥ (the soul) and joy, the requisites of men of Paradise.

At this, the naming of the guardian of Paradise with (the name of) Riẓvān hinteth. From yaḳīn (certainty), is born riẓā ;

So long as, by the light of yaḳīn, the heart is not diffused and dissolved, by it in the heart, appeareth not the containing of events, of calamities, and of joy.

As have said :—

Ẓu-n-Nūn,
Ravīm,
Ḥāriṣ-i-Muḥāsibī.

The repelling of abhorrence (which is the source of the maḳām of riẓā) is the result of the repelling of one's own will.

Ibn 'Aṭā observeth will, in whole ; and in abandoning will in part, regardeth its excellence.

The source of riẓā is yaḳīn and the spreading of the breast is its necessary ; the source of abhorrence is doubt, and the narrowing of the breast is its necessary.

Once in Junīd's society, Shiblī uttered Lāḥaula * * * (there is no power nor virtue, but in God).

Junīd said :—

This is from the heart's narrowness, which is from the abandoning of riẓā.

Shiblī said :—

Truly, thou spakest.

Abhorrence is of two kinds :—

(a) Abhorrence of the heart, which is the opposite to riẓā.
(b) „ „ nafs, „ „ the ḥāl and the maḳām of riẓā.

Possibly in some heart, ariseth this doubt :—

When its preface and source are ḥāl how can the opposite to the ḥāl of riẓā be collected with its maḳām ?

The reply is :—

Only a gift is ḥāl, that, through exceeding fineness and penetrating power, pervadeth all parts of existence ; and thereby no suspicion of the desires of nature remaineth.

But maḳām is mixed with kasb (acquisition) ; therefore is possible the suspicion of the temperament of the wish of nature.

Even as riẓā is the result of yaḳīn, which is the heart's special quality, so special to the heart, is the quality of riẓā.

In it, abhorrence of nafs is not blameable, save when the heart is the possessor of yaḳīn like unto a wide sea, sometimes calm, sometimes rough. When, from the source of divine favour, the winds of circumstances resolve to blow, the heart's sea cometh into tumult ; and therefrom, the excess (foam) of a wave plungeth upon the shore of nafs ; and, in the flowing of nature, goeth flowing. By its means the effects of riẓā and of rest appear in nafs ; and become qualified with the heart's quality.

When these winds take rest, the heart's sea ceaseth from boisterousness ; to its own boundary, the bounty of 'ilm-i-yaḳīn and of rest turneth its face ; and perturbation and abhorrence of nafs return.

In that ḥāl of ignorance (the nature of nafs), 'ilm-i-yaḳīn becometh non-existent nafs putteth on by loan the garment of the heart's feelings, and to (nafs), the heart speaketh.

The riẓā of nafs is the effect of riẓā of the heart, which is the effect of the riẓā of God.

When the glance of the divine Riẓvān taketh attachment to the heart, in it appeareth riẓā. Then the mark of union of the divine Riẓvān with the slave's heart is the union of the slave's parts with Him. Thus speaketh Sahl, 'Abdu-l-lāh.

Since the slave's riẓā is the divine Riẓvān's need,—union with the divine Riẓvān appeareth not in the place void of riẓā. Thus speaketh Rābi'a to Sufyān Ṣūrī.

The maḳām of riẓā is the maḳām of those joined to God,—not the stage of holy travellers, as Bashar Ḥāfī in reply to Fazīl hath said.

Besides that place where one cometh into the place of riẓā of God,—is what maḳām ?

There, where is the glance of riẓā all sins appear good.

More pleasant than that where an abhorrent object reacheth none is what ḥāl ?

Thus speak :—

The Amīru-l-Muminīn and Yaḥyā Ma'āz.

Necessary for the maḳām of riẓā is the ḥāl of love, because when all deeds fall into the place of riẓā, where the Beloved is Agent, all deeds of the Beloved are beloved.

Neither in this, nor in the next, world separate from the slave, riẓā and muḥabbat (love); contrary to fear and hope, which in the next world separate from him.

---

## Muḥabbat (love).

X. 1.

On muḥabbat, is the foundation of all lofty ḥāls, even as on tauba (penitence) is the base of all noble maḳāms.

Since muḥabbat is essentially gift all ḥāls that are founded thereon, they call mawāhib (gifts).

Muḥabbat is the heart's inclination to considering attentively beauty; and is of two kinds:—

i. muḥabbat-i-ʿāmm.
ii. „ „ khāṣṣ.

In the following table, the qualities of muḥabbat are given:—

| Muḥabbat-i-ʿāmm. | Muḥabbat-i-khaṣṣ. |
|---|---|
| (*a*) the heart's inclination to considering attentively the beauty of qualities. | the soul's inclination to viewing the beauty of ẓāt. |
| (*b*) a moon that from viewing the beauteous qualities appeareth. | a sun that, from the horizon of ẓāt, ascendeth. |
| (*c*) a light that giveth decoration to existence. | a fire that purifieth existence. |
| (*d*) a token that saith—"Imitate what is pure; bid farewell to what is not pellucid." | a token that saith—"Live not and consume not." |
| (*e*) the best wine, sealed, tempered (by age). | the absolutely pure fountain. |
| (*f*) a wine (by reason of its temperament, possessed of desires) the porter of purity and of impurity; of fineness and of grossness; of lightness and of heaviness. | a wine (by reason of its being purified from defects) all purity in purity; fineness in fineness, lightness in lightness. |

The fineness and the lightness of this wine affecteth the heaviness and the lightness of the cup; changeth its grossness to fineness, its heaviness to lightness, like the soul that giveth to the eye fineness and lightness.

In the cup of their souls, the lovers of ẓāt drink this wine; and, on hearts and nafs, pour the dregs.

It giveth the lightness :—

(*a*) of agitation to souls (rūḥ).
(*b*) „ shauḳ „ hearts.
(*c*) „ devotion „ nafs.

The relish of this wine affecteth all parts of existence. It giveth :—

(*a*) to the soul, the delight of beholding.
(*b*) „ hearts „ „ remembering.
(*c*) „ nafs „ „ deeds.

"to such a degree that, in nafs, the delight of devotion prevaileth over all natural delights.

From its exceeding pureness and fineness, the essence of the cup becometh in the colour of this wine so effaced that discrimination remaineth not and the form of unity appeareth.

Love effaceth all existence; on the condition that it be established in the ḥāl it giveth its own colour; and, like lightnings and flashings, becometh not quickly extinguished.

Junīd saith :—

Love signifieth the entering into the qualities of the beloved in exchange for the qualities of the lover.

Muḥabbat is verily a link of the links of concord that bindeth the lover to the beloved; is an attraction of the attractions of the beloved, that draweth to himself the lover, and (to the degree that him to himself it draweth) effaceth something of his existence,—so that, first, from him it seizeth all his qualities; and then snatcheth, into the grasp of Ḳudrat (God), his ẕāt.

In exchange, the attraction of love giveth him a ẕāt that is worthy of the description of its own qualities; and after that, his qualities (the enterer of that ẕāt), become changed.

Junīd said :—

" In the exchange."

He said not :—

" In the lover."

For as long as the lover existeth,—not fit to be described with the qualities of the beloved is his ẕāt.

This ḥāl is the produce of muḥabbat and its end. Though its cause appeareth not, its marks are many. To the truth of his muḥabbat :—

every hair on the lover's limbs is a witness.
„ motion of „ mark.
„ resting „ „ sign.

Save by the eye of muḥabbat, one cannot behold this. For the sake of distinguishing the sincere ones from the pretenders, we sum up the ten marks of the lover of God :—

1. In the lover's heart is no love, either for this, or for the next, world, as God revealed to Īsā.

Possibly, in a heart divine love together with compassion (for the people) may be collected; and to some that compassion may show (as) love.

Its mark that it is compassion is this, that, if they leave free to choice the possessor of these two qualities (divine love and compassion),—he abandoneth the people's side.

2. He should not incline to any beauty that they may present to him; nor turn his glance from the beauty of the Beloved (God).

Once a man met a beautiful woman, and to her revealed his love. For trying him she said:—

> Beside me, is one who is more beautiful of face than I and more perfect in beauty. She is my sister.

Back, he looked. Against him, with rebuke, the woman extended her tongue:—

> O boaster! when I beheld thee afar, I thought thou wast a wise man; when thou camest near, I thought thou wast a lover. Now, thou art neither a wise man nor a lover.

3. Means of union with the Beloved, he should hold dear; and be submissive. For that love and devotion are the essence of the love and the devotion of the Beloved.

4. If of the number of hinderers of union with the Beloved, should be his son, of him he should be full of caution.

5. Filled and inflamed with love, he should be at the mention of the Beloved; and of it never be wearied. Every time that mention occurreth, greater should be his joy and exaltation.

The mention of the Beloved, he should hold dear to such a degree that, if, in the midst thereof, he hear his own reproach, therefrom he should gain delight.

6. In respect of orders and of prohibitions, he should preserve devotion to the Beloved; and never oppose His order.

Thus, have said:—

Rābi'a.
Sahl 'Abdu-l-lāh.
Ravīm.

7. In whatever he chooseth, his glance, in desire of the Beloved's consent, should be,—not in desire of another purpose.

Thus, have said:—

Abū Bakr-i-Kattānī.
Shiblī.

8. Much, he should regard a little regard of the Beloved; his own devotion (to the Beloved) little.

Thus saith God's word and the revelation that He sent to 'Uzair.

9. In the ray of the light-splendours of beholding the Beloved, the vision of lovers becometh dulled and dimmed; wherefrom spring jealousy, passion, and sweat.

If he be in the maḳām of tamkīn; and have the power of devouring (suffering) ḥāl; and if astonishment exceed not the soul's boundary, and prevent not the heart from arranging words and deeds,—his soul in beholding is the more astonished as his heart in appearing before another is the more sensible.

If he have not the power of such tamkīn; and, in the power of this ḥāl, the thread of discrimination becometh snatched from his hand, he crieth out:—

> "In me, increase astonishment at Thee."

10. The beholding of the Beloved and union with Him should not diminish his shauḳ.

In his nature, should be evoked a new shauḳ, astonishment, and desire—every moment in beholding; and in every breath in union with the Beloved.

As the degree of propinquity to the Beloved becometh greater, to the degree of sublimity falleth his glance; and his shauḳ, agitation, and desire for union increase.

Even so endless is the Beloved's beauty; and the lover's desire, endless.

Of many marks of love, these are a few; impossible in a book is love's limitation; according to the abundance of marks in love's praise is contrariety of words. According to another description and mark, each one, according to his ḥāl, describeth love.

---

## Shauḳ (desire).

### X. 2.

Shauḳ signifieth:—

> The assault of the claim of delight on account of the Beloved in the lover's heart. Its existence is the requsite of love's truth.

Abū 'Uṣmān Ḥairī saith:—

> Shauḳ is the fruit of muḥabbat (love); who loveth God, with Him desireth union.

According to love's division, shauḳ is of two kinds:—

(*a*) the shauḳ of lovers of qualities the understanding through the Beloved's grace, mercy and kindness.

(*b*) the shauḳ of the lovers of ẕāt through union with, and propinquity to, the Beloved. This shauḳ from exceeding honour is like red sulphur rare of existence. Because generally people are seekers of God's mercy, not of God Himself.

Said a man of heart (a ṣūfī):—

Thou seest a thousand—

| | |
|---|---|
| 'Abdu-r-Raḥmān | the slave of the most Merciful. |
| „ „ Raḥīm | „ „ „ Merciful. |
| „ -l-Karīm | „ „ „ Generous One. |
| but scarcely one 'Abdu-l-lāh | „ „ God. |

The seekers of (God's) mercy are many; few, the seekers of God.

To the seekers of God, paradise is the sight of Him even if by Fate they be in hell: hell, separation from Him, even if they be in paradise.

Thus saith Bāyizīd.

The ḥāl of shauḳ is an excellence such that, to their purpose it conveyeth the messengers of the ka'ba of desire; joined to perpetuality of love, is their perpetuality; ever as long as love remaineth is shauḳ necessary.

Some of the ṣūfīs have denied shauḳ in the stage of being present with, and of beholding, the Beloved.

This denial would have been at the time when shauḳ was special in desire of beholding (the Beloved), which is not necessary; because, beyond the beholding of the Beloved, to special men are other desires, (desirous whereof they are) such as—union, propinquity, and increase of their perpetuality.

Not every one who gained a sight of the Beloved, with the Beloved attained the fortune of union: not every one who became a joiner, gained the stage of propinquity: not every one who became near attained the limit of the degrees of propinquity: not every one who gained that degree, lasting thereon remained.

The shauḳ of these desires, according to the exaltation of its degrees, is much more difficult than the shauḳ of beholding, as some of the great ones of ṭarīḳat have said.

In the Ḥadīṣ of Dā,ūd are words, the meaning whereof is the strengthener of our spirit. Because in ḥāl when the glance is on the Beloved, shauḳ becometh (as is evident to those present and beholding) momently greater.

Then, in connection with what shall have been gained, love is not desirous of beholding, or of being near to, the Beloved; and is desirous in connection with what shall not have been gained.

The shauḳ of beholding is (in existence) the essence of certainty; its acquisition is in this world difficult.

In some places, shauḳ is the cause of death's delay; and in some (where the desired is an order from the Beloved, whose acquisition is as life) it becometh not its cause, but the negation thereof.

In this case, life may be beloved.

The cause of death's delay is not necessary, for shauḳ is the ḥaḳḳu-l-yaḳīn and the maḳām of acquisition.

Possibly the cause of that shauḳ is the beholding of one whose acquisition is in this world difficult.

The word liḳā (beholding) signifieth:—

Mushāhida (manifestation), wuṣūl (acquisition).

In this place, the second meaning is appropriate.

## Ḳabẓ (contraction) and basṭ (expansion).

X. 7.

When the holy traveller of the path of ḥaḳīḳaṭ passeth beyond the maḳām of muḥabbat-i-'āmm (common love), and reacheth to the beginning of muḥabbat-i-khāṣṣ (special love),—he entereth the crowd of the companions of heart and of the Lords of ḥāl; and upon his heart, descendeth the hāl of ḳabẓ and of basṭ.

Ever between these two states, pursuant and expectant the Turner of hearts (God) keepeth his heart, so that out from it He graspeth sensual delights; and it, with His own light, expandeth.

Sometimes in the tight grasp of ḳabẓ, God twisteth his heart so that therefrom becometh expressed the refuse of the existence of delight (ḥaẓẓ); and the effect thereof is shown in tears.

Sometimes in the broad plain of basṭ, God lowereth His rein so that he (the traveller) may establish the marks of devotion and of sincerity.

Thus have said :—

Wāsiṭī and Nūrī.

Ḳabẓ signifieth :—

The extracting of delight (ḥaẓẓ) from the heart, for the sake of holding and capturing its state of joy (surūr).

Basṭ signifieth :—

The flashing of the heart with the splendour of the light of the state of joy.

The cause :—

(*a*) of ḳabẓ is the revelation of the qualities of nafs and the veiling of the splendour of joy's state. The result is the contraction of the heart.

(*b*) of basṭ is the up-lifting of the veil of nafs from before the heart. The result is the expansion of the heart.

Of the qualities of nafs (whereof many are the veil of basṭ) one is ṭughyān (exceeding iniquity).

In the state of the descending of joy, the heart listeneth to nafs; becometh admonished of its state; through joy cometh into exaltation; and through its motion, becometh raised a great darkness like to a cloud, layer on layer, wherefrom springeth ḳabẓ.

To repel this calamity, the heart should at the time of the descending of joy, before listening to nafs, take shelter in God; with truth and penitence, repent, so that He may lower between it and nafs the veil of purity, and preserve it from attachment to nafs and to ṭughyān.

Sometimes to "the first ones," appear in nafs resemblances to :—

| | |
|---|---|
| Ḳabẓ (contraction) | grief. |
| basṭ (expansion) | joy. |

On experiencing either grief or joy, they think that they experience either ḳabẓ or basṭ; and thus, fall into error.

The end of ḳabẓ is basṯ; the end of basṯ is fanā; in fanā, ḳabẓ and basṯ are impossible.

Since ḳabẓ and basṯ are of the crowd of aḥwāl :—
(*a*) in them, "the first ones" share not.
(*b*) from them, "the last ones" having issued from the sway of occupations, have turned.
(*c*) them, "the middle ones" have as their ḥāl.

In the place of ḳabẓ and of basṯ :—
(*a*) "the first ones" have khauf (fear of God), and rijā (hope in God).
(*b*) "the last ones" have fanā (effacement) and baḳā (permanency).

Partners between "the first ones" and "the middle ones" are :—
(*a*) fear and hope according to faith.
(*b*) grief and joy „ „ nature.

"The last ones" by putting off the garment of existence have neither ḳabẓ nor basṯ, neither fear nor hope, neither grief nor joy—except when to the heart's stage shall have reached their nafs; and to it (nafs) become revealed the qualities of the heart; and grief and joy become changed to ḳabẓ and basṯ, and thereby ḳabẓ and basṯ become left in their nafs and are never removed.

## Fanā (effacement) and baḳā (permanency).

X. 8.

Fanā* signifieth :—
the end of travelling to God.

Baḳā signifieth:—
the beginning of travelling in God.

Travelling to God (fanā) endeth when, with the foot of sincerity, the holy traveller travelleth the desert of existence.

Travelling in God (baḳā, becometh verified when, after absolute fanā, they give to the slave an existence purified from the pollution of impurities, so that, in the world of description (the material world), he advanceth in divine qualities.

In the description of fanā and baḳā, the contrarieties of the words of shaikhs agree with the contrarieties of ḥāl of the holy traveller.

According to his understanding and the amending of his ḥāl, the shaikhs have answered each murīd; absolute fanā and baḳā, they have less explained.

---

* Fanā signifieth :—
(*a*) the death of passion, of self-will, of self-consciousness, producing the spiritual resurrection to eternal life (baḳā).
(*b*) the thinking away of self; the emerging from self that veileth man's real essence (God).
(Lahījī in Gulshan-i-rāz).
(*c*) the prayer of rapture, wherein man is effaced from self, so that he is not conscious of his body, nor of things outward and inward, From these, he is rapt,—journeying first to his Lord and then in his Lord.

If it occur to him that he is effaced from self, it is a defect. The highest state is to be effaced from effacement.
(Imām Ghazzālī in Gulshan-i-rāz.)

Some have said :—

| Fanā signifieth :— | Baḳā signifieth :— | The sense is a requisite :— |
|---|---|---|
| (*a*) the fanā of contrarieties. | the baḳā of concordances. | of the maḳām of penitence of Naṣūḥ. |
| (*b*) ,, decline of worldly delights. | ,, permanency of pleasure in the next world. | ,, ,, Zuhd (austerity. |
| (*c*) ,, decline of delights of this and of the next world. | ,, permanency of delight in God. | ,, sincerity of natural love. |
| (*d*) ,, decline of blameable qualities. | ,, permanency of laudable qualities. | ,, purifying and of the glorifying of nafs. |
| (*e*) ,, concealment of things. | ,, presence of God. | ,, intoxication of ḥāl. |

Fanā is of two kinds ;—outward and inward.

(*a*) Outward fanā.

This is the fanā of deeds and is the glory of divine deeds. The possessor of this fanā becometh so immersed in divine deeds that, neither on the part of himself nor on the part of others, seeth he deed, or desire, or will—save the deed, the desire and the will of God.

In himself, no will for any deed remaineth ; he plungeth into no work ; and, from the free manifestation of divine deeds without the pollution of deeds of other than God, gaineth delight.

Some holy travellers have remained in this maḳām, wherein they have neither eaten nor drunk, till God hath appointed over them one who (with eatables, potables, and other things) might support them.

(*b*) Inward fanā.

This is the fanā of qualities and of ẓāt. The possessor of this ḥāl in the revelation of the qualities of the Ancient One is immersed sometimes in the fanā of his own qualities ; and, sometimes, in the manifestation of the effects and of the grandeur of the Ancient One.

Immersed in the fanā of the ẓāt of the Ancient One, he is immersed in the fanā of the ẓāt of Wujūd (the Absolute Existence, God)—until that time when, over him prevaileth the existence of God when his heart becometh cleansed of all temptations and thoughts.

God knoweth that, in connection with that one who shall not yet have passed the stage of fanā, his baḳā is shirk (infidelity) ; and not shirk in connection with that one who, after fanā, shall have reached baḳā.

In this maḳām, the being hidden from feeling (being unconscious) is not a requisite. To some, it may chance ; to others, not. The cause of his not being hidden from feeling is his amplitude of prayer, and capaciousness of mind.

Therein is contained fanā. The presence of his inward (the heart) is immersed in the abyss of fanā : the presence of his outward (the body) is present in what goeth forth from words and deeds.

This may be at a time when he shall have found dwelling in the maḳām of manifestation of ẓāt and of qualities ; and shall have come from the inebriety of the ḥāl

---

(*d*) the proximity to the light of lights wherein the flame of eternal love burneth, ere it transformeth ; consuming self, ere it quickeneth the lover with the embrace of union.
(Gulshan-i-rāz, l. 120.)

of fanā to sobriety. He who is in the beginning of this ḥāl, him, concealeth from feeling the intoxication (of fanā).

Muslim bin Yasār was in prayer in the masjid of Biṣra, when suddenly one of its columns fell. Of the circumstance, all the people of the bāzār knew, yet he in the masjid felt it not.

The baḳā that is in support of outward fanā is this :—

After fanā of desire and of will, God maketh the slave, master of desire and of will, and in absolute sway of the rein (of guidance). Whatever he desireth, he doeth with the will and the desire of God. Even so the giver up of absolute will is in the degree of the degrees of fanā ; the giver up of will wholly in affairs (until he is allowed) and partly in them (until he first returneth in heart to God) is in the degree of the maḳām of fanā.

The baḳā that is in support of inward fanā is this :—

The ẓāt and the qualities of fanā become evoked from the bond of violence in the assembly-place of manifestation in the garb of remaining existence; and from before it, the veil wholly riseth (and departeth).

Becometh neither God the veil of creation ; nor creation, the veil of God. To the possessor of fanā, God is the veil of creation,—as to those who have not reached the stage of fanā, creation is the veil of God.

After fanā, the possessor of baḳā beholdeth each veil in its own maḳām, without one (the veil of the Creator) being the veil of the other (the created).

In him, are collected and included the possessor of fanā and of baḳā. In fanā, he is bāḳī (lasting) ; in baḳā, fānī (effacing).

Outward fanā—

is the portion of the Lords of heart and of the Companions of ḥāl.

Inward fanā

is special to the noble ones, who may have become free from the intoxication of the sway of ḥāl have issued from beneath the veil of the heart ; and, from the society of the heart, have joined the society of the converter of hearts (God).

---

## The aurād (prayers).

VII. 7.

Before the crepuscule, the seeker should have completed his ablution, and should be sitting before the ḳibla in expectation of the prayer of morn.

When he heareth the cry of prayer, he should answer the mu,aẓẓin,—whatever he saith, he should repeat except in :

(*a*) ḥayyi 'alā-ṣ ṣalāt, rise to prayer.
(*b*) „ „ l-falāḥ, „ goodness.

When he should say :—

There is no power nor virtue but in God the great, the mighty !

In every aẕān, he should observe this rule; in the morning aẕān, he should generally say:—

O God! this is the face of Thy day, the back of Thy night, and the sound of Thy prayer.

O Merciful of the merciful! through Thy mercy, me forgive, and my parents, and all the faithful, male and female.

When the morning dawneth, he should utter the renewal of the shahādat—

Welcome to the two kind recording angels! God bless ye! in my record, write that I declare—

that there is no god but God.
" Muḥammad is His prophet.
" paradise is true.
" the fire (of hell) " "
" ṣirāṯ (the bridge) " "
" the question (in the grave) " "
" " balance " "
" " account " "
" " punishment " "
" " book (of record) " "
" " intercession (of Muḥammad) " "

I declare that, in the hour given, God will cause (the dead) to rise from the grave.

O God! to Thee, I entrust this declaration for the day of my need. O God! for its sake,—stop my sin; forgive my sin; make heavy my balance; make me deserving of safety; and forgive me my faults through Thy mercy, O Merciful of the merciful!

Then he should perform two rak'ats of the prayer of the sunnat* of the crepuscule—

with Sūratu-l-Kāfirūn, chapter 109.
" " Ikhlāṣ " 112.

Several times he should repeat:—

the Kalima-i-tasbīḥ.
" " istighfār.

and should say:—

I ask pardon of God for my sin; to God, be glory by the praise of my God.

For the masjid-prayer, he should resolve to go to the masjid. On going out from his house, he should say:—

O God! by the true ingress, make me enter; by the true egress, make me pass out.

---

* There are three kinds of prayer:—
wājib, necessary prayer (five).
sunnat, prescribed "
nafl, voluntary "

On the way to the masjid, he should utter this prayer :—

By the incliners to Thee, by the beggars towards Thee, by this my going and coming out to Thee,—I pray to Thee, O God!

With evil and hypocrisy, I have not issued. To avoid Thy curse and to meet Thy blessing, have I come out. To save me from hell-fire and to forgive me my sin,—I pray to Thee, for none save Thou forgivest sins.

On going into the masjid and planting his foot on the prayer-mat, he should advance his right foot and say :—

In the name of God, to God be praise! peace and blessing on the prophet of God! O God, me forgive and open me the door of mercy.

When he performeth the enjoined observances in the masjid and giveth the salutation,* he should say ten times:—

There is no god but God, the One, with Whom is no partner. Dominion, His; praise, His; life, He giveth and taketh; and is ever living without death. In His hand, is good; over all kings, He is powerful.

Then he should say :—

There is no god but God, the One. Sincerity is His promise; victory, His slave; popular, His army. There is no god but God, the master of grace. To Him, be praise. There is no god but God, save Him, we worship none. Who have faith in Him are saved.

Then he should utter the ninety-nine names† of God; and say :—

O God! bless Muḥammad, Thy slave, news-bringer, prophet, the illiterate but truthful messenger; and this descendant of Muḥammad with blessing such as is Thy will. Give him the means and the blessed degree‡ that Thou promisedest.

Bless his brethren the prophets, the true ones, the martyrs, the pious ones.

O God! to the day of faith (the judgment-day) our chief Muḥammad bless—
among the ancient ones.
„ last generations.
„ those in lofty regions.

O God! bless the soul of Muḥammad among the souls; his body among the bodies; and bestow all the excellences of the blessings of Thy mercy.

His two hands, he uplifteth; and of the above traditional prayer of the prophet (in ẕikr whereof, after this a single section§ will pass) he uttereth as he wisheth.

The Lords of deeds and the companions of stages have cherished this time; on its preservation, established the base of the structure of times and of hours; and in this rule :—

by negation of lusts,
„ abandoning words,
„ assiduity in ẕikr,
by reading without defect,
„ attendance before the ḳibla,

---

* Salām signifies :—

Peace (be) on thee, O prophet, and the mercy of God and His blessing; peace on us and the devout slaves of God; peace on you and the mercy of God and His blessing!

Every prayer must conclude with this salutation.

† See Brown's Darvishes, p. 116.

‡ The degree is the maḳām al Maḥmūd.

§ This is given in chapter vii, section 8 of the Miṣbāḥ.

have ordered seekers and ṣūfīs.

When, by anticipation, he shall have preferred a prayer, best it is that in the masjid, he should sit; be assiduous in ẕikr and in reading; and utter naught till he preferreth the prayer of sun-rise.

On the condition that, sitting, in that place, there shall be no thought of calamity; and that he shall be void of the causes of defect of deeds and of states.

Otherwise, he should return to his dwelling and be engaged in reading till the sun ascendeth.

Of Muḥammad, the story is—

> He who from morning-prayer till sun-rise, sitteth in ẕikr of God is dearer to me than one who saveth four necks (lives).

He should read the following passages of the Ḳurān :—

| | Chapter. | Verse. |
|---|---|---|
| The Sūratu-l-Fātiḥa . . . | 1 | |
| „ Baḳara . . | 2 | 1-5, 164-165, 255-257, 284-286. |
| „ Imrān* . . | 3 | 190-200, 18-19, 26-27. |
| „ Kahf† . . . | 18 | 107-110. |
| „ Ḥadid . . | 57 | 1-6. |
| „ Ḥashr . . . | 59 | 21-24. |

Then he should utter :—

| | |
|---|---|
| Thirty-three times the Subḥāna-l-lāh, | glory be to God! |
| „ „ Alḥamdu-li-llāh, | praise „ |
| „ „ Allāhu Akbar, | God is great! |
| Once Lā ilāha illa-l-lāh, | there is no god but God. |
| His is no partner; | |
| He is God. | He is immortal. |
| „ single. | „ imperishable. |
| „ one. | „ eternal. |
| „ divine. | „ perpetual. |
| „ unity. | |

His is order; His is praise; He is powerful over all.

---

* After this are omitted four passages not identified (see below).

† „ „ three „ „ „ „

*Verses of the Ḳur,ān.*

| From | To |
|---|---|
| " Verily your God." | " of the benefactor." |
| " Verily, to you the prophet come." | the end. |
| " Upon God, I call." | „ |
| Verily those that have faith. | „ |

| | |
|---|---|
| and Ẕu-n-Nūn. | " the best of heirs." |
| Praise to God. | the end. |
| To thy God, praise. | „ |

Till near sun-rise he should be assiduous:

in reading.
„ praying.
„ aẕkār (ẕikrs).

Then he uttereth the seven prayers, whereof the ten-fold utterance is obligatory, —that is, the ten aẕkār (repetitions).

| | | Chapter. |
|---|---|---|
| i. | the Suratu-l-Fātiḥa | 1 |
| ii. | „ Falak* | 113 |
| iii. | „ Nās* | 114 |
| iv. | „ Ikhlāṣ | 112 |
| v. | „ Kāfirūn | 109 |
| vi. | Āyatu Kursī | 2 v. 255 |

vii. glory to God; praise to God; no god but God; God is great; there is no power nor virtue but in God, the great, the mighty.†

O God! upon Muḥammad and his offspring send Thy blessing:
O God! me, forgive and my parents and all the faithful, male and female:
O God! towards me and them, do so, soon or late, in this and in the next world, as befitteth Thee; towards us, do not as befitteth us,—for Thou art the gentle Pardoner, the generous Bestower, the merciful Merciful.

This ended, he should engage:—

in the tasbīḥ, repeating subḥān allāh, glory to God.
„ istighfār „ astaghfir-ul-lāh, I ask God to forgive me.
„ tilāwat, reading the Ḳurān.

till the sun riseth a spear's length. Then, in the aforementioned way, he performeth the prayer of sun-rise.

If he have an important worldly matter, in it (for himself, or for his family) he engageth.

If God shall have given him the bounty of leisure, he should regard as booty the being engaged in worship of God; should without defect be assiduous in deeds and in devotion, till the time of the prayer of ẕuḥā‡ cometh, when he performeth it.

If still he have power for deeds, and no langour enter his soul,—he should be assiduous in deeds. If not, he should rest himself for a while.

---

* Together, these two are called—ma'ūẕatain, the two ma'ūẕ "shelter in God."

† The clauses are:—

*1st*—the tasbīḥ.
*2nd*— „ taḥmīd.
*3rd*— „ tahlīl.
*4th*—the takbīr.
*5th*— „ hawla.

‡ Ẕuḥā (or chāsht) is the middle hour between sun-rise and noon.

Deeds are of two kinds :—

(*a*) outward :—

ṣalāt, prayer.
tilāwat, reading.
ẕikr, repeating God's name.

(*b*) inward :—

muḥāẕira, being present before God.
murāḳiba,* fearful contemplation.
muḥāsiba, calling one's self to account.

The arranging of deeds is in this wise. As long as possible, the seeker should unite outward deeds with inward deeds; and in order advance ṣalāt, tilāwat, and ẕikr—on the condition of the heart being present with God, and of its being in fearful contemplation.

If, through languor union with an inward deed (muḥāẕira, murāḳiba) be impossible, he should be content with an outward deed.

Murāḳiba is that contemplative state wherein he ever regardeth God, his preserver and watcher: and this is the essence of ẕikr.

If, in respect of murāḳiba, he be languid; and temptations and thoughts prevail,—he should awhile rest himself in sleep so that nafs may rest from languor and torment; and, again, with joy may turn to deeds. Otherwise, through sorrow, nafs, with confused tale, entereth the heart; complaineth; prevaileth over it; and therein causeth hardness.

Before the declining of the sun (from the meridian), he should be awake for an hour, to arrange for ablution, so that at the time of noon, he may have finished his ablution; and may, engaged in ẕikr and tilāwat, be sitting before the ḳibla.

When the sun declineth from the meridian, he performeth :—

four rak'ats,
one salutation,

and, thereby, becometh prepared for the prayer of ẕuhr.

After that—

he performeth the sunnat of ẕuhr.
„ sitteth expectant of the jamā'at.
„ engageth in tasbīḥ, and in istighfār.

It is laudable if, between an enjoined observance and the sunnat of the morn, he utter a prayer.

The ṣalāt-i-ẕuhr being ended, he uttereth :—

| | | Chapter. | |
|---|---|---|---|
| the Suratu-l-Fātiḥa | | 1 | |
| „ | Āyatu-Kursī | 2 | 255. |
| „ tasbīḥ, | Glory to God. | | |
| „ taḥmid, | Praise „ | | |
| „ takbīr, | God is great. | | |
| „ tahlīl, | There is no god but God. | | |

* See pp. 59, 64, 69, 86.

It is an excellence if, here, he should utter the āyāt (verses) and the prayers previously mentioned after the ṣalāt of the morn.

Alive with holy deeds in the afore-mentioned way, he should make the time between ẓuhr (noon) and 'aṣr (afternoon).

This is for that one who hath no other occupation, and who passeth his time in devotion.

When 'aṣr cometh, he preferreth four ruk'ats of the sunnat; and readeth :—

| | | | Chapter. |
|---|---|---|---|
| in the 1st rak'at the | Suratu-l-Zilzāl* | | 99. |
| „ 2nd „ | „ | Ādiyāt | 100. |
| „ 3rd „ | „ | Ḳāri'a | 101. |
| „ 4th „ | „ | Takāṣur | 102. |

When he performeth the ordinance of 'aṣr no time remaineth for the ṣalāt of nawāfil (works of supererogation); it is the time of ẓikr and of tilāwat. At this time, naught is more excellent than the society of :—

a learned zāhid, possessed of zuhd, for the blessing of whose breathings he may borrow the splendours of advantages; and—in respect to abandoning the world, to perpetuity of devotion and of desire,—may increase his resolution.

When he wisheth to come out from the stage he saith :—

In the name of God: what God pleaseth; God is my sufficiency; there is no power nor virtue but in God the great, the mighty. O God, towards Thee, I go out; and me, Thou makest go out.

He uttereth :—

| | Chapter. |
|---|---|
| the Suratu-l-Fātiḥa | 1. |
| „ Falaḳ | 113. |
| „ Nās | 114. |

Between 'aṣr (afternoon) and maghrib (evening-prayer) he uttereth a hundred times each of the following prayers :—

(*a*) There is no god but God, who is single, whose partner is none; His is the dominion; His the praise; powerful is He over all things.

(*b*) the tasbiḥ.†
„ taḥmid.
„ tahlīl.
„ takbīr.

(*c*) Glory to God, and to Him, praise; glory to God, the mighty, and to Him, praise; I ask forgiveness of God.

(*d*) There is no god but God the ruler, the Just, the Visible.

---

* The significations are :—

| | |
|---|---|
| zilzāl | the earthquake. |
| ādiyāt | „ war-horses that swiftly run. |
| ḳari'a | „ striking. |
| takāṣur | „ emulous desire of multiplying. |

† See p. 113.

(*e*) O God! upon Muḥammad and his offspring, send benediction.

(*f*) I ask forgiveness of God, the mighty,—save who is no God,—the Etern al, the Ancient penitence, I offer.

(*g*) Whatever pleaseth God: there is no power but in God, the great, the mighty—save who is no god—the Eternal, the Ancient, penitence, I offer.

(*h*) Whatever pleaseth God; there is no power but in God.

Daily, once, at the beginning, and at the ending, of day, he should say:—

O God me Thou createdest, guidedest, fedest, quenchedst, causedest to die, causedest to live: Thou art my God; save Thou none is mine; save Thou is no God; single, Thou art; no partner is Thine.

Whatever pleaseth God; there is no power save in God:
" " from God, are all favours:
" " in the hand of God, is all good:
" " save God, none wardeth off sin.

Before sunset, he must perform ablution; and seated before the ḳibla, be ready for the approach of night.

Till the sun setteth, he should utter:—

(*a*) the seven prayers whereof the ten-fold utterance is obligatory.
(*b*) ,, tasbiḥ.
(*c*) ,, istighfār.

At sun-set, in answer to the aẕān, he uttereth:—

| | Chapter. |
|---|---|
| the Suratu-l-Shams | 91. |
| ,, ,, Lail | 92. |
| ,, ,, Falak | 113. |
| ,, ,, Nās | 114. |

O God! the face of Thy night this is, and the back of Thy day.

Between the aẕān (of sunset) and the iḳāmat, as his time is little, he quickly performeth two ruak'ats of the sunnat; and uttereth:—

| | Chapter. |
|---|---|
| in the 1st ruk'at, the Suratu-l- Kāfirūn | 109. |
| ,, 2nd ,, ,, Ikhlāṣ | 112. |

He reneweth "the shahādat," and saith:—

Welcome to the angels of the night; welcome to the two kind angels.

In the masjid, he joineth the two 'ishā (evening prayers) until he joineth the blessing of being in the masjid (i'tikāf) and of the union of the two 'ishā.

It therein he see increase of safety of faith, of perfection, of sincerity, and of tranquillity,—he may go to his own corner; and (of all the prayers which he performeth between maghrib and 'ishā) may utter:—

| | Chapter. |
|---|---|
| (*a*) with two rak'ats | |
| the Sūratu-l-Burūj | 85. |
| ,, ,, Ṭāriḳ | 86. |

| | Chapter | |
|---|---|---|
| (*b*) with one rak'at. | | |
| the Sūratu-l-Baḳara,* | 2 | v. 1—16. |
| „ „ Ikhlāṣ† | 112. | |
| (*c*) the Āyatu-l-Kursī‡ | 2 | „ 255. |
| „ Sūratu-l-Ikhlāṣ† | 112. | |

Well it is if he unite (*b*) and (*c*) with (*a*).

After performing the enjoined duty of 'ishā and the two rak'ats of the sunnat he goeth to his dwelling or to his khilvat-place.

Before sitting down, he performeth four rak'ats with :—

| | Chapter. |
|---|---|
| the Sūratu-l-Luḳmān | 31. |
| „ „ Yāsīn | 36. |
| „ „ Dukhan | 44. |
| „ „ Mulk | 67. |

If he wish to shorten the prayer, he uttereth :—

| | Chapter. | |
|---|---|---|
| the Āyatu-l-Kursī‡ | 2 | v. 255. |
| „ Sūratu-l-Ḥadīd§ | 57. | |
| „ „ Ḥashr‖ | 59. | |

Then he performeth eleven rak'ats, and uttereth—

the Sūratu-l-Ṭāriḳ 86.

and delayeth not, save when he is engaged in devotion of vigilance of his own nafs, wherein delay is excellent.

When he wisheth to sleep, he should (as to purity and to ẕikr) be as before stated; when he awaketh and wisheth to make the tahajjud, he maketh it standing as before stated.

Some short-sighted ones (whose vision may not have found the collyrium for the observing of the beauty of perfection of rule) may regard the repairing of times according to rules,—the portion only of 'ābids.

They see no great need of it for the Lords of stages and for the Companions of union.

Possibly this is the mark of him who, in search of, and in love for, God, is sincere :—

That he regardeth not much the expenditure of his own times and the being immersed in deeds and in devotion; and becometh not vexed.

---

* After the Sūratu-l-Baḳara, cometh a passage from—
"Your God is God the One,"
to
For this tribe that hath come to reason,
which passage in the Ḳurān I have been unable to identify.

† This is to be repeated fifteen times.

‡ And "The prophet believeth."

§ The beginning.

‖ „ end.

For when, in respect of its Beloved, true love gaineth the opportunity of happiness and of meeting and the possibilities of the good fortune of prayer; and, in His presence, hath the power

| | |
|---|---|
| of weeping. | of paying homage (with the ground kiss). |
| „ flattering. | „ doing service. |

it recogniseth its own exceeding hope and great prosperity.

---

## Ru,yat (beholding God).

I. 6.

Clearly beholding God is :—

(*a*) in this world, difficult, because bāḳi is not contained in fāni.
(*b*) in the next world, promised to the faithful (muslim) and denied to the kāfir.

The faithful (muslim) seeth God :—

(*a*) in this world, with the eye of faith and with the glance of vision.
(*b*) in the next world, with the glance of sight and of vision (as in the Hadīṣ).

In the matter of seeing, the purport of this resemblance is the glance of the next world with the glance of vision in this world—not the (vain) resemblance of God (possessed of glory) to the moon (void of glory); because this spectacle resembleth no other spectacle.

The truth of true faith is this :—

In his own belief, the faithful reacheth to the degree of yaḳin; and as to this, belief is diverse.

In this world, a crowd :—

(*a*) know by 'ilm-i-yaḳīn; and the promise of their 'ainu-l-yaḳin is in the next world.
(*b*) see with 'ainu-l-yaḳin „ „ „ ḥaḳḳu-l-yaḳin „ „ „

Hence said he what he said :—

"In my heart, my God, I saw."

This is faith. For Ma'āẓ used to pass by the door of the house of the ṣaḥāba and used to say :—

"That I may have faith for an hour,—come."

When 'ainu-l-yaḳīn reacheth to perfection, it gaineth the degree of beauty of vision wherein he seeth no increase of form as Amīru-l-Muminīm 'Alī hath related of this maḳām—

"If rent were all the veils, not at all would increase my yaḳin."

The error of the crowd that denied the seeing (of God) in the next world, two-fold is its error :—

(*a*) obligation to God's word—"Him, the eye understood not."
(*b*) the idea of the next world (founded) on this world.

As to (*a*)—

Seeing is one thing (possible), understanding another (difficult). The sun's form, one can see; it, one cannot comprehend.

As to (*b*)—

With seeing of this world, the seeing of the next world hath no connection.
What connection hath fānī with bāḳī?

The mistake is this, that the crowd thought that even as in this world so in the next world, for seeing the five following conditions are necessary:—

| | |
|---|---|
| a side. | an air. |
| „ description. | a splendour-light. |
| „ quality. | „ surrounding of light. |

Vain imaginings, are all these fancies; and great is this error that, in respect of his own ḥāl and maḳām, a person conjectureth in a degree superior thereto.

To-day, the affairs of the next world gaineth that one, who, from the world and from its delights, shall wholly have turned his inclination.

He is—

(*a*) in heart, in the next world, in the hidden world, dwelling in ḳudrat.
(*b*) in body, in this world, in the world of shahādat and of ḥikmat.

This crowd performeth deeds for cash and giveth not itself to credit.

What, from beholding the promise, others have to-morrow, is for them the essence of cash to-day.

Despite this, for them also is a promise, which is the cash of another crowd; and for it, cash reacheth the Absolute Banker (whose promise is not the cash of another; and that is, Muḥammad, whose cash is the promise of other prophets).

The promise of saints is the cash of prophets; the promise of the faithful muslim) the cash of saints.

According to his own ḥāl, Muḥammad hath a promised maḳām, the signification whereof is the —

Maḳām-i-Maḥmūd, the praised maḳām.

In it, with him none hath partnership. In this sense, the signifier is the word that occurreth in invitation to faith; and thereto the speaker is the word of the Kalām-i-Majīd (the Ḳurān).

---

## The witnessing of prophecy; and its ending (with Muḥammad).

I. 8.

Through the witnessing by God and the proving by endless miracles, people of faith have had—faith in Muḥammad's mission; and in the demand of the traditions of the Kalām-ī-Majīd, by the revelation of the faith, whereby all other religious rites and orders are abrogated.

The perfection of prophecy in Muḥammad's mission placed, on the door of other prophecy, the seal of decline. After him, closed became the path of prophecy; and all invitations (to faith).

Who from the path of following him turneth his face; and considereth not necessary to himself the rules of his sharī'at, is the friend of Shaiṭān, the enemy of the Merciful, and of the crowd of infidels.—Them, God requite!

If from the miracles* other than by the prophets, something becometh apparent, it, they should call deceit, not miracle† (of the prophets).

At one time when Fir'aun used to go by the Nīl-bank—as he went, the Nīl went; as he stood, the Nīl stood.

Not of the crowd of miracles (of the prophets) was this, though doubtless to him and to his people it appeared as the essence of power. Nay, it was divine deceit that daily, in his own kufr, he might become more firm; and, from the acceptance of faith, more astray.

Possibly, by the blessing of following Muḥammad, some of the miracles other than by the prophets may be revealed to the auliyā (saints); and to them they may be a blessing, whereby greater may become their yaḳīn.

Not necessary is it that the truth of the ḥāl of a walī, or of a sincere one, should be manifested by miracles (of the prophets). Because it is possible that the rank and the ḥāl of the master of miracle may be lower than the rank and the ḥāl of him, who is not master of miracle.

By reason of the manifestation of miracle, is commonly the strengthening of manifestation and the aiding of the faith of the master of miracle.

To the crowd (whose power of yaḳīn is in perfection) is no need of the effects of ḳudrat free from ḥikmat.

For this reason, hath come the tale of:—

| karāmat | miracle (of the prophets). |
|---|---|
| khwāriḳ-i-'ādāt | „ (of other than the prophets). |

On the part of the ṣaḥāba, seldom; on the part of modern shaikhs, often,—despite the fact that superior to their ḥāl, is the ḥāl of the ṣaḥāba.

The cause is that, mention whereof hath passed. Nay, in their opinion, through beholding the lights of absolute ḳudrat through ḥikmat, the glance of their vision is neither strange nor rare; and, in the strengthening of their yaḳīn, is no excess of effect.

---

* خوارق عادات

† كرامات

When something became disclosed to those, for whom was no continuance of manifestation,—by it, they become impressed; and the power of their yaḳīn, greater.

As the prophets are special by waḥy (revelation), the auliyā (saints) are from others of the faithful distinguished, by ilhām-i-rabbānī (divine inspiration).

To them, either in khwāb or in wakefulness, God bestowed good inspiration; a part of the parts of prophecy is true khwāb (sleep, dream).

---

## Ma'rifat-i-dil (deep knowledge of the heart).

III. 6.

The ma'rifat (knowledge) of the qualities of the heart are difficult, and its signification abstruse—

by reason of the continuance of its power in the forms of ḥāl; and its advancement in the degrees of perfection.

Hence they call it—

قلب ḳalb (the heart).

„ ḳullab (a cheat).

Since ḥāl is the gift of God and His gifts are boundless, endless are the power and the advance of the heart in degrees of perfection and in ascents of the beauty and of the grandeur of eternity without beginning.

Contained, in the limits of number and in the number of limit, are not its qualities and its ḥāls.

In limiting and numbering it, whoever spake knoweth of very truth, that the establishing of the limit of understanding and the making it dear becometh not the portion of his own capacity.

In the ocean of ma'rifat-i-dil thousands of divers of the seas of ma'ārifat have dived;—its abyss, none hath reached, or renounced its rarities and wonders.

Not every one, who found a trace thereof, thereof news gave back to the heart. From it, to whom fell the precious jewel—it, he placed on the platter of desire.

The meaning of dil (the heart) is that point, wherefrom the circle of existence came into motion and wherewith it found perfection. With it, is joined the mystery of eternity without beginning; and in it, the source of sight reached the limit of vision, and therewith glorified became.

The beauty and the grandeur of the aspect of bāḳi; the throne of the Merciful; the stage of the Ḳurān and of the Furḳān; Barzakh,* between the being absent and the being present; rūḥ (the soul) and nafs; the seas of the country and of dominion; the observer and the observed of the king; the lover and the beloved of God; the bearer of the load and the load of the mystery of the deposit of God's grace—all are its (the heart's) qualities.

The purport of the marriage of rūḥ and of nafs (is) the result of its (the heart's) existence; and the object of the links of the country and the dominion of God (is) the reverberation-place of vision and the pasturage of beholding (Him).

---

* See the Ḳurān, iii, 24; ix, 114.

Its form (is) pictured with the essence of love; and its vision, illumined with the light of beholding.

When, free from the soul, became nafs, on both sides love and contention appeared. From the marriage of the two loves (rūḥ and nafs), was born the heart's form; like to Barzakh, it intervened between the sea of rūḥ and the sea of nafs; to both inclined; and between them became the hinderer of contention.

That the heart's form appeared from love's source is proved thus—

> Wherever it seeth a beauty, with it it allieth itself: wherever it findeth an associate, with it, it intertwineth.

Not without a chosen one, nor a beloved, nor a heart-adorner,—ever is it. Firm is its base on love, and love's existence on it.

In their existence, the heart is like unto the throne of the Merciful. The throne is the heart of the greatest in the great world; the heart is the throne of the least in the least world (Ādam).

Included, beneath the sway of the throne's surrounding, are all hearts,—even as in the sway of the greatest rūḥ (God), are the parts of rūḥ; and, in the sway of universal nafs, the parts of nafs.

A form and a truth, hath the heart ever as hath the throne. Its form is that piece of cone that, in the left side of the body, is a deposit: its truth is that divine grace mention whereof hath been made.

Between this truth and its form, rational nafs and the animal rūḥ intervene; because the heart's truth is purely grace, and its form the essence of grossness. Between absolute grossness and grace, resemblance is in no way.

The rational nafs and the animal rūḥ (which have, each, a face to the world of grace; and a face to the world of grossness) intervene between the heart's form and its truth,—so that every trace (that may issue from the heart's truth) may first reach nafs; may by affinity take its aspect of grace; and may, to the animal rūḥ, convey its aspect of grossness.

Even so, by affinity, the animal rūḥ taketh its form of grace; intrusteth to the heart's form the aspect of grossness; and, therefrom, becometh diffused in the quarters of the body.

Even so the grace of mercy first is from God; becometh spread upon the truth of the throne; reacheth from it to all thrones; joineth by their means to the throne's form; and, hence, reacheth the quarters of the material world.

The affinity of the throne's form is to its truth. Because every bounty (whereby truth reacheth the material world) first reacheth its form, and thence penetrateth to other bodies.

So is the affinity of the heart's form to its truth.

All hearts find bounty from the throne :—

(*a*) its truth from the throne's truth.
(*b*) „ form „ „ form.

At a time when, by means of prosperity, opposition as to God between the heart and the throne appeareth, nothing of creation is greater than the throne. Of its greatness God's word speaketh.

Muḥammad hath said the hearts are four :—

(i) the heart, pure, luminous, wherein the lamp is kindled. This is the heart of the faithful mushin.
(ii) „ dark, head-lowered. This is the heart of the kāfir.
(iii) „ addicted to hesitation between kufr and faith. This is the heart of the hypocrite.
(iv) the heart, inclined, possessed of sides, whereof one side is the place of faith; and the other, of hypocrisy.
In it, are the aid of faith from the holy world, and the purification like to freshness that increaseth from pure water; and in it, are the aid of hypocrisy from the world of pollution, and a stain like a wound that increaseth from purulence and ichorous pus.
Whichever of these two is superior, ordereth the heart.

The source of contrariety of these four kinds of heart is the result of contention between rūḥ and nafs.

To its own world, rūḥ wisheth to draw nafs ; and nafs, rūḥ. Ever in this contention they are. Sometimes rūḥ prevaileth and draweth nafs from the low centre to the lofty maḳām, sometimes nafs prevaileth, and draweth rūḥ from the summit of perfection to the abyss of loss.

Ever obedient to that side that prevaileth is the heart until when dominion becometh established wholly on one. In following it, the heart accepteth contentment.

On these two attractions, are established happiness and misery.

If the happiness of eternity without end and the favour of eternity without beginning arrive and give to rūḥ (the soul) the aid of grace, whereby it gathereth strength ; conquereth nafs ; escapeth from contention ; advanceth from the descending-place of creation to the rising-place of ḳidam ; and, turned wholly away from nafs and ḳalb (the heart), approacheth to the viewing of God—then dil (the heart) in its following from the maḳām of ḳalb (the conversion whereof is necessary) ascendeth to the maḳām of rūḥ and in rūḥ's dwelling resteth.

Then following dil (the heart), nafs issueth from its dwelling (which is the world of nature) and reacheth the maḳām of dil (whose child it is).

Such is the heart of the faithful wherein is no atom of shirk (partnership with God) and kufr (infidelity).

If, otherwise, be the state and the effect of misery and the hardness of eternity without beginning arrive and make rūḥ captive to dil and nafs victorious, so that it gathereth strength, and, to its own world, draweth ḳalb and rūḥ—rūḥ descendeth from its own maḳām to the place of ḳalb; ḳalb entereth from its own maḳām the place of nafs; and, in nature's soil, firm becometh nafs.

Such is the heart of the ḳāfir, who is lowered of heart, black with kufr,—altogether seized.

If, on either side, be not total victory, the inclination of dil is generally:—

(*a*) to nafs, if nafs be powerful and dil hesitating in the middle.
Such is the heart of the munāfiḳ (hypocrite).

(*b*) to rūḥ (or to both sides), if rūḥ be powerful.
Such a heart is inclined and hath two faces—one towards faith, the other towards hypocrisy.

---

## Ma'rifat-i-murīd va murād va sālik va majzūb.

## Deep knowledge of the murīd (the follower, the lover, the disciple), of the murād (the followed, the beloved, the shaikh), of the holy traveller, and of the attracted one.

III. 9.

Ṣūfīs assign two meanings:—

to murīd, the follower, the lover (the disciple).
„ murād, „ followed, „ beloved ( „ murshid).

The murīd (disciple) is called muḳtadī (the follower) because:—

The eye of his vision becometh, with the light of guidance, the see-er; and gazeth at his own defect. The fire of desire of perfection kindleth in his nature; and never resteth except by the acquisition of the murād (the followed) and of propinquity to God.

Impressed with the travelling of the man of desire, whoever was; and, in the two worlds, hath a desire other than God, or resteth a moment from desire for the murād,——for him, illusory is the name of desire.

Thus say:—

Shaikh 'Abdu-l-lāh Ḥāfiẓ.
Abū 'Usmān Ḥairī.

The murād is called muḳtadā (the followed) because:—

The power of his sway (over murīds) hath reached to the degree of perfecting imperfect ones to the diversity of ways of capacity; to the ways of directing and of instructing with the glance of the eye.

Like this is the person, or the holy traveller, (who is) the attracted one, who, with the foot of travelling, hath traversed all the deserts and the dangerous places of sensual qualities; and then, with the aid of divine attraction, passed from the degrees of the ḳalb (heart) to the ascents of rūḥ (the soul); reached to the world of kashf (revelation) and of yaḳīn (certainty); and is ever in beholding (God).

Or like this, is the (God) attracted one, (who is) the holy traveller, who first, with the power of attractions, hath traversed the plain of the maḳāms, reached to the world of revelation and of beholding; and then, with the foot of travelling, beheld the stages and the halting-places; and found, in the form of 'īlm, the truth of ḥāl.

To these two, is preserved the rank of being a shaikh, or of being a muḳtadā (a followed).

Neither of the two following hath the right of the dignity of being a shaikh.

(*a*) The imperfect holy traveller, who from the strait place of effort to the plain of manifestation, hath not reached.

(*b*) The imperfect attracted one, who, in respect to the subtleties of holy travelling and to the truths of maḳāms, of stages, and of dreadful places,—hath not gained knowledge.

To them, becometh not committed :—

The ruling over the capacity of the murīd and the instructing him in the rules of ṭarīḳat.

For this reason, more than its good is the evil of every control that they exercise.

---

The existence of the murīd and his capacity of perfection is like unto an egg, wherein is existent the capacity of being a bird.

If it be worthy of the power and of the impressing of the blessing and of the protection of a matured bird (wherein the vehemence of the power of begetting is overpowering),—while in the egg, the power of the spiritual life and the specialities of its perfection of flying penetrate. At last, off from itself the egg pulleth the egg-garment; putteth on the honour-robe of being a bird; and conveyeth itself to the perfection of capacity.

On the contrary, if he place the egg beneath a (young, immature) bird, that hath not the power of flying,—a time lapseth, and in the egg the capacity of the existence of flying becometh corrupted. Then the egg is not worth restoring.

Even so, if—beneath the sway of a perfect shaikh (who shall have attained to the degree of perfecting imperfect ones; and in whom, are joined together the travelling on, and the flying on, the Path, and attraction) the sincere murīd make obedient his own existence—the bird of truth, "God created Adam in His own form," issueth from the egg of his existence; flieth in the liquid air of divine essence; and reacheth the degree of producing.

If beneath the sway of the imperfect holy traveller, or of the imperfect attracted one, the murīd come, corrupt in him becometh the capacity of the perfecting of humanity; and he reacheth neither to the perfection of man, nor to the stage of perfection.

Even so, in the material world, the demand of God's mature ḥikmat and current sunnat is this—

that, despite the capacity for producing, appeareth not the permanency of species, except after union of the two producers with the bond of lust, by the means of the deed, active and passive; and by the impressing and the impression.

So, in the spiritual world, the mystery of the ḥaḳīḳat of man (which is purely service) cometh not into existence—

> except after the union of the murīd and of the murād with the bond of love; and the murīd's acceptance of the murād's sway. This is "the second birth."*

Though in the ḳudrat of God, possible is the existence of the son without the father,—yet, in ḥikmat, it is prohibited just as is prohibited the spiritual birth without the union of the murīd and of the murād.

In ḳudrat it is possible (as is shown by the existence of some attracted ones); in ḥikmat, difficult.

Further, in birth without the father, calamity may be expected as in the birth of 'Īsā, who (in divinity and in humanity) became the source of error of the Christians—Him, they called—"the Son of God."

If an attracted one become master of revelation, not through the directing of a consummately perfect shaikh,—not secure are others from calamity.

In the sense of lover, murīd is:—

> the traveller, who is (God-) attracted.

In the sense of beloved, murād is:—

> the (God-) attracted one, who is the traveller.

Among them, restricted is the sense of shaikh.

Whose labour (as to revelation and manifestation) is preceding is lover; whose revelation (as to the form of effort) is preceding is beloved. In this way, the sense of murīd and murād is the essence of murād.

The Ḳurānic verse comprehendeth the explanation of the ḥāl of the lover and of the beloved.

Divine will, not the slave's acquisition, is the cause of choice: the condition (of acceptance) of guidance is the forerunner of repentance (which is the slave's deed).

In this form, the choice is the ḥāl of the beloved. Only by arrangement and by degrees, are the guidance of the ḥāl of the lover, and the travelling of lovers in the regions of maḳāms.

Until he fulfilleth the lowest maḳām, he reacheth not to the lofty maḳām.

They ascend:—

| | degree. | | degree. |
|---|---|---|---|
| from the | 1st | to the | 2nd. |
| ,, | 2nd | ,, | 3rd. |
| ,, | 3rd | ,, | 4th. |

Thus, by arrangement, they travel all the maḳāms. Then, changeth, travelling to attracting; endeth, travelling in flight; joineth, labour with manifestations; and reacheth, the being absent to beholding (God) face to face.

---

* See p. 67.

In this maḳām, do they write for the lovers the mandate of khilāfat; give the honour of being a shaikh; and order power over the murīd.

For this degree is the middle maḳām :—

(*a*) between the hidden and the manifest.
(*b*) „ God „ man.

In this maḳām, like to the throne of the merciful is the slave's existence that hath one side towards the hidden world; and the other towards the material world.

With the former, he taketh the bounty of God's mercy from the hidden world; with the latter, he conveyeth it to the material world and to the people.

---

When at the beginning of ḥāl, beloved ones take the path by the aid of attraction they traverse the regions of maḳām with a single attraction, and, therein, are comprehended the acquisition of all deeds of beloved ones.

Included in the purity of their ḥāl, is the purifier of the crowd of maḳāms.

The binding by maḳāms is for common lovers, who have not yet reached the world of kashf; whose travelling is in the removing of the darkness of the qualities of nafs; and from whom, in every maḳām, becometh effaced the darkness of a certain quality till that time when by this effacing, their nafs gaineth, with divine light, full refulgence.

As in nafs the inclination of nature is a darkness (which, in the maḳām of sincere penitence, becometh effaced); and delight in the world is a darkness (which, in the maḳām of austerity, becometh effaced); and poverty of trust on the surety of provision of God is a darkness (which, in the maḳām of rīẓā, ariseth and departeth)—accordingly, in every maḳām, a darkness becometh effaced till all the darknesses of nafs (by the travelling of the crowd of the crowd of maḳāms) arise and depart; and from the veil of darkness, becometh revealed the beauty of the face of yaḳīn.

By reason of the preceding of revelation on the path, when all the quarters of existence and of the interior (before the travelling of the stages of maḳāms, of travelling, of effort) are, with the light of yaḳīn, illumined; and cut off from them are the darknesses of the qualities of nafs.

In them, is existing the abstract of all maḳāms; separate from all zāhids they are despite delight (in the world); reliant on God, despite attention to the chattels of the world; and contented with God, despite abhorred sins of nature.

Because on God is their existence; not on themselves.

The absolute murād (the followed, the beloved, the murshid) and the absolute maḥbūb (beloved) is Muḥammad, the Sayyid of created beings—

The purpose of creation was his existence; created beings are all his offspring.

To none save to him, did they give the honour robe of being "a beloved." Even to the tābi'īn advance from the maḳām of being a lover to being a beloved is only by implicitly following Muḥammad.

Then from Muḥammad came the address in respect of Mūsạ, who had the degree of being "a lover (of God)" and who wished to be "a beloved (of God)."

When 'Īsạ desired this degree, at a time when He was desirous of Muḥammad God kept him detained some years in the sky, till after the mission of Muḥammad, so that—

> by God's order He might descend (to earth), and (by reviving the faith of Muḥammad and by following the sunnat of prophecy) reach the maḳām of being "a beloved (of God)."

God, none reacheth by being a lover,—only by being a beloved: God, none reacheth save by God.

Abū 'Alī Daḳḳāk hath said:—

> As Mūsạ was a murīd (lover), he said:—"O God! open me my heart."
> As Muḥammad was a murād (beloved), to him, God said:—"Thy heart, opened we not?"

Mūsạ said:—

> "Let me see."

Came the answer—

> "Me, thou shalt never see."

To Muḥammad, God said:—

> At thy God, shalt thou not look? (Yea, thou shalt).

In the attraction of truth, the similitude of the love of the Ancient One (God) is Muḥammad—even as, in the attraction of iron, is the quality of the magnet.

As the magnet giveth its own quality (the attraction of iron) to its own attracted and beloved one, so that it can attract another (piece of) iron—so, in its own attracted one, the speciality of every attracter permeateth.

From the magnet of love for the Ancient One (God), the rūḥ (soul) of Muḥammad (which is the first attracted and beloved one) acquired the speciality of the attraction of the souls of the faithful (muslims).

From the quarters and regions of the world, to himself Muḥammad drew thousands of souls of the ṣaḥāba, each one of whom found a portion of that speciality suitable to his capacity.

To himself, he drew the souls of the tābi'īn.

So, œon after œon, womb after womb, from the souls of the tābi'īn to the souls of the shaikhs and of the firm 'ulmā,—that speciality became transported; of the murīd to the murād, the chain (of attachment) became arranged; and every murīd, a murād became.

Such is the effect of following Muḥammad.

By perfection of following and by the link of union with the souls of shai<u>kh</u>s, whoever gained union with the soul of Muḥammad—in him, appeared love for God; and the degree of being a beloved (of God) and of being a murād.

For, according to arrangement, the souls of shai<u>kh</u>s are united with the soul of Muḥammad; thereby, in all permeate—love, following (the followed), and love for God.

The murīd, whose soul with the soul of the consummately perfect shai<u>kh</u>, (who shall have slipped out from his own desire; and gained from another shai<u>kh</u>, the heritage of love for God) uniteth not,—never reacheth the degree of being a beloved (of God), nor gaineth the maḳām of sway over another (the murīd).

---

## I'tiḳād (belief), the place whence it is taken, and the binding of one's self to the true faith.

I. 1.

The words i'tiḳād and ittiḥād signify:—

the binding of a form of 'ilm in the heart of the existence of mysteries.

Its place of origin, in the beginning of ḥāl, is the repetition of the hearing of news; and the continuance of the following of impressions as in children's pure nafs, which, by the passing of time, becometh the cause:—

of iniquities of ideas and fancies.
,, the following of the people's faith.

In their mind, the form of those beliefs becometh, like the (imperishable) sculpture on stone,—firm to such a degree that, in it, the power of another form appeareth impossible.

Whom, they see declining from the sunnat of their own—

faith, and the good of the religious order,

they charge with perversion and error.

Of them, is a crowd that hath, according to its own idea, held to the arguments of its own religion; and of itself imagined the verifying of, and the expelling (of deniers) from, its own circle of following.

If verily they look, they see themselves even so in the degree of following their own Imāms and 'Ulamā, from whom by reason of good opinion (and by the fancy of goodness of that opinion), they may have accepted arguments; from whom fancies and understandings may have issued; and with whom, the thought of yaḳīn and by the abundance of verification, they may have become pleased.

By reason of diversity of opinion, is the contrariety of desires, wherein human nafs is innate; and the existence of disputing and of forbidding worldly positions and demands (by the disease of seeking which, hearts are commonly distressed).

From the ancient to the modern ones, hath arrived this contrariety in the happy state.

Gradually, in the midst, the parties became diffused and dispersed; drew to enmity and hate; and it, by way of heritage from ancestors, descendants have taken.

Œon after œon, became pressed together its darkness (of hate), till it reached the limit of enmity, and ended in execration and kufr.

Then wherever, the past favour of eternity without beginning joineth, and wisheth to bestow faith upon the slave—

it releaseth him first from effects, customs, and manners; conveyeth him to the purity of the first creation; teareth up from his heart the root of obstinacy and of desire; till he becometh worthy of the form of true faith; and clear to him becometh the manifestation of the pure God.

In the time of the society of Muḥammad, by the blessing of the effects of descent of waḥīy (revelation), and of the ray of light of prophecy the nafs of the people had become eradicated from the darkness of customs; and hearts, purified from the pollution of nature and from the impurity of desire, turned away from this world, turned to the next world, seekers of God, with the light of faith,—had beheld through the veil the form of the hidden.

Therefore free was their belief from the reproach of contrariety; and their heart, from the ills of desire.

One of heart, of opinion, of tongue were all.

When the sun of prophecy became veiled in the veil of the hidden; and the light of purity, concealed in the veil of grandeur,—the darkness of desire of the land of nafs of the people (who, by the light of prophecy, had gained effulgence) became effaced in its light.

By the sun's being veiled and hidden, it again cast its shadow; and, little by little, forth from the concealed ambush, came the darkness of its desire.

Hearts turned their face from the moderation of steadfastness to turning aside; contrariety, to the degree of turning wholly away, appeared; and open to shaiṯān, became the path of sway.

According to the distance from the time of prophecy and of being veiled, the light of innocence daily became greater through the darkness of the descendings of nafs in the world; and contrariety commonly appeared.

Who is the seeker of the true faith, should follow the first crowd of the "companions"; should turn his heart from love for the world, so that, by the light of yaḵīn, the eye of his vision may be opened; and to him may be discovered the pure God.

This appeareth only—

by true purity.
" excellent refuge in the giver.
" the complaining of the evil of nafs.
" keeping one's self pure of sin by God's grace.

For, the associate of answer, God maketh every question that is through sincerity and perturbation.

To whom, God gave the favour of change of desire away from the world, the root of contention He plucked up from his heart and made it the glancing place of His mercy.

Its mark is this—

> By the glance of mercy, he becometh not joined with the veiled ones; nor with them treadeth the path of contention.

This is of the specialities of the ṣūfīs, whose hearts have wholly turned to the ecstasy of the sweetness of love (for God) away from the love for the world; whose veins of contention have become extirpated; and who, with the glance of mercy, have gazed at the commonality of the people, gained safety from enmity, and who are entitled—firḳa-i-nājiya.*

---

## 'Ilm-i-farīza (the knowledge of God's ordinance).

II. 3.

That 'ilm, the desire whereof is for all muslims an ordinance of God, is, in the opinion of the 'ulamā, contradictory.

Some have said it is :—

(*a*) the 'ilm-i-ikhlāṣ (sincerity).

Because even as devotion to God is God's ordinance, so sincerity in devotion is also God's ordinance; as for 'ilm, practice is necessary, so practice is necessary for the 'ilm-i-khlāṣ.

(*b*) the 'ilm-i-āfāt-i-ikhlāṣ (the calamities of sincerity); or the quality of nafs, the revelation whereof is the power of ikhlāṣ.

Then the 'ilm-i-ikhlāṣ is dependent on the 'ilm of the qualities of nafs. Dependent on it whatever may be a necessity is on it also necessary.

(*c*) the 'ilm-i-waḳt (period); or the knowing in what thing (deeds or words) it is best to be daily engaged.

(*d*) the 'ilm-i-ḥāl (mystic state); or the knowing the ḥāl (that may be between the slave and the Lord God), and the rule which is special to that ḥāl; and the learning its excess (or defect) at any period.

(*e*) the 'ilm-i-khawāṭir (thoughts); attached thereto is the distinguishing between the sources of the acts of thoughts and the goodness and evilness of acts.

All this is faẓīlat (excellence), not farīẓa (God's ordinance).

Not lawful is the abandoning of farīẓa. If 'ilm-i-farīẓa be one of those 'ilms, not lawful to muslims, is its abandoning.

---

* This is the name of an Arab tribe.

What Muḥammad hath said is enjoined to all muslims; the knowing of it is to all muslims impossible.

Not every nature can be prepared for these 'ilms; not lawful is unbearable trouble.

Most true is the ḳaul (word) of those of former times.

The ḳaul of Shaikh Abu Ṭālib-i-Makkī is—

It is the 'ilm of the source of Islām; or the five columns—

| | | |
|---|---|---|
| i. | the kalima-l-shahādatain, | the two creeds. |
| ii. | „ ṣalāt. | prayer. |
| iii. | „ zakāt | alms. |
| iv. | „ ṣaum | dream. |
| v. | „ ḥajj | pilgrimage. |

| | | |
|---|---|---|
| It is the | 'ilm-i-bay' | (purchase). |
| „ | sharā | (sale). |
| „ | ṭilāḳ | (divorce). |
| „ | nikāḥ | (marriage). |

Enjoined on high and low, is the knowing of these; for the understanding of them is, for all reasonable men, possible.

The (totality of all ḳauls is the) ḳaul of Shaikh Shahābu-d-Dīn 'Umar-i-Sahrwardī—

It is the 'ilm-i-mutafarẓ (the enjoined 'ilm); or the 'ilm of orders and of prohibitions (of God).

Because though the slave is ordered as to doing, and prohibited against abandoning, them,—incumbent on him is their 'ilm, so that the practice of them may be established.

The rules of the shar', as regards orders and prohibitions, are of two kinds:—

(*a*) the comprehender of the chosen common people,—

| | |
|---|---|
| the 'ilm-i-mubāni-i-islām. | the 'ilm-i-nikāḥ. |
| „ bay'. | „ ṭilāḳat. |
| „ sharā. | |

which are incumbent on all muslims by reason of:—
requisites.
necessity.
need.

| | |
|---|---|
| (*b*) the 'ulūm-i-faẓā,il (excellences). | the 'ilm-i-ḥāl (state). |
| „ 'ilm-i-ikhlāṣ (sincerity). | and other 'ilms already mentioned. |
| „ „ khwāṭir (thoughts). | |

These are enjoined on some special folk, who have the capacity and the power of knowing them; and not enjoined on common folk who have not the power.

For some special ones, whose capacity is fit, these 'ilms are of the number of God's ordinances. By them, they are ordered and prohibited.

Some of the ṣaḥāba have grieved and said :—

> We have the power not to bring into action impure thoughts ; impure thoughts, we have not the power to prevent. If as regards them, go a reckoning and a requital, difficult is the work.

Came this ayat—

> Save to its limit, nafs, God troubleth not.

Whoever cannot perform the ordinance is by it not ordered; and for the abandoning of it not reproved.

Whoever can restrain impure thoughts,—on him, is enjoined the ordinance.

The shaikhs, who have made yaḳīn of something and reckoned it God's ordinance, have spoken according to their own state.

This limit is the comprehender. Those 'ilms, which others have mentioned ; and according to their own ḥāl, reckoned God's ordinance, they have called—

the 'ilm-i-dirāsat (teaching).
„ „ wirāṣat (heritage).

---

## The ḥāl of man.

III. 10.

According to diversity of degrees, the ranks of men are of three kinds :—

i. The wāṣil (those joined to God) and the kāmil (the perfect).
The واصل (wāṣil) are the mukarrab (those near to God) and the sābiḳ (those gone before others in faith) . . . . . . . The Ḳurān lvi 10—11

ii. The سالك (sālik) holy travellers of ṭarīḳ (the path) of perfection.
These are the pious ; the aṣḥāb-i-yamīn (companions of the right hand) „ 8

iii. The مقيم (muḳīm) dwellers of the essence of defect.
These are the wicked ; the aṣḥāb-i-shumāl (the companions of the left hand) „ 9

The men of wuṣūl (union with God) are of three crowds :—

(*a*) The انبيا (ambiya), prophets, whom, after union and perfection, God sent to the people for the sake of perfecting the imperfect ones ; and whose existence He made the link of the hidden and the material world to invite people to Him, and to keep prosperous the realms of God and of the angels.

(*b*) The متصوفه (mutaṣawwifa), shaikhs, who, by perfection of following Muḥammad, have gained union (with God) ; and who were, after that, ordered to invite the people by the ṭarīḳ of following Muḥammad.

Consummately perfect are these two crowds, to whom, after their being immersed in the essence of jam' (collected), and in the abyss of tauḥīd (unity of God), the grace of eternity without beginning bestowed freedom and salvation from the belly of the fish of fanā (effacement) to the shore of tafraḳa (dispersed) and to the plain of baḳā (permanency),—so that, to salvation and to degrees, they might guide the people.

(*c*) The jamā 'at (crowd), to whom, after arrival at the degree of perfection, the trust of perfecting (the imperfect ones) in reference to inviting the people (to Islām) passed not; who became immersed in the sea of jam' (collected) and in the belly of the fish of fanā (effacement), who became naught so that neither news nor trace of them reached to the shore of tafraḳa or to the region of baḳā; who became threaded on the thread of the dwellers of the towers of ghairat (jealousy), and of the inhabitants of the land of ḥairat (astonishment); and to whom after perfection of union the power of perfecting the imperfect ones was not entrusted.

The men of sulūk (the path of travelling) are of two kinds :—

(*a*) The seekers of lofty purpose, and the murīds of the face of God.
(*b*) „ „ paradise, „ „ „ next world.

The seekers of God are :—

(*a*) The متصوفه mutaṣawwifa.

These are that crowd that have gained freedom from some of the qualities of nafs; become qualified with some of the ḥāls and some of the qualities of the ṣūfīs; and become the beholder of the excess of their ḥāl.

Yet with the proud trailing residue of the qualities of nafs are they left distressed; and therefore deprived of the acquisition of the end of the man of propinquity to God and of ṣūfiya (ṣūfī,ism).

(*b*) The ملامتيه (malāmatiya), the reproached.

These are that crowd who, in the observance of the meaning of ikhlāṣ (sincerity) and in the preservation of the rule of ṣidḳ (truth), have expended much effort; who in the concealing of their devotion and in the veiling of their almsgiving from the people's glance regard necessary great effort; who neglect not the minutest matter of holy deeds; who regard an enjoined duty all the excellences and the nawāfil; whose religious order is at all times the verifier of the sense of ikhlāṣ; and whose taste is for the singularity of God's glance upon their deeds and ḥāls.

As the sinner is full of caution, as to revealing his sins, so (lest there be suspicion of hypocrisy) as to revealing their devotion, do they practise hypocrisy that the order of ikhlāṣ may suffer no injury.

Although they are precious of wujūd and exalted of ḥāl, yet from their glance not wholly rent is the veil of creation. Therefore are they left veiled from beholding the beauty of tauḥīd (the unity of God) and the essence of tafrīd (inward solitude), because the concealing of deeds and of their ḥāl from the people's glance is known and allowed in the sight of the people and of themselves, who are the forbidders of the sense of tauḥīd.

Nafs is of the crowd of strangers. As long as on their own ḥāl, they keep their glance, not wholly have they expelled strangers, from the viewing of their own deeds and ḥāls.

The difference between the mutaṣawwifa or ṣūfiya and the malāmatiya is this :—

From the malāmatiya, the attraction of the grace of the Ancient One hath wholly uptorn the existence of ṣūfiya; and from the glance of their witnessing uplifted the veil of creation and of egotism.

In making their devotion, in issuing their alms, the malāmatiya see not in the midst themselves and the people. They are secure from the knowledge of the people's glance; and bound to the concealing neither of their deeds nor of their ḥāl.

If good they see in revealing their devotion, they reveal it; otherwise, they conceal it.

The mutaṣawwifa or ṣūfiya are—

مخلص (mukhlaṣ), saved.

The malāmatiya are—

مخلص (mukhliṣ), sincere.

The description of their ḥāl is:—

"Them, by sincerity, we (God) saved."

---

The seekers of the next world are four crowds—

زهاد (zuhhād, sing. zāhid), zāhids, dry austere men.
فقرا (fuḳarā, „ faḳīr), faḳīrs.
خدام (khuddām, „ khādim), servants of God.
عباد ('ubbād, „ 'ābid), those dedicated to God.

The zuhhād are those who with the light of faith and of certainty behold the beauty of the next world; clearly see this world in the form of ugliness; turn their desire from inclining to the worthless decoration of the fānī (perishable); and incline to the true beauty of the bāḳī (imperishable).

Against the صوفيه (ṣūfiya), the opposing of this crowd is—

because the zāhid is, by the delight of his own nafs, veiled from God; and because paradise is the maḳām of delight of nafs.

By beholding the beauty of eternity without beginning and the love of eternal ẓāt, the ṣūfī is veiled from both worlds.

As in respect to this world, he may have expended delight, so in respect to the next world, is his delight.

The Ḥadīṣ saith:—

Unlawful for the people (of the next world) is this world; unlawful for the people (of this world) is the next world; unlawful for the people (of God) are both worlds.

In the degree of zuhd (austerity), is the ṣūfī above the degree of the zāhid far wherefrom is the delight of nafs.

---

The fuḳarā are those who possess naught of the chattels of the world; who in desire of excellence and of the divine Riẓvān (God), have separated from their native land; and who have abandoned accustomed objects.

The cause is one of the following three things:—

(i) the hope of lessening the fearful reckoning of punishment (on the day of judgment). For necessary is the reckoning as regards lawful deeds; and, punishment as regards unlawful deeds.

(ii) the hope of excellence of reward and of excelling on entering paradise.
Glad tidings, brought Jibra,il one day to Muḥammad:—
"By half a day (equal to five hundred years), will the faḳīrs of thy ummat (tribe) enter para-
"dise before the rich of thy tribe."

(iii) the desire of tranquillity of heart, and of freedom of mind—for the sake of much devotion; and therein the presence of the heart.

Against the malāmatiya and the mutaṣawwifa, the opposing of the faḳīr is—

Because the faḳīr is the seeker of paradise and is desirous of his own delight. They (the malāmatiya and the mutaṣawwifa) are the seekers of God and desirous of propinquity to Him.

Above this degree in faḳr, is a maḳām superior to the maḳām of the malāmatiya and of the mutaṣawwifa.

> 'Tis the special description of the ṣūfī. Though the degree is above the degree of the faḳīr, yet the abstract of the maḳām of faḳr is included in his maḳām. The cause is that, for the ṣūfī, the traversing of the maḳām of faḳr is of the crowd of enjoined conditions; every maḳām, wherefrom he advanceth, its purity he rendeth and thereto giveth the colour of his own maḳām.

In the maḳām of the ṣūfī, is another description for the faḳīr :—

> On his part, the denial and the absence of possession, of all deeds, ḥāls, and maḳāms.
>
> On his part, he beholdeth no deed, no ḥāl, no maḳām; and regardeth them not special to himself, Nay, himself of himself he seeth not.

Then his, is—

> no wujūd (existence).
> „ ẕāt (essence).
> „ quality.

He is mahv in mahv (obliteration in obliteration); fanā in fanā (effacement in effacement).

Such is the truth of faḳr, in excellence whereof, the shaikhs have spoken. What, in the sense of faḳr, before this has been mentioned,—is the impression and form of faḳr.

The superiority of the maḳām of the ṣūfī above the maḳām of the faḳīr is because—

> The faḳīr is ruled by the desire of faḳr and of the delight of nafs. The ṣūfī hath no special desire; in faḳr or in wealth, effaced is his desire in the desire of God—his desire is the essence of the desire of God.
>
> If he choose the form of faḳr and its way, it becometh not veiled by his own desire and choice; his desire is the desire of God.

Some have said :—

> Who is void of impression and of quality is the ṣūfī: who is void of things material, is the faḳīr.

Abū Al 'Abbās-i-Nihavandī saith :—

> The end of faḳr is the beginning of taṣawwuf.

Some of the shaikhs have said :—

> As cautious of wealth, should be the faḳīr as the wealthy one of faḳr.
>
> By the entrance of wealth, the faḳīr feareth that faḳr may become abhorrent to him; by the entrance of faḳr, the wealthy one, that wealth may become abhorrent to him.

Once a wealthy one brought ten thousand dirams to Ibrāhīm Adham and asked him to accept them.

Ibrāhīm refused, saying—"With ten thousand dirans, thou wishest to efface, from "the record-book of fuḳarā, our name."

Between faḳr (poverty) and zuhd (austerity), the difference is this :—

Possible without zuhd, is faḳr. Thus, with firm resolution a person abandoneth the world through the desire of yaḳīn ; yet, in him, is left the heart's delight.

Possible without faḳr, is zuhd. Thus is a person possessed of chattels, wherefrom his delight is turned.

Faḳr hath a custom,—the want of property. Its truth is the expelling of qualities from orders ; and the denying to one's self the choice of a thing.

Faḳr is the form of zuhd and its sign. The meaning of zuhd is the expending of desire (for God) away from the world.

When, beneath the towers of pomp, God wisheth to veil, from the glance of strangers, some of His saints, He outwardly clotheth them with the garment of the wealthy one (which is the form of desire), so that them, the outward people may regard as of the crowd of desirous ones of this world ; and thus, from the glance of the unprivileged, the beauty of their ḥāl may be concealed.

The kernel of the ḥaḳīḳat of faḳr and of zuhd is the special description and requisite of the ḥāl of the ṣūfī. The custom of faḳr is the choice of some of the shaikhs of the ṣūfīs ; and in it, their purpose is—the following of the prophets, the abandoning of the world, the inciting and the inviting of seekers with the form of faḳr and with the tongue of ḥāl.

In this sense, their choice is proved by the choice of God, not by the desire of the delight of the next world.

---

The khuddām are those, who choose the service of fuḳarā and of the seekers of God ; who, after the performance of the ordinances of God, have expended their time in ceasing to labour, and in making tranquil the heart as to solicitude for matters of livelihood and for capacity for the next world ; who prefer this service to nawāfil, and who in their need enter on every way not forbidden by the shar'—in acquisition, in beggary, and in receiving gratuitous income.

In taking and giving money, their glance is on God.

In taking money, they regard the people the link of God's giving to them, and in giving money, they regard them as the means of their acceptance (with God).

On account of the honour of this maḳām, appeared similitude in respect to the crowd of the ḥāl of the khādim and of the shaikh. In respect to the khādim, they have established no difference from the shaikh.

The difference is this—

The khādim is in the maḳām of the abrār (the pious).

” shaikh ” ” muḳarrab (those near to God).

In the choice of service, the purpose of the khādim is the reward of the next world; otherwise not bound by service is the khādim.

Standing in the purpose of God not in his own purpose is the shaikh.

---

The u'bbād are those, who, ever, on the portions of devotion and on the rules of nawāfil, display assiduity for the sake of the reward of the Nīl of the next world.

Existent in the ṣūfī, is this description but free from the impurities of desire. For they worship God for God, not for the reward of the next world.

Between the 'ubbād and the zuhhād, the difference is this—

With the existence of (despite) desire for the world the form of 'ibādat (devotion) is possible.

Between the 'ubbād and the fuḳarā, the difference is this—

With the existence of (despite) wealth, a person may possibly be 'ābid (dedicated to the service of God).

Then, it became manifest—

(*a*) that the wāṣil (those joined to God) are three crowds.
(*b*) „ „ sālik (the holy travellers) „ six „

Each one of these nine crowds hath two similitudes—

(*a*) محق (muḥiḳḳ), the verifier.
(*b*) مبطل (mubṭil), „ abolisher.

---

To the prophets of both crowds, the similitude of the verifier is—

the shaikh of ṭarīḳat (the Path) and the 'ulamā of ṣūfiya,—who, by following Muḥammad, invite the people through the desire of vision.

The similitude of the abolisher is this—

In calumny, he layeth claim to prophecy; and falsely and slanderously attributeth to himself waḥy (revelation).

Him, they call—

متنبي (mutanabbī), "one who calleth himself a prophet."

After the expiration of the time of mission, in the brain of a jamā 'at (assembly), the bird of this desire wished to lay an egg. In the end, to the wind of destruction, they gave their head, and rolling fell into hell.

---

To the ṣūfīs, the similitude of the verifier is—

mutaṣawwifa, who are exceedingly informed and desirous of the ḥāl of the ṣūfīs; and by the residue of their attachments to the qualities of nafs are detained from the maturity of purpose and forbidden it.

To the ṣūfīs, the similitude of the abolisher is—

a jamā'at (assembly), who in life reveal themselves ṣūfīs; who are void of the power of their belief, deeds, and ḥāl; and who, having taken off from their neck the halter of devotion, graze free from encumbrance in the meadow of revelation.

They say—

the binding to the orders of the sharī'at is the portion of the common folk, whose glance is restricted to outward things. Loftier than that is the ḥāl of the special folk and of the man of ḥāḳiḳat. For they (the common folk) give attention to outward customs, while their solicitude for viewing the inward presence is not great.

This crowd, they call—

باطنيه bāṯiniya.*

مباحيه mubāḥiya.

---

To the majẕūbān-i-wāṣil (the joined attracted ones), the similitude of the verifier is—

a crowd of the men of sulūk, whose travelling is yet in the traversing of the stages of the qualities of nafs; and whose existence, from the burning of desire's ardour, is in agitation and perturbation.

In the maḳām of fanā, before the revelation of the tidings of the morn of the manifestation of ẕat, of resting, and of dwelling,—sometimes a flash of the flashings of that manifestation glittereth on the glance of their witnessing; and from the breeze-place of fanā, a breath of the breathings of union joineth the perfume-place of their heart.

So, in the flashing of the lights of lightning, the darkness of the qualities of their nafs becometh folded; and to their heart, from the heat, the bubbles of that breath give fire of search, agitation, shauḳ of the soul, and restfulness.

When that lightning expireth and that breath ceaseth, the manifestation of the qualities of nafs, the heat of desire, the agitation, and the shauḳ return; and the holy traveller wisheth to be wholly drawn out from the clothing of his own qualities, and to be immersed in the sea of fanā, so that he may rest from the ruining of his existence.

When that ḥāl hath not become his maḳām, and sometimes it descendeth on him, his interior becometh wholly informed and desirous of this maḳām.

His name was—

the similitude of the verifier to the joined attracted ones.

To the joined attracted ones, the similitude of the abolisher is—

a crowd, who lay claim to being immersed in the sea of fanā, and to being annihilated in the essence of tauḥīd: who, to themselves, assign not any moving or any resting.

They say—our moving is like unto the moving of doors, which without a mover is impossible. Though this sense is true, it is not the ḥāl of that jamā'at (assembly).

From this matter, their purpose is :—

(*a*) the framing of excuse for sins.
(*b*) „ assigning of it to desire for God.
(*c*) „ repelling from themselves reproach.

---

* The bāṯiniya (Ismā,liya, the Assasins) were founded in the eleventh century by Ḥasan Sabā Shaikhau-l-jabāl.

This crowd, they call—

زنادقه (zanādiḳa zanādīḳ, sing. zandiḳ)—infidels.

To Sahl Àbdu-l-lāh, they said :—

A certain one saith—The connection of my deed with the desire for God is as the connection of the motion of the door with its mover.

He said :—

If the speaker be one who preserveth the sources of the sharīa't and the limits of orders of worship,—he is of the crowd of the ṣādiḳ (sincere).

If he be one who, in opposition of the rules of the shar', hath no fear of falling into destruction, he speaketh so that he may make apparent the way of assigning his deeds to God, and of causing to fall from himself reproach—together with the being up-torn from faith and religion,—he is of the crowd of zanādiḳa.

---

To the malāmatiya, the similitude of the verifier is—

a crowd, who, for the repairing and the destroying of the people's glance, show not much consideration. Much of their effort is in ruining customs and habits, and in loosening the bonds of rules of association; the source of their ḥāl is naught save freedom of heart and disposition of heart; and on their part, appeareth neither the gazing at the usages of the zuhhād and the 'ubbād, nor the issuing of acts of nawāfil and of devotion.

No bond do they make for the resolution of deeds; they persevere only for the performance of the enjoined ordinances; not ascribed to them is the amassing of the chattels of the world; contented with goodness of heart, they desire no increase of substance.

Them, they call—

قلندریه (ḳalandariya), ḳalandars.

Through the absence of hypocrisy, this crowd resembleth the malāmatiya.

Between the malāmatiya and the ḳalandariya the difference is—

the malāmatiya seek union with all faẓā,il (excellences) and nawāfil (works of supererogation); but keep them concealed from the people's gaze.

the ḳalandariya pass not beyond the farā,iẓ (enjoined ordinances); and, as regards the revealing, or the concealing, of their deeds from the people's gaze, are unfettered.

The crowd, at this time called ḳalandariya, have taken from off their neck the halter of Islām; and are void of these mentioned qualities.

For them, the name of ḳalandariya is illusory; fit is the name—

حشويه (ḥashwiya), the padded ones.

To the malāmatiya, the similitude of the abolisher is—

a crowd (also of the zanādiḳa) who claim sincerity, and greatly strive in revealing iniquity. They say :—

From this, our purpose is the reproach of the people, and the taking away of the glance (of approval) of man; no need of the people's devotion, hath God.

By their sin, un-injured they consider the sin restricted to the people's injury, and devotion among laudable actions.

---

To the zuhhād, the similitude of the verifier is—

a crowd whose delight hath not wholly been expended away from the world; and who from it desire at once to turn.

These, they call—

متزهد (mutazahhid), self-denying.

To the zuhhād, the similitude of the abolisher is—

a jamā'at (assembly), who (for the acceptance of the people) abandon the world's decoration; from off all the world's chattels, take up their heart; and thereby desire the acquisition of rank among men.

It is possible that their ḥāl may be obscure:—

(*a*) to some. They think that they have wholly turned away from the world; and that they themselves, by abandoning wealth, have purchased rank.

(*b*) to themselves. They think that (since outwardly they are not engaged in desire for the world's chattels) they have wholly turned from the world,

This crowd, they call—

مرايه (mar'iya) acting hypocritically.

---

To the fuḳarā, the similitude of the verifier is—

He whose exterior is painted with the custom of faḳr, and whose interior is desirous of the ḥaḳiḳat of faḳr. Yet hath he inclination to fanā and, with difficulty, endureth faḳr; regardeth the true faḳr of the fuḳarā a special favour from God; and therefore ever preferreth portions of thanks.

To the fuḳarā, the similitude of the abolisher is—

He whose exterior is painted according to the custom of faḳr; and whose interior is, as to its ḥaḳiḳat (truth), void of information.

His purpose is purely the revealing of claim, of mandate, and of the people's acceptance (of him).

Him, they call—

مرايه (mar'iya), acting hypocritically.

---

To the khuddām, the similitude of the verifier is—

He, who ever remaineth standing in the service of the slaves of God; who, in his heart, wisheth to do them service unmixed with the suspicion of worldly design or rank; and ever to free his resolution from doubts of inclination and of desire.

Yet to the ḥaḳiḳat (truth) of zuhd, he shall not have reached.

At one time by reason of the superiority of the light of faith and by the concealing of nafs, some of his powers fall into the place of merit.

At another time, by reason of the superiority of nafs, his service is mixed with desire and hypocrisy. The crowd who are not in the place of merit, he preferreth, with the expectation of laudation, to full service; and some, who are worthy of service, he excludeth.

Him, they call—

متخادم mutakhādim.

To the khuddām, the similitude of the abolisher is —

He who in service hath no resolution for the next world. Nay, the people's service, he hath made the snare of worldly advantages, so that thereby he may attract bequests and chattels. If, in the acquisition of his design, he see not effected his purpose, he abandoneth it.

Then is his service restricted to desire for rank, for wealth, for numerous followers and approvers, so that thereby, in assemblies and companies, he may seek precedence and glorification.

In every service, his glance is on his own delight.

Him, they call—

مستخدم (mustakhdim) an employer of many servants.

---

To the 'ubbād, the similitude of the verifier is :—

(*a*) He, who desireth his own times immersed in devotion; but by reason of the residue of the pretensions of nature, and of the want of purification of nafs, languor momently falleth on deeds, or prayers, and on devotion.

(*b*) Or he who hath not yet found the delights of devotion; and who, in them, standeth with difficulty.

Him, they call—

متعبد (muta'abbid), devout.

---

To that one of the crowd of mar,iya, the similitude of the abolisher is —

He, whose glance in devotion is on the people's acceptance (of him); and, in whose heart is no faith as to the reward of the next world.

So long as he seeth no stranger attentive to his own devotion, in it he remaineth not.

---

## The Ādāb of Muḥammad's Mission (of prophecy).

VI. 3.

Known it is that, in the opinion of men of investigation and of sincere lovers, the beloved of the beloved is the beloved.

Who loveth not the beloved of the beloved, its sign is that, with design, his love is distempered.

Verily, such a one is the lover of himself, not the lover of the Beloved; he loveth the Beloved for the reason that he regardeth Him the source of pleasure and the place of delights to himself,—not, really and truly.

Sincere lovers, who have become free from the sickness of hawā (desire) and the design of nafs (lust), and pure of the impurities of existence,—desire themselves for the sake of the Beloved, not the Beloved for the sake of themselves; desire for His sake the sacrifice of their own existence,—not, for themselves, His existence; and prefer to their own purpose His purpose,—nay, no purpose is theirs save the Beloved's purpose.

As the beloved of the beloved may be beloved, so the means of union with the Beloved is the beloved.

Manifest, it is to the man of faith and of yaḳīn that Muḥammad is the beloved of God and the agent of the King, great and holy. Then demandeth love for God sincerity of love for Muḥammad.

When it became known that wherever love may be, necessary is the observance of ādāb to the beloved (Muḥammad), to men of faith (especially to the Lords of revelation and of beholding), were requisite the observance of ādāb to him, and the preservation of the magnificence of his mission.

Though in form and body, Muḥammad is hidden and concealed from the glance of outward beholders,—in quality and spirituality, he is clear and revealed to the Lords of vision. The form of his sharī'at is the mould of his spirituality.

Then as long as is left his sharī'at in the body,—in truth, his form is present; and continuous and perpetual is the aid of his life for souls and for nafs. The verifier of this is the ancient word.

Though the sharī'at is in this way the link of the bounty of life, in another way it is the means of the acceptance of life. Muḥammad calls the causing of his sunnat to live (in men's hearts) the causing himself to live.

Thus, for the nations, his sharī'at and sunnat are life-giving and life-accepting.

The source of doors (of opening) and the column of ādāb,—after the strengthening of love's links, and the perfecting of love's conditions,—is ever viewing the person of the beloved, and the contemplating of hearts.

As, in all his ḥāls, outwardly and inwardly, the slave seeth God known and informed,—so informed and present, he should regard Muḥammad in respect to his own exterior and interior.

Towards Muḥammad, the beholding of his form of grandeur and of dignity may ever be the guide to the preservation of ādāb; towards him, he may be ashamed of opposition, secretly or openly; and of the subtleties of the ādāb of his society, he may let go no subtlety whatever.

The greatest part of ādāb is this—

In his heart, he should not conceive that to any created being should be possible that perfection, rank, and loftiness of degree that are Muḥammad's; that to God, any travellers can find the path except by his guidance; that to any Walī, should be the power of perfecting and directing another save by borrowing from the light of his power; that to a maḳām, should reach an arriver, who may be independent of his aid, although in his stage of propinquity, he may have attained to perfection.

The distributed bounty of all existing things is the purified soul of the prophet (Muḥammad) and his holy nafs. Without his means, no aid floweth from God.

Who by Shaiṭān's deceit becometh haughty and proud, and in whose mind the idea of power and of wealth gathereth—becometh doubtless the rejected of ulūhīyat God), and the banished of the court of rubūbiyat (God); and, wrapped with groans, returneth from the maḳām of propinquity (to God) to farness (from Him).

Let us flee to God for shelter.

---

Another ādāb is—

After establishing the rule of belief, and after perfect following of his sunnat and ṭarīḳat, it is necessary that, learned in following his sunnat, he should make every effort; in it should regard negligence unlawful; and should verily know that the degree of being a beloved he cannot gain save by observing the sunnat and the nawāfil (works of supererogation).

He should not imagine that fulness of nawāfil is the degree of lovers and of murīds; independent of it, is the beloved or the murād, for whom the performance of the enjoined ordinances is sufficient.

The sign of being a beloved is service in the following of the sunnat and of the nawāfil. At the inn of the narrow path, they keep every sunnat of Muḥammad's sunnats, distributed from the sea of the existence of prophecy,—by whose aid, bounty, and currency flourish, in the soil of nafs and of the heart, the bubbles of love, the tulips of truths, and the odoriferous plants of yaḳīn.

With Muḥammad, whoever hath connection, apparently or really, as :—

the sādāt (plural of sayyid).
„ 'ulamā
„ mushā,ikh (plural of shaikh).

Who are, outwardly and inwardly, the offspring and the heirs of 'ilm (knowledge) and of prophecy,—all, for the sake of love for Muḥammad, he should love; and their honouring, regard necessary.

In all ḥāls—

of اعتقاد belief,
„ قول ḳaul,
„ فعل deed,

he should associate the reverencing of Muḥammad with the reverencing of God; and devotion to him, the requisite of devotion to God.

Not true, nor acceptable, is faith in God and in His Unity,—without association with faith in Muḥammad, and with confession as to his (prophetic) mission.

Not the ṭarīḳ of union with God, is the performance of the enjoined ordinances without the sunnat of tradition.

In nearness to God, to liken his similitude to two bows' length is fit.*

---

* From God, Muḥammad is not farther than two bows' length.

They call the honouring of him, the essence of the honouring of God ; devotion to him the essence of devotion to God.

> Who submitted to Muḥammad, submitted to God ; with thee who made bai'at, bai'at made with God (see the Ḳurān).

As in speaking and in books, they mention the name of God with magnifying and reverencing, so should they mention the name of Muḥammad—

| | |
|---|---|
| with salawāt, benedictions. | ta'ẓīm, reverence. |
| „ taslīmāt, salutations. | tamkīn, honour. |

---

## Ādab (duties, observances) towards God.

VI. 2.

The preservation of ādāb is both love's fruit and also its seed. As love is more perfect, greater is its solicitude for the preservation of ādāb towards the beloved ; as the form of ādāb is more evident to the lover, for him greater is the glance of the beloved's love.

Then every slave, in whose heart love for God shall be firmer, his solicitude is greater for the preservation of ādāb towards Him ; and more powerful for the purifying of the exterior and of the interior in a way, that to himself may represent to his sight in the form of the sick for God (not in the garment of the sinner).

Although his propinquity to God is greater, stronger are the desires in his nature for the subtleties of (additions to) ādāb.

For doubtless, than the work of servants and of followers (who, in the thread of the remote and of the stranger, are disobedient), the work of others (wazīrs, courtiers, others) near to the majesty of kings—is more difficult and dangerous, and more are their desires for accessions of ādāb.

There are seven ādāb of God.

1. By viewing another, they should not keep back the glance from beholding the beauty of God.

In the Ḥadīṣ, it is said :—

> When, for prayer, the slave arose, verily present with God he was. Then if at another he look, the Provider of the world saith :—
>
> O slave ! at whom lookest thou ? Than I, who is better ? O son of Ādam ! to me turn thy face ; for to thee better than that whereat thou lookest, am I.

2. Though propinquity to the King (God) and his honouring ; and through gaining the power of conversing with, and travelling in, God, the slave should not forget his own (low) degree, nor transgress beyond the limit of service and of the revealing of his faḳr and misery—that to rebellion he become not addicted.

> Once Maḥmūd (of Ghuzni) desired (to prove) the trust of (his favourite slave) Ayāz.

When he was present, he saw that, on a nail, before him, Ayāz had suspended a rent postīn (sheepskin coat) and an old blanket.

He asked, saying :—What is this ?

Ayāz replied :—

When the hand of power threaded me on the thread of service, it drew from off my head this garment of poverty, and clothed me with the honour-robe of liberality.

Them, for repelling forgetfulness and forbidding disobedience (the requisites of the nafs of man), I arranged before my face, so that at them, momently, I might look ; (by repeating and calling to mind) recollect past events ; my own (former) degree (of poverty) forget not ; and of the cap (of sovereignty), of the bejewelled girdle, and of the gold-woven cloth (which, through the graciousness of the king, I have obtained) become not proud.

In respect to the sayyid of both worlds (Muḥammad), the Kalām-i-Majīd giveth news. Of his observing these two ādāb in the presence of God.

Although in inclining to God, Mūsā was not accused of dimness of sight, yet by reason—

(*a*) of abundance of descent of ḥāl,
(*b*) „ the delight of the samā' of God's word,
(*c*) „ „ ẓauḳ (delight) at the sources of propinquity,
(*d*) „ intoxication of the heart from drinking cups of tauḥīd,

forth from his hand, he gave the thread of discrimination ; transgressed the limit of worship ; and, through joy, entered upon asking (God).

Opposed to his desire, the back of its hand dashed the word of God :—

"Me, thou shalt never see."

Immediately, came this voice :—

Between the dust (of man) and the Lord of Lords,—what ?

3. The ear's listening to the word of God, and truly hearing orders and prohibitions against the abandoning of listening to the ḥadīṣ of nafs. The hearing of the word of God worketh in that way that whenever on his own tongue, or on another's tongue, in prayer or out of prayer, a phrase or a verse of the Ḳurān-i-Majīd goeth,—it, he heareth from a true speaker ; and knoweth his own tongue or another's tongue (to be) the means whereby God conveyeth to his ear His own word—as, by the (burning) olive bush, He conveyed to Mūsā His own ancient address.

The purifying of the stations of 'ilm, and the congratulating of the subtleties of the understanding of words of the Ḳurān by the moderating of nafs, and the abandoning of listening to the ḥadīṣ of nafs is attainable ; and its purport is this āyat—

"When the Ḳurān is being read, to it listen and refer if thou wishest to be pitied (by God).

4. The ādāb of asking and of address. As, from the form of order and of prohibitions, the sense of the question is farther, nearer it is to ādāb.

In asking the Pardoner (God) and (seeking) mercy from his tribe, Ibrāhīm preferred, out of the form of order, the words of prayer, saying :—

Me, those have sinned against; but, the most merciful pardoner, Thou art.

He said not :—

Them, pardon and forgive.

In the desire of repelling torments from nations, and of asking pardon from God he kept out from the form of order his address, saying:—

Them, if Thou torment—they are Thy slaves; them, if Thou forgive, the precious Wise One, Thou art.

He said not :—

Them, torment not ; but forgive them.

Out from the voice of order, Ayūb kept his desire of recovery—

Me, ailment hath afflicted ; the most Merciful of the merciful, Thou art.

He said not :—

On me, have mercy!

In answer to God's address—

Art Thou He who told the people—" As gods besides Allah, accept Me and My mother ? "

'Īsạ said :—

Verily, Thou toldest the people ; to the people, Thou madest known.

5. Concealing nafs in the fold of diminution, and depreciating one's own existence in the manifestation of the effects of God's power, when he mentioneth a favour of God's favours to himself.

Muḥammad said :—

At the earth, I glanced—east and west.

He said not—

I saw.

By not mentioning the deed, to himself he concealed his own existence; and thus was nearer to ādāb.

6. The preserving the mysteries of God.

When the slave gaineth knowledge of a mystery of the mysteries of God ; and becometh the place of deposit and one with whom is desposited aught,—its revealing he should hold unlawful.

Otherwise, far from the degree of propinquity, he goeth and becometh the place of punishment.

In the Ḥadīs̤—

The betraying of secrets is kufr.

7. The observing the times :—

| of asking. | of resting. |
|---|---|
| „ praying. | „ keeping quiet. |

This sense is dependent upon the ma'rifat of the times :—

of grace (of God).
„ mercy „
„ bast̤ (expansion of heart).

In the times of grace, is the plunder of leisure—

for praying.
„ asking.

In the times of wrath, of severity, and of ḳabẓ (contraction of heart), is the season :—

of being silent.
„ abstaining from asking.

Who preserveth not this ādāb; who, at the time of prayer, is silent; who, at the time of being silent, is vociferous,—his time is the time of hate.

At the time of prayer, the slave should ask (of God) according to his ḥāl and maḳām.

If he be in the first of the maḳāms of propinquity and, notwithstanding that, in respect of joy, he be not permitted,—not possible is it that on the carpet of joy, he should place the foot of inquiry.

Against asking for trifling matters, cometh the forbidder,—the majesty of God's grandeur.

One day, Shiblī sent to one of the sons of the world; and, from him, desired something of the world.

That one replied :—

From God, desire this world also, since, from Him, thou desirest the next world.

Reply, Shiblī sent back :—

Thou art ignoble; ignoble is this world : God is noble; noble is the next world.
The ignoble from the ignoble, I seek; the noble from the noble.

If he be at the end of propinquity, and in respect to joy permitted by God, it is lawful to travel the path of joy—in praying and asking.

In the beginning of ḥāl, on account of the world's contempt and reproach, Mūsā used not to seek from God worldly needs; otherwise, the need of the next world and of asking trifling matters in the veil of grandeur would have been until that time when God conveyed him to another degree in propinquity (to Himself), superior to that (previous) degree; and, in the asking of mean matters, permitted him saying :—

> O Mūsā! ask of Me, even if it be the salt of thy (worthless) ferment (the dust elements of the body).

When he became necessitous for food, Mūsā said :—

> O God! on me whatever thou causeth to descend is the best for the faḳīr.

Known, it became that there is an ādāb for every—

> waḳt (period).
> ḥāl.
> maḳām.

Hence, is the ḳaul of Abū Ḥafaṣ Ḥuddād :—

> All ādāb is taṣawwuf; for ādāb is all waḳt, ḥāl, and maḳām. Who performed the ādāb of waḳt reached the pinnacle of manliness; who wasted the ādāb was far from propinquity (to God) and rejected of His acceptance.

Whoever guardeth as to keeping these seven ādāb, the hope is that, from observing the subtleties of the other ādāb, he will not be portionless.

In short, from off the slave, the ādāb of God should fall in no ḥal except in the ḥāl of fanā and in the immersion in the essence of jam'. For the observance of ādāb demandeth change of wujūd and acquireth duality.

In the ḥāl of fanā, the slave's existence (the demander of change) becometh upplucked. Hence the ḳaul—

> Saith God the great, the praised—
> Necessary is ādāb for him who observeth ḳiyām in My name and with love for Me; necessary is destruction for him to whom is revealed the truth of My ẕāt. Ādāb or 'aṭab (destruction),—either of the two,—he can choose.

The explanation is :—

> The glory of God's ẕat demandeth fanā; in fanā, ādāb weakeneth; the glory of names and of qualities demandeth existence; in existence, the protection of ādāb is necessary.

Junīd saith :—

> When love becometh true, dropped are love's conditions.

Because the end of love's demand is this—

> When the lover becometh fānī in the beloved, and the twofold custom ariseth (to depart); the way of ādāb becometh the change of existence. Nay, in a ḥāl such as this, the observing of ādāb is the abandoning of ādāb.

Once Abu-l-'Abbās bin 'Aṭṭār, while in the midst of some of his ṣaḥāba, extended his foot, denying :—

> In the midst of people of ādāb, the abandoning of ādāb is ādāb.

Once when Muḥammad was sitting with Abū Bakr and' Umar, a part of his auspicious thigh became exposed.

Suddenly 'Uṣmān approached Muḥammad, covered his thigh saying :—

Him, whom the angels regard I must regard.

Though this ḥāl pointeth to 'Uṣmān's esteem in Muḥammad's opinion ; yet compared with that ḥāl (which was between Muḥammad, Abū Bakr, and 'Umar) it was lower—for nearer to concord was that ḥāl.

---

## Ādāb-i-Ma'īshat (the rule of livelihood).

VI. 7.

Diverse, according to contrariety of degrees, are the ḥāls of the متصوفه (mutaṣawwifa) in causation and in reliance (on God).

(*a*) Some, through weakness of ḥāl, for the amending of time, in search of daily food rely on chattels. These are called متسبب (mutasabbib).

(*b*) Some, through power of ḥāl and denial of will, suffice themselves with the surety of God ; on Him, rely ; and in no way seek reliance on daily distributed food (through man's effort). These are called متوكل (mutawakkil).

(*c*) Some strive in kasb (acquisition) ; some in beggary ; some (for the amending of their time) now in kasb, now in beggary.

Ibrāhīm Adham, sometimes for the maintenance of the ṣaḥāba, used to obtain a morsel of lawful food by watching over sown fields, or by reaping ; and sometimes when alone, at the time of need and to its extent, used to travel the path of beggary. Awhile, he was a dweller in the jām' (masjid) at Biṣra and used to break his fast every three nights ; on the night of breaking the fast, he used to come forth, and to take morsels from the doors of houses ; to the eating of these morsels, he restricted himself.

Abū Ja'far-i-Ḥaddād (Junīd's murshid) used to go forth, every two or three nights, in the first two watches (of the night); and to the extent of his need, at doors, used to beg.

In the beginning of ḥāl, Abū Sa'īd-i-Kharāz used, when he was very necessitous to hold forth the hand (of beggary); and to say :—

"The prophet of God !"

So long as the necessity for concord was not complete, they have not seen this crowd in beggary whereof they are full of caution. Because of it the sharī'at hath cautioned them in the way of inciting and of terrifying.

(*a*) Inciting.

In the history of Ṣaubān, it is related that one day Muḥammad said to the aṣḥāb :—

Who in one thing will join me,—him, in Paradise, I will meet.

I said:—

O prophet of God! I will.

He said:—

Of the people, ask naught.

(*b*) Terrifying.

In the Ḥadīs, it is said:—

Urge not thy prayer (of beggary) till God permitteth; till only a piece of flesh remaineth on thy cheek.

The ādāb of the beggar is:—

So long as no necessity ariseth, he should not enter upon beggary. As long as he hath power, he maketh nafs desirous of patience of its handfuls till from the hidden, the door openeth.

When, in places of need, by giving patience, nafs displayeth levity, true wealth from all exterior to God is acquired.

The second crowd متوكل (mutawakkil) on account of perfection of being engaged with Him,—viewing the grandeur of tauḥīd and the light of yaḳīn,—seek the causing in no cause of the causes of daily food; and from no created being, seek aid,—so that the Causer of causes (God) may as He desireth convey to them daily food.

One day, they inquired of Bāyizīd, saying:—

Thee, we see engaged with none: whence is thy livelihood?

He replied:—

The (unclean) dog and the (filthy) pig, my Master feedeth, wherefore should he not feed Abū Yazīd?

Some are those who, whatever they ask, ask of God, so that He giveth them one of these things:—

(i) the giving of the desired object.
(ii) „ power of patience.
(iii) „ erasing of desire from the heart.

Some ask naught, either from the people, or from God; because in His 'ilm, they have effaced their own 'ilm and desire; they know that in their affairs, more comprehending is the 'ilm of the Eternal than their own 'ilm; attachment to their affairs, on the part of Universal Desire (God) is greater and more complete than partial desire on their part; therefore on account of His 'ilm, they are independent of begging.

They call the mutawakkil "the companions of gratuitous income"; because their taking is from the income received gratuitously from the hidden. Although he seeth that, from the hidden is gratuitous income without their nafs being desirous, they accept it, even if, in need of it they be not.

Some are slow in taking and in giving; because, in both ḥāls, they have suspected the residence of desire in their own nafs.

Some are slow in taking, not in giving; because in giving they less regard the pleasure of nafs.

Some are slow in giving, not in taking; because in taking they regard only the will and the act of God,—in giving, their own will and act.

Some are slow neither in taking nor in giving; because their existence is annihilated in the light of tauḥīd, their giving in divine causes, is their safety from the calamity of desire. In the world, the existence of this crowd is more precious and less often found than (rare) red sulphur.

The ādāb of:—

the mutasabbib (or tārik).
„ mutawakkil.

is this, that before arrival at the degree of the glory of ẕāt, of qualities, and of deeds (which are the source of glories), they haste to taking gratuitous income and to giving it without the connection of a new permission, or of a ready knowledge.

Before the rules of the maḳām of freedom, they plant not the foot, in the footplace of the free.

In respect to the Aṣḥāb of tamkīn and to the Lords of yaḳīn, they regard not their own ḥāl without a true proof.

By the residence of the veil of seduction, the truth of the shaikh's ḥāl may appear to him obscure; but at the time of examination (the fact) that the cash of his ḥāl is counterfeit is not concealed to the assayer of vision.

As long as he is bound by the residence of the residence of his own habits, for him is not reserved the maḳām of freedom.

Shaikh Ḥamād used to eat no food unless, in dream or in sleep, he saw the order:—

(*a*) Certain food of such a quantity from such a one,—take.
(*b*) „ „ „ to Ḥamād take.
Then he used to take it.

To one of the crowd of his own murīds, Shaikh Abdu-l-Ḳādīr-i-Ḥiblī sent, despite that the depositor was absent, saying:—

In thy presence, a certain one hath a desposit; thence, some gold and some food thou shouldest send me.

That murīd came before the shaikh and said:—

Rule over the deposit, how is it lawful for me to exercise? If they ask thee, thou wilt give a decision that it is not fit (to do so).

With compulsion, the shaikh ordered him (to take from the deposit).

Immediately after that, from the master of the deposit arrived a letter saying so much gold and so much food, take up from the deposit; and take to Abdu-l-Ḳādir.

Its quantity was exactly as the shaikh had stated.

Then in respect to his delaying in (the matter of) submission (to his order) the shaikh reproved that murīd and said :—

> Void of the truth of 'ilm, thou thoughtest was the commanding of the fuḳarā.

The truth of gratuitous income is this :—

> From God, they should take it, not from the people—whether its cause be the hand of man, or not; whether it be known or not—on the condition that in its preface there be no wishfulness.

The Shaikhu-l-Islām relateth that once to Shaikh Abū-l-Sa'īd a man came, and said :—

> I wish to make a fixed quantity of a daily allowance that they should bring for thy use; but I think that the ṣūfis have said : "Sinister, is what is known."

The Shaikh said :—

> This, we say not : because the known that God willeth for us,—in it, His deed we see; and it auspicious, not sinister, we regard.

---

## Ṣalāt (prayer).

VII. 5.

When a person wisheth to begin the ṣalāt (namāz, prayer), its sunnat is that, in its preface, if it be an enjoined ordinance, he should prefer the iḳāmat.*

Generally in the ṣalawāt—except in the nawāfil of safar in respect to the rāḥila—the condition is :—

> In body, he should look towards the ḳibla and in heart, towards the Master of the ḳibla; from the wickedness of the temptations of Shaiṭān and from the thoughts of nafs should take shelter in God; and to himself should utter :—
>
> the Suratu-n-nās, chapter 114, the Ḳurān.

---

| * The aẓān | | the iḳāmat. |
|---|---|---|
| (a) 4 takbīr | | " |
| (b) 4 Shahādat | 2 of God | " |
| | 2 " Muḥammad | " |
| (c) 4 Ḥayy-i-'alā | 2 for ṣalāt | " |
| | 2 " falaḥ | |
| (d) | | 2 iḳāmat. |
| (e) 2 takbīr | | " |
| (f) 2 tahlīl | | 1 tahlīl. |

After the four ḥayy-i-'alā the sunni muslims add twice—

As ṣalātu khairun min-an-naum (prayer is better than sleep).

The shī'a muslims say :—

(a) Ḥayy-i-'alā khair il 'amal (rise for the best deed, prayer).

(b) Either one (or two) shahādat of the vilāyat (walīship) of Ali after the two shahādats of Muḥammad.

> Both hands, he should uplift in such a way that the two palms are level with (and parallel to) the two shoulders, the two thumbs near to the two lobes of the ear, and the finger-tips level with the the ears.

According to the appointing, he should in his heart, perform the established ṣalāt; if he urge it also orally it should be continuous as in the namāz (prayer) of morn. He should say :—

> "I utter the enjoined prayer of this morn."

In confirming resolution in his heart, he lowereth his hands and saith :—

> الله اكبر Allahu Akbar, God is greatest,

so that the first portion of the takbīr may agree with the falling of the two hands. With the takbīr should be associated—the end of the takbīr, the end of the falling of the hands, and the niyyat.

In الله, he observeth the maddā (the lengthening of alif); in the zamma (ـُ) of the ه he exaggerateth not.

In اكبر he addeth not an ا (alif) between the ب (bā) and the ر (rā), but maketh it majzūm.

In letting fall the hands, he avoideth swinging so that he may be with deliberation, dignity, and khushū' (humility).

---

At the time of takbīr, he should be the beholder of God's majesty.

In his glance, the people should appear contemptible and feeble; he should not turn his attention as to their being informed about his ḥāl. Thus, may he come into the crowd, of the ṣādiḳ (the sincere ones) and draw not on himself the line of falsehood.

The most excellent of the takbīrs is the first takbīr (the iḥrām) as Junīd saith :—

> Of every thing is a chosen part; the chosen part of the prayer is the first takbīr.

The first takbīr is the place of resolution; resolution is the life of practice. Whenever resolution is for God, and free from the impurities of causes,—its order is applicable to (other) parts of deeds.

If through the beholding of shaiṭān, through error or neglect, practice becometh defective,—resolution hath no great effect.

From Ibn Salim, Abū Nasr Sirāj quoteth :—

> Resolution is to God, for God, from God; otherwise is destroyed whatever is added to the slave's prayer after the resolution, even if it be to God and for God.

After the takbīr, and the falling of the hands, he should advance his hands mid-way between his breast and his navel; should place the right hand on the left hand, the fore-finger and the middle-finger on the left wrist; should seize with the three other fingers both sides of the end of the wrist; should lower his head; should keep his glance on the place of prostration; should stand so that his stature may be firm and erect; should not bend his knees; should keep his feet apart to the extent of four fingers; should make effort to keep his feet parallel to each other; should not lift a foot; should not place one foot on the other.

In the sharī'at, zaghn (the lifting of the feet) and ṣafd (the joining of the feet) are prohibited.

Thus, he standeth, and saith :—

> To Him, who created the heaven and the earth, obedient and faithful, my face, I turn: not of the crowd of mushrik (believe's in partnership with God) are we; verily, from God, the Provider of the world, are—my prayer, my devotion, my life, my death. His, is no partner; to this belief, we are commanded: of the crowd of mushirs, are we.

In the preface to the talāwat (reading) to this extent (if he have not the power of prolonging it) he should not abridge the enjoined ordinances.

If he have the power of prolonging the reading, he should, after reading the āyat of tawajjuh, utter the prayer istiftāḥ (asking aid) :—

> To Thee, O God—glory! to Thee, praise! Auspicious is Thy name, lofty Thy rank; save Thou, is no God. O God! Thou art king; there is no God but Thou my Lord; Thy slave, I am; I have oppressed my nafs; I confess my sins; my sins, forgive. Verily none forgiveth sins save Thou; lead me to goodness of heart; to goodness of heart, verily none leadeth save Thou; pass over my sins; over sins, verily none passeth save Thou; I stand in service of Thee; by Thee, I stand; in Thy hands, is all good and evil none.
>
> To Thee, I cry; to Thee, I approach; Thee I extol; of Thee, I ask forgiveness; to Thee, I repent; from the accused shaiṭān, I flee to God. In the name of God, the merciful, the compassionate.

After this, he will utter the Fātiḥa and that Sura that he desireth; between them if there be an Imām, he should delay awhile and slowly utter :—

> O God! between me and my sins, place distance—as distance, Thou hast placed between the east and the west; cleanse me from my sins as, out of the filthy garment, Thou hast made the white garment. O God! with water, with snow, with hail,—wash out my sins.

This prayer, he should (if alone) utter before the Fātiḥa. In uttering, in praying —he should be fully present (conscious). The words of the Ḳurān that he urgeth on his tongue,—their meanings with the desire of being present (conscious), he should comprehend.

Thus, the speech of the tongue (which is the interpreter of the heart) may be the author of the speech of the heart. For the credit of the heart's speech is not the tongue's. If the tongue's speech be not the author and the interpreter of the heart's speech, the prayer-utterer is neither the speaker in the way of needs to God, nor the hearer in the way of understanding Him.

In respect to the hearing together the word of God, the men full of presence (consciousness) and the Lords of propinquity, are comprehenders of three ḥāls, only found among them.

i. Regarding the outward signification of the world of dominion. This is the special power of nafs, so that it may stand in the place of its ḥadīs̤.
ii. Regarding the inward signification of the world of angels. This is the special power of the heart, so that it may forbid the heart from turning to the world of dominion.
iii. Regarding the pomp of the Speaker (God) from the world of jabarūt. This is the special power of the rūḥ (the soul), so that it may protect men from turning to other than God; and may reach a place where the soul is so immersed in the sea of shuhūd that the prayer-utterer is hidden from feeling (consciousness).

One day, Muslim bin Yasār was offering prayer in the masjid of Biṣra. Suddenly a column fell, and of the fall thereof all the people of Biṣra knew; but he, in the masjid, knew of it naught.

Awhile, he should rest; and then proceed to the rukū' (bowing the body from the hips).

In the rukū', he should keep his stature well-bowed, the neck and the back straight; should place the palms of the two hands, with extension of the fingers, on the two knees; should not bend the knees; should keep in the state of standing, the lower half of the body (hips downwards), and his glance on the feet.

When he establisheth himself in the rukū', he should, three times, say :—

To my God, the greatest,—glory; to Him, praise.

If he say it ten times, it is full.

Then, he saith :—

O God! to Thee, I bow; to Thee, I make humble my limbs; to Thee, I incline; to Thee applied are my ear, my eye, my flesh, my limbs, and tendons.

Restricted to it, he should keep all his spirit; for these significations become the qualities of his ẕāt.

When from rukū', he uplifteth his head, he saith :—

Him, who praiseth Him, God heareth.

When he standeth erect, he saith :—

O God! the praise of the heaven and of the earth—to Thee!

After that, if it be in the second raka't of the enjoined ordinances of the morning, or of the witr of the latter half of the month Ramaẓān, he should utter the prayer of ḳunūt.*

O God! guide us whereto Thou wishest to guide; protect us whereto Thou wishest to protect; cause us to love what Thou wishest us to love; make auspicious to us what Thou

* The up-lifting of both hands and joining them before the face, at a distance of a foot, palm upwards, parallel to the prayer-mat.

> hast bestowed. Save me from the evil of what I have neglected; give benediction to Muḥammad, the noblest of the prophets; forgive and pity, for Thou art the Most Merciful.

Before standing in ḳiyām, he should go to sujūd (prostration). The Ḥadiṣ saith:—

> Him, who raiseth not erect his spine between rukū' and sujūd, God looketh not at.

Then into sujūd, he goeth; and, as he goeth, uttereth a takbīr. He placeth on the prayer-mat first the lower limbs, then the upper limbs.

That is—

He placeth on the ground first the knee, then the hand, the forehead, and the nose; keepeth open the eyes, and his glance on the tip of his nose; placeth on the prayer-mat his two bare palms; keepeth the head right between the two hands; placeth on the prayer-mat his hands parallel to the shoulder and the tip of the elbow against his side; holdeth joined together the fingers opposite the ḳibla; extendeth on the prayer-mat the wrist; and saith three times:—

> To my God, the loftiest,—glory; and praise to Him.

If he say it ten times, it is full. Then he saith:—

> To Thee, I prostrate myself: in Thee, faith I have; to Thee, I bow. Auspicious, is God the best of makers.

---

In the presence of God, a crowd in sujūd seeth its own nafs fallen on the dust of fanā.

By reason of the residue of existence, this crowd is affected by the majesty of pomp, and humility is the custom of its ḥāl.

A crowd of the men of revelation and of beholding, in the state of sujūd becometh described with the truth of fanā; in the light of the shuhūd of the ẕāt of Wāhīd (God the One), seeth the existence of created beings, high and low, obliterated,—like to the obliterating of the shadow in the sun's light; and seeth itself entered in sujūd into the spaciousness of fanā on the border of the sheet of the grandeur of God.

By reason of fanā, this crowd is not impressed with the form of the grandeur of zāt; in the essence of affection it is plucked forth from the garment of submission.

Besides these two crowds of the manifestations of the mysteries of sujūd, is a crowd (in which, for the sake of prolonging prayer, and of the loftiness of being described with baḳā after fanā,—are collected affection and fear).

This crowd is:—

(*a*) in heart and in nafs submissive through the manifestation of the fire of grandeur (of God).

(*b*) in soul and with head uplifted and exalted, through the viewing of the light of affection of the beauty (of God).

---

Then, he uplifteth his head from sujūd and uttereth the takbīr; sitteth erect on the left foot; uplifteth the right foot so that its toes are opposite the ḳibla; placeth his hands on the knees without an effort of joining, or of separating, them; and saith:—

O God! me, forgive; on me, have mercy; me save; pass over my sins.

Again into sujūd, he goeth; and when from it he raiseth his head. If again he wisheth to rise, for the sake of sitting at ease, he sitteth and lightly riseth. In the last tashshahud (p. 45), he sitteth on the prayer-mat on the left foot; placeth his hands near the tip of the knee on the thigh; draweth to the palm the fingers of the right hand, except the forefinger; keepeth expanded from the palm the fingers of the left hand; and saith:—

O prophet! auspicious blessings, holy benedictions from God; to thee, salutation and the mercy of God and His peace; on us and the pious slaves of God, salutation.

I declare that there is no God but God; I declare that Muḥammad is His slave and His prophet. O God! on Muḥammad and his offspring, bestow Thy benediction; on Muḥammad and his offspring, have mercy; Muḥammad and his offspring, congratulate as Thou hast bestowed benedictions, congratulations, and mercy on Ibrāhīm and his offspring.

Verily, Thou art glorious and honourable. O God! me forgive what is past, last, secret, and open and what Thou knoweth more than I. Verily! Thou art the first and the last. There is no God save Thou.

When, in shahādat (p. 89), he reacheth to —— (illa-l-lāh), he uplifteth the forefinger, and inclineth it to the right side.

At the end of tashshahud (p. 45), for loosening the knot of the iḥrām (p. 154), he again giveth the salutation (p. 111); turneth his face to the right side, so that the people on the right may clearly see over his cheek.

In that state of resolution of issuing from—

ṣalāt,
salām (p. 111),

he bringeth into his heart those present of the angels, of the faithful jinn and men; and a moment delayeth.

Again, he turneth his face slowly to the left side, and giveth another salutation (p. 111).

Of this form, motion, resting, words, and deeds (which in the form of ṣalāt are mentioned) are some enjoined ordinances and some sunnats.*

---

* These are described in the Miṣbāḥu-l-Hidāyat, chapter 7, section 6.

# The (mystic) rose of the Ḳādiris.*

(Brown's darvishes, pp. 89—93.)

Every ṭariḳ (path) hath its sign; the sign of the Ḳādiris is a rose which is green, because the word حي (the Living one) was manifested in green colour to one of the shaikhs. It hath :—

| White rings.† | | | Series of leaves. | | Colours. | | Petals. | |
|---|---|---|---|---|---|---|---|---|
| | Number. | Signification. | Number. | Signification. | Number. | Signification. | Number. | Signification. |
| outside | 1 sharīʿat (muslim law). | is my word . | 1 five leaves . | five virtues of muslims. | 1 yellow | sharīʿat . | seven . | the seven beauteous names of God. |
| outside | 2 ṭarīḳat (the path). | „ „ practice | 2 six „ . | six characteristics of faith. | 2 white. | ṭarīḳat. | | |
| inside . | 3 ma'rifat (divine knowledge). | „ the chief of all things. | 3 seven „ . | seven verses of the ḳuran . | 3 red . | ma'rifat. | | |
| inside . | 4 ḥaḳīḳat (truth). | „ my condition. | The whole series (18 leaves). | Muḥammad brought mercy to eighteen worlds. | 4 black | ḥaḳīḳat. | | |

Shaikh Ismā,ilu-r-Rumī, successor to 'Abdu-l-Ḳādir, adopted this rose as emblematic of the seven names‡ of God uttered during the ẕikr :—

| Name of God. | Signification. | Colour of its light. | Number of times the name must be repeated. |
|---|---|---|---|
| Lā ilāha illa-l-lāh . . . . | no god but God . . . . | blue . | 100,000 |
| Allāh . . . . . . . | Allāh, (the beauteous) name . | yellow . | 78,586 |
| Hū . . . . . . . | He . . . . . . . | red . | 44,630 |
| 5 Hay . . . . . . . | the Living One . . . . | white . | 20,092 |
| 6 Wāḥid . . . . . . | „ One . . . . . | green . | 93,420 |
| 'Azīz . . . . . . . | „ Dear One . . . . | black . | 74,644 |
| Wadūd . . . . . . | „ Loving „ . . . . | none . | 30,202 |

The seven colours are emblematic of the lights (splendours) of the seven names; its eighteen gores (tark), of the numerical value of the two letters in :—

حي (the Living One).§

---

* This order was founded by shaikh Abdu-l-Kâdir-ī-Gīlānī (*b.* 1078, *d* 1166), His titles were :—
(*a*) Pīr-ī-dast-gīr, the hand-seizing Pīr.
(*b*) Muḥyu-d-Dīn, collected in faith.
(*c*) Ghauṣu-l-Aʿẓam, the greatest Ghauṣ.

† The white colour signifieth submission to the shaikh. The first three circles signify the acquisition of ḥāl, that is, of ḥaḳīkat. The green cord surrounding the rose signifieth "the living one."

‡ The ninety-nine beautiful names of God are given in Brown's Darvīshes (p. 116).

§ ح = 8
ي = 10
Total 18

In the centre of the rose, is the seal of سليمان (Sulaimān), the signification whereof is :—

س freedom from defect.
ل gentleness of disposition.
ي power of spiritual vision.
م familiarity with his companions.
ن prayers and salutations belong to God (the Ḳurān i. 4).

The rose is embroidered on felt of camel's hair, emblematic of the felt khirḳa that Muḥammad gave to Uvais Ḳarnī, Sulṭān of faithful lovers.

In the word گل (gul) the rose, the letters گ and ل are the first letters of the two lines of the Ḳurān, xxxix. 37.

The origin of the rose of the Ḳādirīs is as follows :—

Shaikh 'Abdu-l-Ḳādir Gilānī, under the direction of Ḳhzir (Elias), proceeded to Baghdād.
When he arrived, Shaikh 'Alī,u-l-Vāhidī-al-Ḳādirī sent him a cup full of water, which meant the Baghdād being full of holy men, there was no room for him.
Whereupon 'Abdu-l-Ḳādir put a rose into the cup, which meant that Baghdād would find a place for him.
Then all present exclaimed :—
"The shaikh is our rose!"

---

## The bai'at (the pledge) of the murīd.

(Brown's Darvishes, pp. 94, 95; 97-101; 103, 215, 216.)

As appointed by its Pīr (founder), the mubāyi'at (the pledging) of a murīd of the Ḳādirīs is as follows :—

The murīd sitteth with his right hand* in the right hand of the shaikh (the murshid); expresseth his repentance, and his readiness to take the 'ahd (the pledge).

The shaikh addresseth him thus :—

The Faḳīr must be of an active mind, brilliant in thought, of good repute, near in approach to God, of a good heart, of a meek demeanour, of serious deportment, of a mind easy to acquire knowledge, prepared to teach others who are ignorant, disposed to trouble no one, though they trouble him.

It is incumbent on him to speak only of those things which belong to his faith; to be generous of his means; to avoid what is forbidden and wrong; to be careful in refraining from what is doubtful; to aid those who are strangers; to be a parent to the fatherless;

---

* The two thumbs must be raised against each other. This is the bai'at, the pledge.

The bai'at (the giving of the hand) of the murīd taketh place several years after his admission to the Order of Darvishes. The period dependeth on the shaikh (murshid) and on the degree of knowledge (ma'rifat) and acquisition (kasb) of the murīd.

The shaikh, or the murīd, is held to see in a vision either the Prophet 'Alī or the Pīr (founder of the Order).

This ceremonial is a secret which the murīd takes an oath never to divulge.

to be of a pleasant countenance; to be gentle of heart and joyful of spirit; to be agreeable and happy.

Even in poverty, not to expose his secrets to others, nor to divulge them; to be gentle in conduct and in intercourse; to be bountiful of his benefits, kind in language, few in words; to be patient with the ignorant, and to refrain from doing them any wrong; to show respect to great and small; to be faithful to those who confide in him, and to keep aloof from all duplicity; to be strict in his religious duties; to refrain from sloth and slumber; to speak ill of no one; to be sedate, easily satisfied, and thankful for benefits bestowed; to be much in prayer and fasting, truthful of tongue, permanent in abode; to curse no one; to be without calumny, hatred, of a grave heart, and careful of the perfect performance of the religious duties of the Order; and to be as correct in thought as in deed.

Having uttered this counsel, the shaikh, holding the murīd's hand in his own, reciteth from the Ḳurān :—

i. Sūratu-l-Fātiḥa.
x. „ „ Yūnas.
xlviii. „ „ Fatḥ (first 10 verses).
xxxiv. „ „ Aḥzāb (the 56th verse).
xxxvii. „ -s-Ṣaffāt (the 180th—182nd verse).

Then the shaikh offereth the istighfār (prayer for pardon) :—

O great God, I beseech Thee to pardon me,—Thou, like to whom is none other.

"To Him, I repent of my sins; Him, I ask to pardon me, to accept my repentance, to lead me "in the true path, and to have mercy on all those who repent of their sins. Accept my "oath of fealty, the oath which Muḥammad administered to the aṣḥābs (companions)."

Then the shaikh addresseth the murīd :—

All muslims are bound to offer up their devotions, to give alms and religious advice, to disbelieve any association with God (Father, Son and Holy Ghost), to abjure wine, not to waste their means, not to commit adultery, not to kill forbidden food, not to calumniate any one.

These I command you to observe as implicitly as the dead body is submissive in the hands of the preparers for interment.

Rebel not against what you know hath been commanded thee of God; commit not what is forbidden; make no innovations in your prayers; commit no sins, distinguish between the wrong and the true path.

Bear your shaikh ever in mind in this world and in the next.

The Prophet is our prophet, and the Shaikh 'Abdu-l-Ḳādir-i-Gīlānī is our Pīr (founder); the oath of fealty is the oath of God; this hand is the hand of Shaikh 'Abdu-l-Ḳādir-i-Gīlānī, and the hand of the Director of the True Path is in yours;

I am the Khalīfa of 'Abdu-l-Ḳādir; he accepted this hand; with it, I accept you (as his disciple).

The murīd replieth :—

I also accept you (as my murshid).

The shaikh respondeth :—

I therefore do now admit you.

Then the shaikh pronounceth the ẕikr, which the murīd repeateth three times after him; and directeth him to recite with him the Fātiḥa (Ḳurān i.); and, the salāt va salām (the prayer of peace for the Prophet).

The murīd kisseth the hand of the shaikh, and of all the darvīshes present.

This act is called muṣāfaḥat (taking by the hand).

The shaikh offereth up the istighfār (the prayer for pardon of the sins of the murīd) and addresseth the assembly:—

"The acceptance of this initiation by the murīd is a source of future advantage to him. The prayer which we have offered for him is for the submission of his body to his spiritual will, just as when the angels, before addressing the Creator, prostrate themselves humbly before Him,—so hath the murīd by his acceptance of this bai'at (giving of the hand) submitted to my rule."

Our shaikh ('Abdul-l-Ḳādir) hath said—It is not proper for the shaikh to sit in the post of pillage, nor to gird on the sword of benevolence until he becometh qualified by the following twelve qualities:—

| Name of person. | Quality. |
|---|---|
| Allāh (God) . . . . . | to cover up and to forgive. |
| Muḥammad . . . . . | to intercede and to accompany. |
| Abū Bakr . . . . . | truthfulness and benevolence. |
| 'Umar . . . . . . | to command and to forbid. |
| 'Uṣmān . . . . . | to feed the poor and to pray when others sleep. |
| 'Alī . . . . . . . | to be knowing and brave. |

If these qualities be not possessed by the shaikh, he is unworthy of the submission of the murīd.

When he doth possess them, follow under his banner. When he doth not, Shaiṭān hath made him his friend; and he will participate neither in the benefits of this life nor of the next.

The prophet hath said:—When to one of his murīds a shaikh giveth spiritual advice; and by it, he refuseth to abide—God abandoneth him.

Shaikh 'Abdu-l-Ḳādir hath said:—When any one of my murīds is oppressed with affliction, let him walk three paces to the eastward and say:—

O Thou, much desired: Thou, the aid of all in the hour of trouble, in the deepest of darkness, as in the dangers of the desert, Thou seest all things.

In the hour of shame and confusion, me only Thou canst protect.

When I am overcome with affliction, in the hour of danger, me Thy supreme intelligence will support.

O Thou, ever present, Thee I implore to free me from grief.

The ceremony may be varied as follows :—

When a murīd wisheth to enter an Order he is received in an assembly thereof.

The shaikh toucheth his hand, and breatheth three times into his ear—

Lā ilāha illa-l-lāh (there is no god but God).

which he commandeth him to repeat daily 101, 151, or 301 times (talķīn).

The murīd voweth to spend his time in khilvat; and to repeat to the shaikh his mushāhida (manifestations).

According to these mushāhida, the shaikh knoweth the time when he may breathe into his ear successively—

| | |
|---|---|
| Yā Allāh . . . . . . | O God. |
| „ Hū . . . . . . | „ He. |
| „ Ḥaķķ . . . . . . | „ Just One. |
| „ Ḥayy . . . . . . | „ Living „ |
| „ Ķayyūm . . . . . | „ Existing „ |
| „ Ķāhhār . . . . . | „ Avenging „ |

This exercise (chilla) requireth six to ten months according to the murīd's capacity.

When he reacheth the last maķām he hath acquired takmīl-i-sulūk (the perfection of travelling in the Path), and is fit for admission. During this novitiate, they call the murīd—kūchak.

The murīd liveth in the world and gaineth his livelihood. The shaikh attendeth only to his takya convent and trusteth to God for his support.

The shaikh instructeth the murīd that there are :—

| | Number. | | Number. |
|---|---|---|---|
| مقام station . . . . . . | 40 | اقليم clime . . . . . . . . | 7 |
| درجه degree . . . . . . | 360 | كره globe . . . . . . . . | 4 |
| منزل stage . . . . . . | 28 | عالم world . . . . . . . . | 18,000 |
| دايره circle . . . . . . | 12 | آيت Ķurānic verse . . . . . | 7 |
| ساعت hour . . . . . . | 24 | حرف letter . . . . . . | |
| فصل section . . . . . . | 4 | فاتحه Ķurānic openings . . . | 7 |

The darvīsh reacheth ḳuwwat-i-ruḥī-i-bāṯinī (the power of the inward soul) through:—

tawajjuh, turning the face devoutly in prayer to God.
murāḳiba, fearful contemplation of God.
taṣarruf, self-abandonment to pious reflection.
taṣawwuf, mystic spiritualism. (See pages 133—135, 138).

The exercise of this power is called ḳuwwat-i-irādī (the power of the will) which is traced to divine power, man's soul being connected with the supreme Soul (God).

There are three ẕikrs:—

ẕikr-i-khafī (the silent ẕikr) when in solitude.
,, jahrī (the audible ,, ) ,, ,, society.
,, allāh, the ẕikr of God (Ḳurān, xxiv. 37).

Ṯarīḳat is composed of columns, of precepts, and of principles as below:—

*Tarīḳat.*

| | Columns. | Precepts. | Principles. | Result. |
|---|---|---|---|---|
| 1 | توبه repentance . . | علم knowledge . . | احسان benevolence . | معرفت divine knowledge. |
| 2 | تسليم resignation . . | سخاوت generosity . | ذكر repetition (of God's name). | حلم meekness. |
| 3 | ديانت fidelity to the Order. | قرب nearness to God . | ترک معاصي abandoning sin. | صبر patience. |
| 4 | خشوع و خضوع humility (of limbs and of the heart). | دين faith . . . | ترک دنيا abandoning the world.* | طاعت submission. |
| 5 | رضا contentment . . | تفكر meditation . . | خوف خدا fear of God | ادب manners. |
| 6 | خلوت retirement . . | توكل reliance on God . | عشق خدا love for ,, | صدق sincerity. |

## Ẕikr, Murāḳiba, Tauḥıd, Daur and Ḥālat.

(Brown's Darvīshes, pp. 215—227.)

The statutes of nearly all the darvīshes require them to repeat daily:—

Lā ilāha illa-l-lāh, no god but God.
Yā Allāh O God!

---

* Muḥammad said:—

This world is forbidden to those of life in the next world; life in the next world is forbidden to those of this world; both are forbidden to the slaves of God.

| Yā Hū | O He. | |
|---|---|---|
| „ Ḥakk | „ Just | One. |
| „ Ḥayy | „ Living | „ |
| „ Kayyūm | „ Existing | „ |
| „ Kahhār | „ Avenging | „ |

These names (asmā-i-ilāhī) refer to :—

(*a*) sab' samā (the seven heavens).
(*b*) anvār-i-ilāhī ( „ divine splendours).

The exercises of murakiba (fearful contemplation), and of tauḥīd (the unity of God) are as follows :—

(*a*) on their heels, elbows touching, the darvīshes sit in a circle; and simultaneously make slight movements of the head and of the body.

(*b*) or they balance themselves slowly right to left, left to right; and incline the body forwards and rearwards;

(*c*) or, seated, they begin these motions in measured cadence with a staid countenance, eyes closed, or fixed upon the ground; and continue them on foot.

The convent-hall (wherein these exercises are carried out) is of wood; and is called the tauhīd-khāna, (the house of unity).

---

## The daur (rotatory dance).

The Darvīshes holding each other by the hand put forward the right foot, increasing at every step the strength of the movement of the body.

They uncover their hands, take off their turbans; form a second circle within the first; intertwine their arms; lean their shoulders against each other; raise the voice; and unceasingly utter—

Yā Allāh! Yā Hū!

They do not stop till strength is exhausted. Each one leaves when he pleases.

To the Shaikh seated before the kibla, the darvīshes offer praise.

The four senior darvīshes approach the shaikh; embrace each other; and place themselves, two on his right, two on his left.

The other darvīshes, arms crossed, heads inclined, advance. Each one boweth to the tablet whereon the founder's name is inscribed; putteth his hands over his face and beard; kneeling before the shaikh, kisseth his hand; and taketh his place on the pūstīn (sheep-skin) spread in a half circle in the hall.

The circle being formed, they all chant together—

| | |
|---|---|
| the Takbīr. | Allahu Akbar. |
| „ Fātiḥa. | The Kurān,i. |

The shaikh repeatedly pronounceth the words :—

Lā ilāha illa-l-lāh! No god but God!

Balancing themselves from side to side and placing their hands on their face, breast, abdomen, and knee—the darvīshes exclaim :—

Allāh!

One of the darvīshes on the shaikh's right chaunteth the—

Ḥamd-i-Muḥammad.

while the other darvīshes, moving their body to and fro, continue to exclaim—

Allāh!

After a few minutes, they rise, approach each other, press their elbows against each other, balance from right to left and then from left to right — the right foot being firm; the left foot in periodical movement, the reverse of that of the body.

All observe great precision of measure and of cadence. In the midst, they cry:—

Yā Allāh! Yā Hū.

Pale of face, languishing of eye,—some sigh, some sob; some weep, some perspire great drops.

In the middle of a hymn, chaunted alternately by the two darvīshes on the shaikh's right, they accelerate their movements. One putteth himself in the centre to incite them by example.

During this hymn, the darvīshes take off their turbans; bear their shoulders against each other; and compass the hall at a measured pace, striking their feet against the floor, and all at once springing up and exclaiming:—

Yā Allāh! Yā Hū!

When they would stop from sheer exhaustion, the shaikh, making violent motions, inciteth them anew.

The two senior darvīshes take his place, double the quickness of the step and the motion of body, and all dance till entirely exhausted.

---

## Hālat (Ecstasy).

Two darvīshes take down from niches cutlasses; heat them red hot; and present them to the shaikh.

After breathing over them prayers and invoking the aid of the Pīr of the Order, the shaikh raiseth them to his mouth, and then giveth them to the darvīshes, who eagerly ask for them.

Transported by frenzy, the darvīshes seize upon the glowing irons, gloat upon them, lick them, bite them, hold them between the teeth, and cool them in their mouth!

Others stick cutlasses into their sides, arms, and legs.

If they fall under their sufferings they cast themselves, without a complaint, or a murmur or a sign of pain, into the arms of their Brothers.

Some minutes after this, the shaikh visiteh each; breatheth upon his wounds, rubbeth them with saliva, reciteth prayers, and promiseth speedy cure.

It is said that twenty-four hours afterwards, nothing is to be seen of their wounds.

They call the red hot irons gul (the red rose), because the use of them is as agreeable to the soul of the darvīsh as the perfume of the rose is to the voluptuary.

---

## The dance of the samā'.

The darvīshes (nine to thirteen) sit on sheep-skins on the floor at equal distances from each other. Thus for half an hour,—arms folded, eyes closed, head bowed,—they remain in profound meditation.

The shaikh on a seat, on a small carpet, breaketh silence by a hymn in honour of God. Then he inviteth the assembly (majlis) to chaunt with him the fātiḥa*:—

"Let us chaunt the fātiḥa, in glorifying the holy name of God; in honour of the blessed religion of the Prophets, especially of Muḥammad Muṣṭafā, the greatest, most august, magnificent of all heavenly envoys; in memory of the first four Khulafā; of the sainted Fātima; of chaste Khadīja; of the Imāms Ḥasan and Ḥusain; of all the martyrs of the memorable day, (battle of Karbalā, 680 A.D.); of the ten evangelical disciples, the virtuous sponsors of our Prophet; of all his zealous and faithful disciples; of all the imāms, mujtahids, of all the 'ulamā, of all the auliyā, of all the holy women of Islām.

"Let us chaunt in honour of Ḥaẓrat-i-Maulāna, the founder of our Order, of Ḥaẓrat-i-Sulṭānu-l-'Ulamā (his father), of Sayyid Burhānu-d-Dīn (his teacher), of Shaikh Shamsu-d-Dīn (his consecrator), of Vālida Sulṭān (his mother), of Muḥammad 'Alīu-d-Dīn (his son and vicar), of all the successors, of all the shaikhs, of all the darvīshes, and all the protectors of our Order, to whom the Omnipotent designeth to give peace and mercy.

"Let us pray for the constant prosperity of our society; for the preservation of the very learned and venerable General of our Order, for the preservation of the reigning Sulṭān, the very majestic and clement sovereign of the Islām Faith, for the prosperity of the Grand Vazīr and of the Shaikhu-l-Islām, and of all the Muḥammadan soldiery and of all the ḥujjāj to Makka.

"Let us pray for the repose of the soul of all the pīrs, of all the shaikhs, and of all the darvīshes of all other Orders; for all good people.

"Let us pray for all muslims of one and of the other sex, of the east and of the west, for the maintenance of all prosperity, for preventing all adversity, for the accomplishment of vows, and for the success of praiseworthy enterprise.

"Finally, let us ask God to deign to preserve in us the gift of His grace, and the fire of His love."

After this, all chaunt together; the shaikh reciteth the fātiḥa and the ṣalawāt.

This being ended, the darvīshes, standing in line to the shaikh's left, arms folded, head bowed, slowly approach.

---

* The shaikh reciteth first the fātiḥa, then uttereth the following prayer.

The first darvīsh having arrived nearly opposite to the shaikh profoundly saluteth the tablet, wherein is inscribed the founder's name; advancing by two leaps to the shaikh's right side he turneth to him, saluteth him, and beginneth to dance.

The dance consisteth in turning on the left heel, in advancing slowly, and in making the turn of the hall with closed eyes and opened arms.

This, in succession, all the darvīshes do.

Interrupted by two short pauses, during which the shaikh reciteth prayers, the dance lasteth for two hours.

Towards the close, the shaikh joineth in the dance; then returning to his seat, he reciteth Persian verses for the prosperity of religion and of the state; and saith:—

Let us pray for the Sovereign of the muslim and most august of Monarchs of the house of 'Usmān, Sultan, son of a Sultān, grandson of a Sultān * * * * and for the darvīshes, present and absent; for all friends of our Order; for all the faithful, dead and quick, in the east and in the west.

The fātiha is chaunted; the samā, concluded.

Government of India Central Printing Office.—No. 100 D. O.—2-5-91.—1,004.